HOW TO PAINT

TREES,
FLOWERS
AND
FOLIAGE

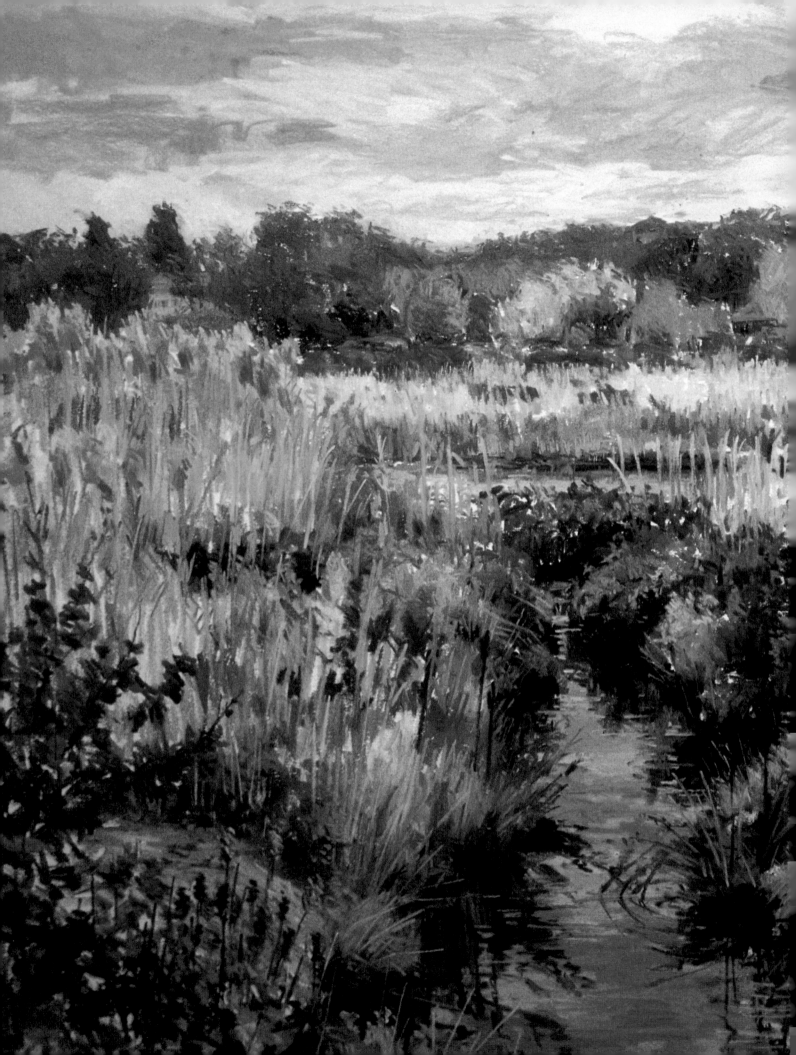

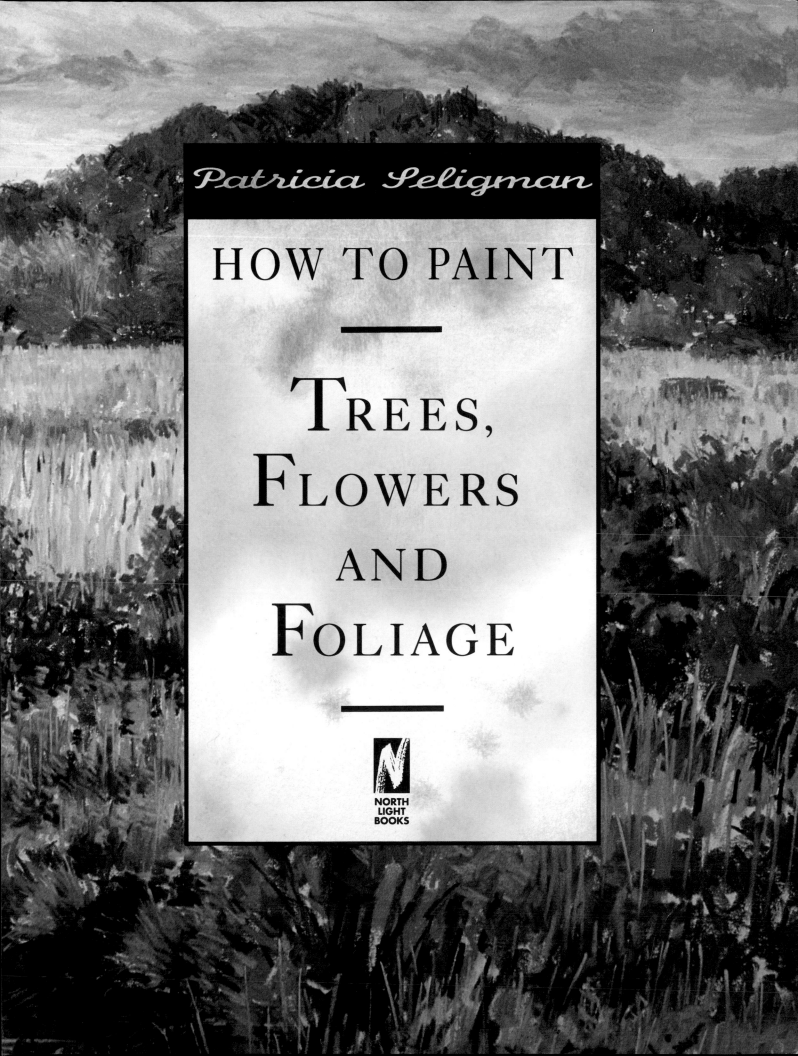

Patricia Seligman

HOW TO PAINT

TREES, FLOWERS AND FOLIAGE

NORTH LIGHT BOOKS

CONTENTS

A QUARTO BOOK

First published in the U.S.A. by
North Light Books, an imprint of
F&W Publications, Inc
1507 Dana Avenue
Cincinnati, Ohio 45207

First published 1994
Copyright © 1994
Quarto Inc

ISBN 0-89134-562-0

This book was designed and produced by
Quarto Inc
6 Blundell Street
London N7 9BH

Senior Art Editor Penny Cobb
Designer William Mason
Editor Hazel Harrison
Senior Editor Kate Kirby
Photographers Paul Forrester,
Chas Wilder
Picture Manager Giulia Hetherington
Picture Research Laura Bangert
Editorial Director Sophie Collins
Art Director Moira Clinch

Typeset in Great Britain by
Poole Typesetting Ltd, England
Manufactured in Hong Kong by Regent Publishing
Services Ltd
Printed in China by Leefung-Asco Printers Ltd

Title page: Corn Hill Salt Marsh in Autumn,
pastel, Simie Maryles

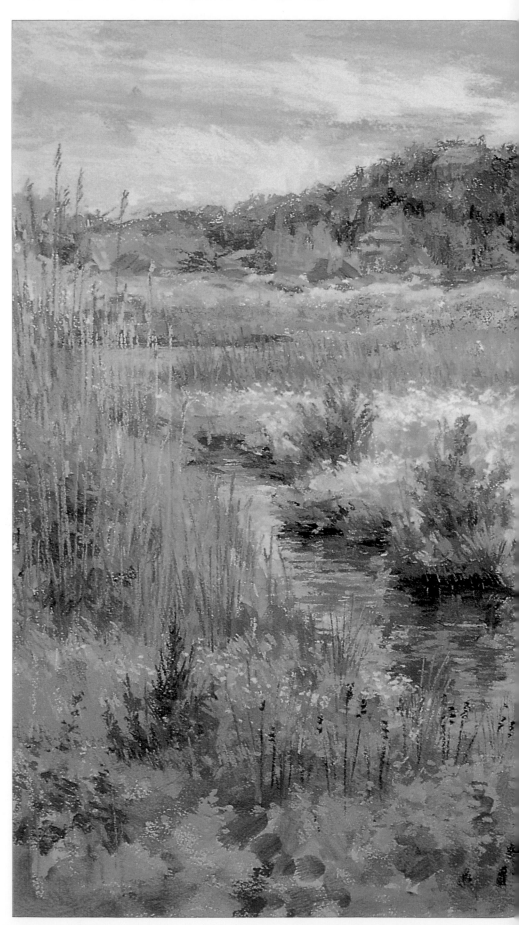

INTRODUCTION 6

Chapter One: Foreground

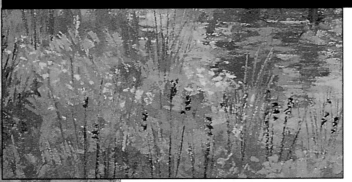

ABOUT LOOKING 12
CHOOSING AN APPROACH 14
DETAIL AND EDGE QUALITY 18
CONTRAST AND COLOR 36
SCALE AND PROPORTION 44
IN THE FIELD 46

Chapter Two: Middle Ground

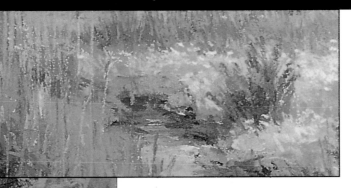

ABOUT LOOKING 52
CHOOSING AN APPROACH 54
DETAIL AND EDGE QUALITY 62
CONTRAST AND COLOR 76
SCALE AND PROPORTION 86
IN THE FIELD 92

Chapter Three: Distance

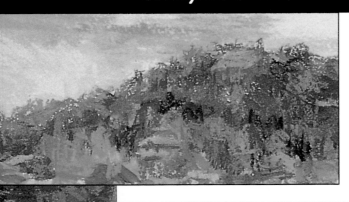

ABOUT LOOKING 98
CHOOSING AN APPROACH 100
DETAIL AND EDGE QUALITY 104
CONTRAST AND COLOR 110
SCALE AND PROPORTION 116
IN THE FIELD 118

Chapter Four: Putting it Together

CHOOSING AN APPROACH 124
THE PAINTING PROCESS 132
MAKING ADJUSTMENTS 138

INDEX 142
CREDITS 144

Corn Hill in May

Simie Maryles • pastel

Introduction

TREES AND FLOWERS ENTICE US WITH THEIR BEAUTY, BUT MUST TAKE THEIR PROPER PLACE IN YOUR COMPOSITION

TREES AND FLOWERS are an integral part of the natural scenery and in many cases are the very things that attract you to a certain landscape subject. It is hard to resist the lure of a poppy field, a bluebell woods, or the glowing colors of autumn foliage. Foliage and flowers can become a subject in themselves, painted in close-up detail in a botanical manner, or as an indoor set-up – a branch of still-life painting. Here, however, we are concerned more with sweeping impressions in which trees, flowers, and foliage are seen in their natural context, whether a garden, a backyard, or a wide panorama stretching away into space. The book deals with the common problems of all landscape painters – and how to create a con-

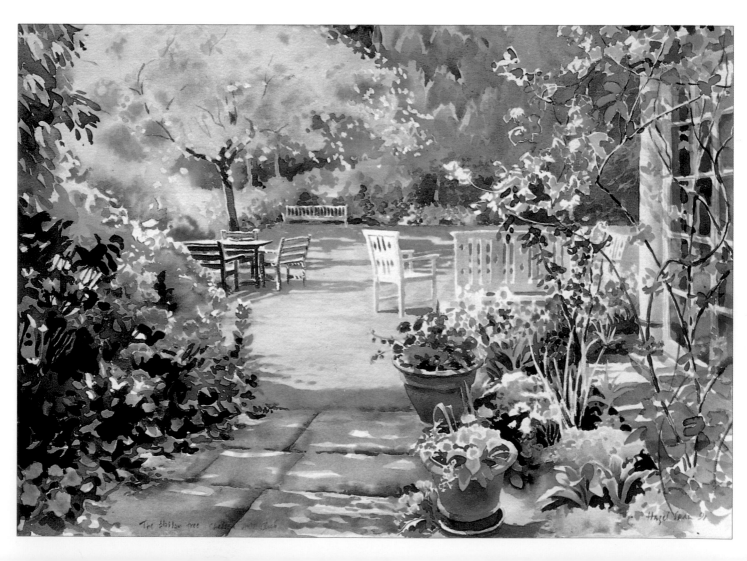

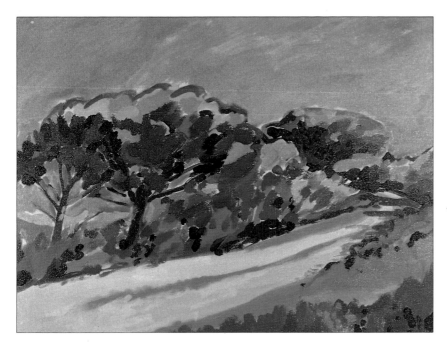

Midday in Provence

Gerry Baptist • acrylic

Keeping the colors bright and the tonal values to the higher end of the scale helps to suggest the light and the heat in this sunbaked landscape, and the juxtaposed complementary colors create a vibrant impression.

▽ **Hogweed, Norfolk**

Maurice Read • watercolor

When you look closely at the picture, you can see how the artist has created an impression of the cow parsnip flowers with a few strokes of color. Even though the focus is on the flowers in the foreground, the view stretches out behind into the far distance.

vincing impression through considered use of color and brushwork.

Almost everything you choose to paint creates problems of some kind, and trees and flowers are no exception. One difficulty is that they can entice you into an over-detailed approach and overly bright colors.

About this book Every artist dealing with the real world is concerned with creating an illusion of three-dimensional space on a two-dimensional surface, and often this is the main problem. If you are painting a tree some way away from you, it is essential to understand how to create an impression – to capture the essence of the tree without elaborate detail. Similarly, you must be able to judge the kind of treatment needed for flowers in the foreground, where you usually require more detail, but not so much that the painting looks labored and overworked.

To simplify things, the book is divided into four chapters, the first three dealing in turn with each of the main divisions of the picture space – the foreground, the middle ground and the distance. But this is in a way an unnatural division, because your painting should not

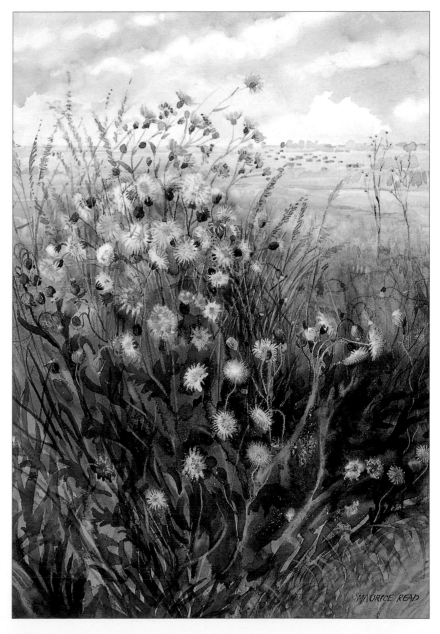

◁ **Chelsea Garden**

Hazel Soan • watercolor

Sunlight and soft shadow, the artist has caught the mood of a tranquil garden setting. The positioning of the bench in the background leads the eye and invites the viewer into the picture.

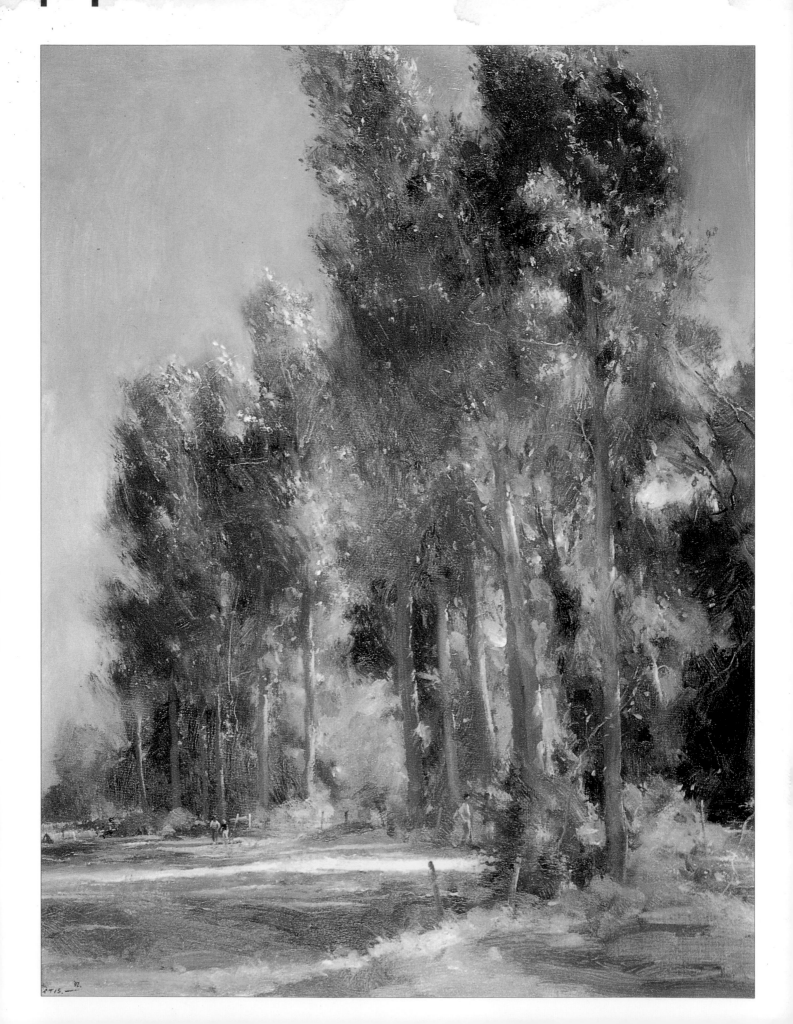

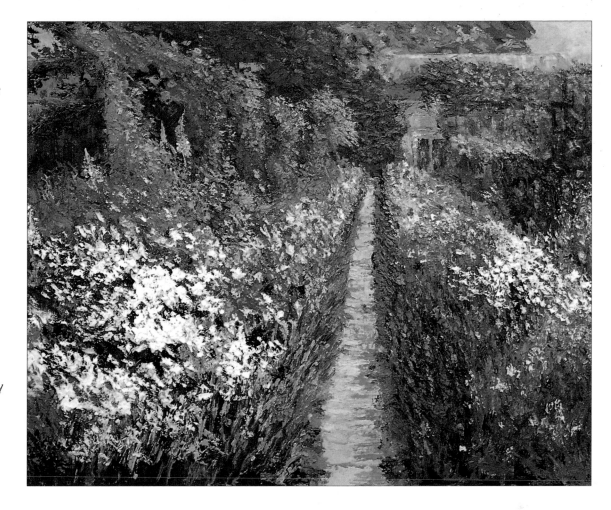

Poplars in a Breeze

David Curtis • oil

The movement of the foliage is built up in the brushwork and the subtle greens, enlivened with superimposed dabs of vibrant highlight.

Monet's Path

Urania Christy Tarbet • oil

The artist has managed to describe several different plant species, all of which are instantly recognizable to the viewer.

be seen as a series of separate parts, so the fourth chapter looks at the picture as a whole, explaining ways to unify the foreground, middle ground, and distance through color, control of tonal values, and understanding of the techniques relating to your chosen medium.

Within each chapter – or division of space in pictorial terms – certain subject headings are repeated, as they represent the key problem areas. **Choosing an Approach**, for example, covers topics such as sketching, exploring your subject, and deciding on the composition. **Detail and Edge Quality** concerns the degree of detail to include and explains the importance of hard and soft edges in describing trees and flowers. **Contrast and Color** shows you how to introduce additional excitement and interest into your landscapes, and how to create the illusion of space by observing and using the effects of aerial perspective, while **Scale and Proportion** explains how to use simple perspective and contrasts in scale.

The book covers all the painting media – watercolor and gouache paints, oils and acrylics, and pastels – and provides a series of hints on both "standard" and "special" techniques. For example, you will discover how to choose the best brushes to describe certain leaf and flower shapes, how to use thick paint (impasto) to suggest edges, how to overlay pastel colors to create subtle color effects, and how to suggest texture by such methods as spattering and sponging in watercolor.

There are also sections which give more detailed information on trees and flowers, which will help you to recognize their important characteristics. Even when you are dealing with trees in the distance, say a line of willows along a river bank, you will want to give an impression of a particular species of tree. To do this, you will have to learn what makes one tree different from another – perhaps it is shape, or color, or a combination of both. Too often trees are painted with brown trunks and mid-green leaves, but nature is far more inventive, and the play of light and shade creates yellows and blues even when foliage is technically green. Flowers, too, reveal subtle cadences of color when you observe them closely – red roses are by no means red all over.

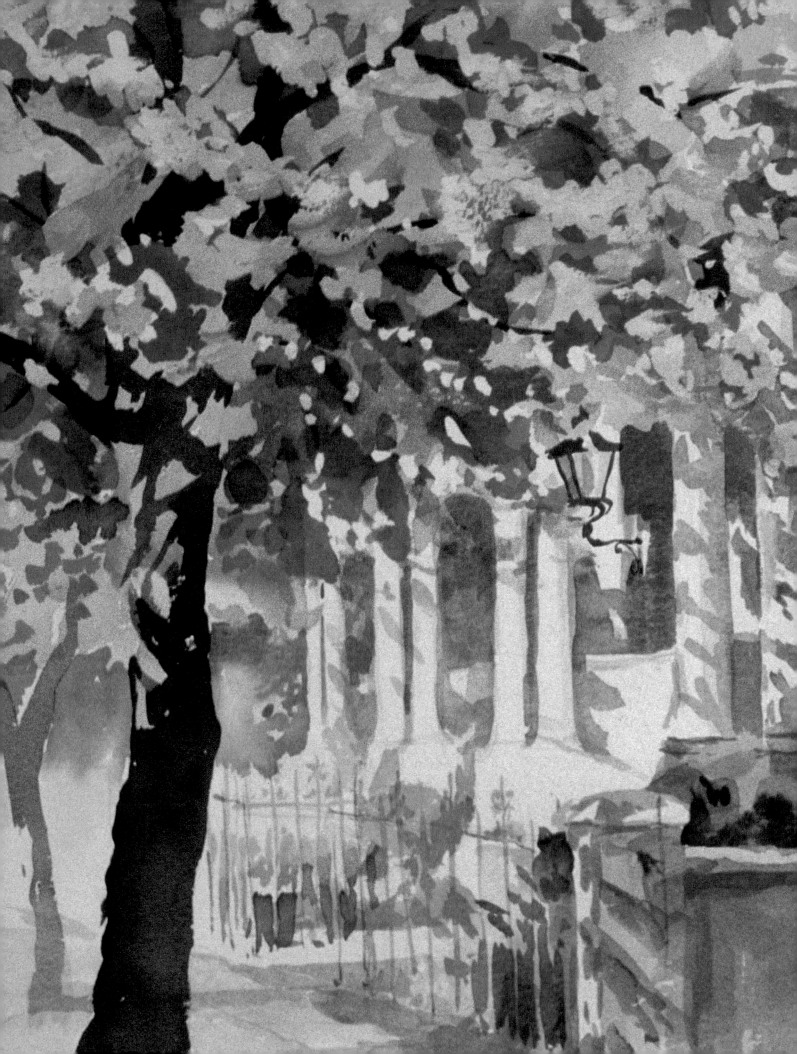

Chapter One

FOREGROUND

———

ABOUT LOOKING   12

CHOOSING AN APPROACH   14

DETAIL AND EDGE QUALITY   18

CONTRAST AND COLOR   36

SCALE AND PROPORTION   44

IN THE FIELD   46

WHEN YOU LOOK AROUND you, your eyes constantly change focus as they collect different visual information. Imagine you are looking out on a country scene, for example. First you would take in the overall view, and then perhaps something in the foreground might claim your attention. Having studied this, your eyes may be directed to the middle distance, touching on some feature such as a small farmhouse in a grove of trees, before moving on to distant hills or clouds on the horizon. You cannot give all these areas of interest the same degree of emphasis, so you will need to decide on the main point of focus. In this chapter, we focus on the foreground of the painting, showing how the artist can make the most of this area of the picture space.

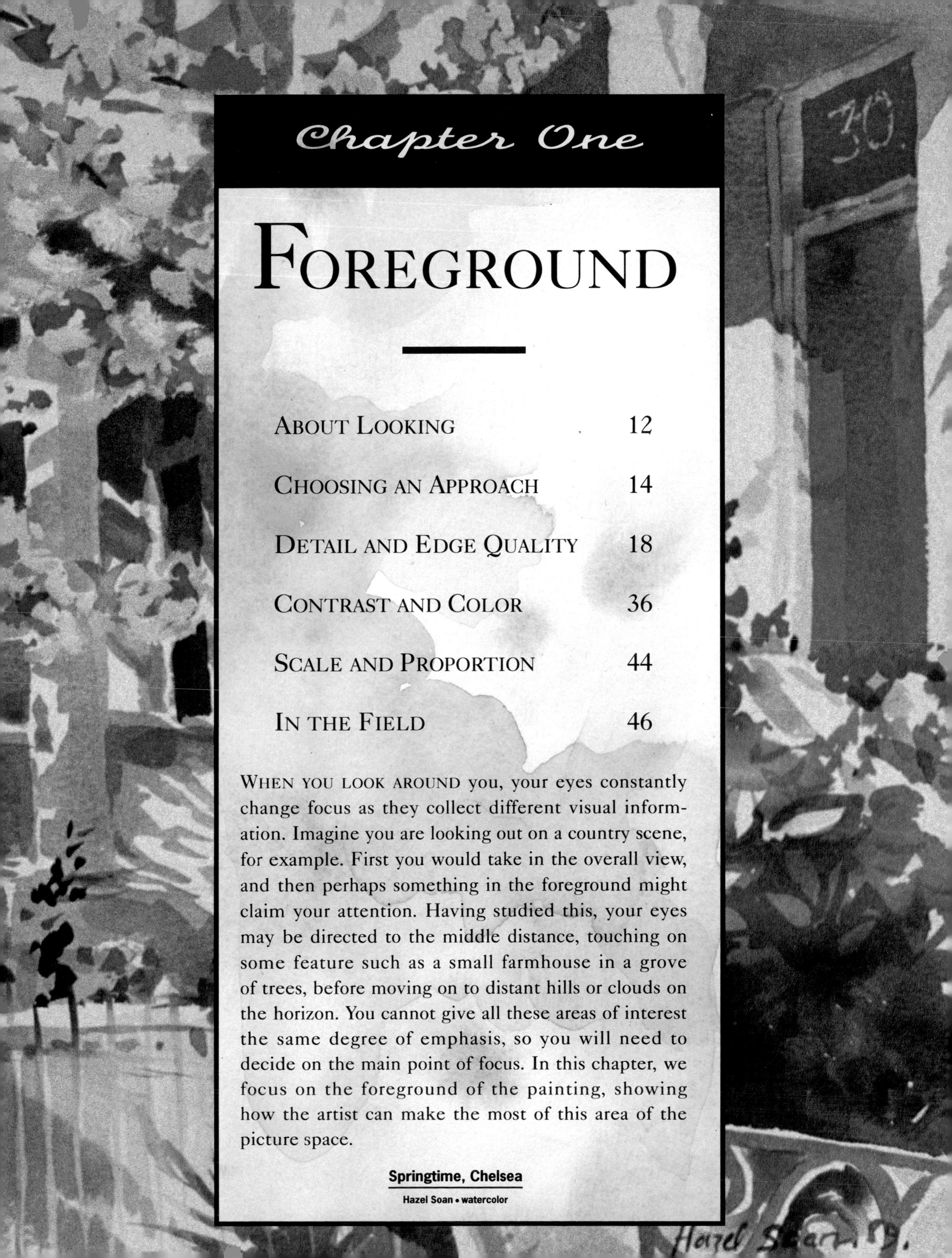

Springtime, Chelsea

Hazel Soan • watercolor

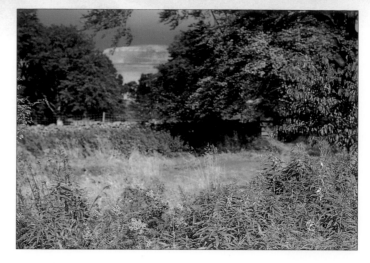

About looking

A VIEW IN CLOSE-UP

ON THESE PAGES we show you how you can interpret and edit the scene in front of you by looking at it from different angles and viewpoints. Here we focus on the foreground, but the same scene is viewed in the chapters on the middle ground and distance. These photographs also show how changes in season, weather, and light will affect the scene dramatically. A camera is a useful aid for the artist, enabling you to make a quick record of what you see, but it is wise to make sketches and written notes as well wherever possible.

On these two pages the focus is on the foreground.

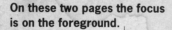

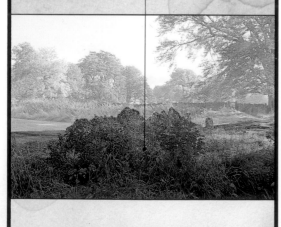

▲ *By focusing your camera on the foreground so that the middle ground and distance are slightly blurred, you can create some of the effects the artist would need to introduce into his painting – harder, crisper outlines in the foreground contrasted with softer edges in the distance.*

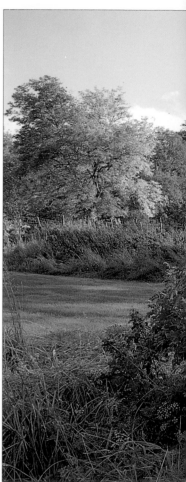

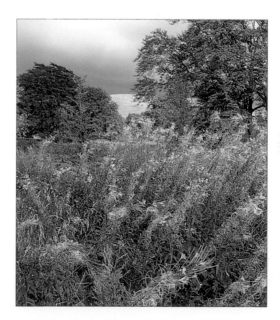

▲ *Moving back, these diagonal spires of seeded rosebay willow herb make a graphic introduction to the background.*

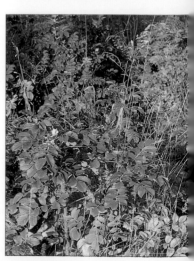

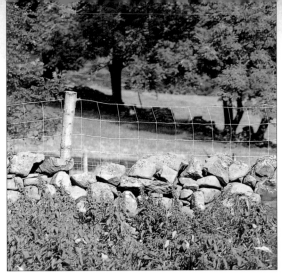

◄ By moving further into the landscape, the wall and fence in the middle distance now become an excellent foreground "frame" for the rest of the scene.

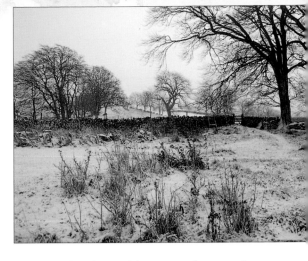

▲ Viewed in winter with snow on the ground, the same scene takes on a very different appearance. The reddish dried grasses could be exaggerated to create foreground interest and lead the eye to the more distant line of trees.

▼ The yellow mimosa on the right will help to focus the eye on the foreground flowers. By slightly rearranging things, the artist can make a more striking pattern.

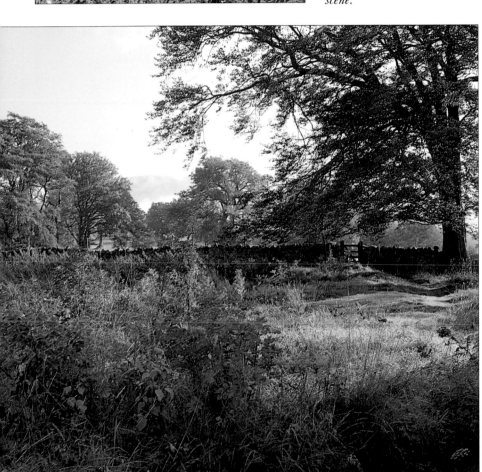

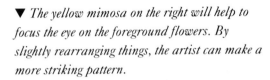

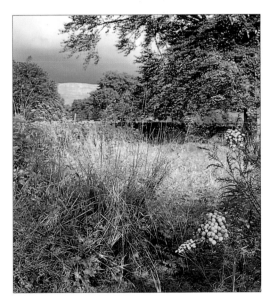

◄ Focusing in on the interwoven rose hips and dry grass in the foreground provides a strong pattern element.

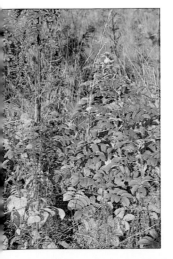

► With the scene lit from the back, the dynamics are altered dramatically, with the sense of distance considerably reduced. The season is early spring with the trees coming into leaf and the lush willow herb in the foreground making a bank of subtle greens.

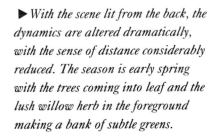

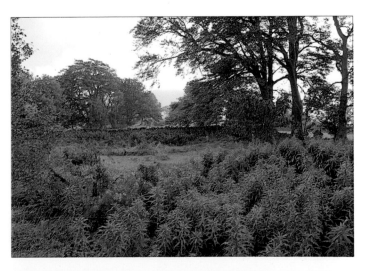

EVERY LANDSCAPE VIEW HAS a foreground, but the foreground can play many different roles in the overall scheme of the painting. It can be generalized, even deliberately played down, to keep it from dominating the painting. Shapes and colors in the foreground can be used to lead the eye into the painting – perhaps a branch, some foliage, or a path that seems to point into the middle distance, where the center of interest may be. The foreground can also help you create a sense of space. Meadow flowers dotting a field, for example, may seem unadventurous, but would immediately create the illusion of depth and recession. The foreground can even be the subject and focus of the painting – a flowerbed or a screen of trees.

Choosing an Approach

ENCOURAGE THE VIEWER TO EXPLORE EVERY PART OF THE PAINTING THROUGH CLEVER COMPOSITION

Introducing the painting A clever artist can compose his or her painting so that when you look at it your eye is encouraged to explore every part of it. This can be done in various ways, one of which is the careful placing of

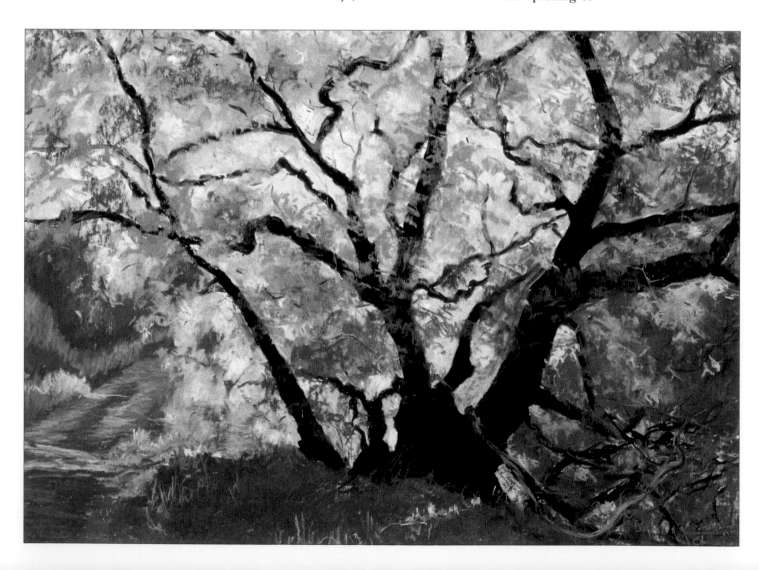

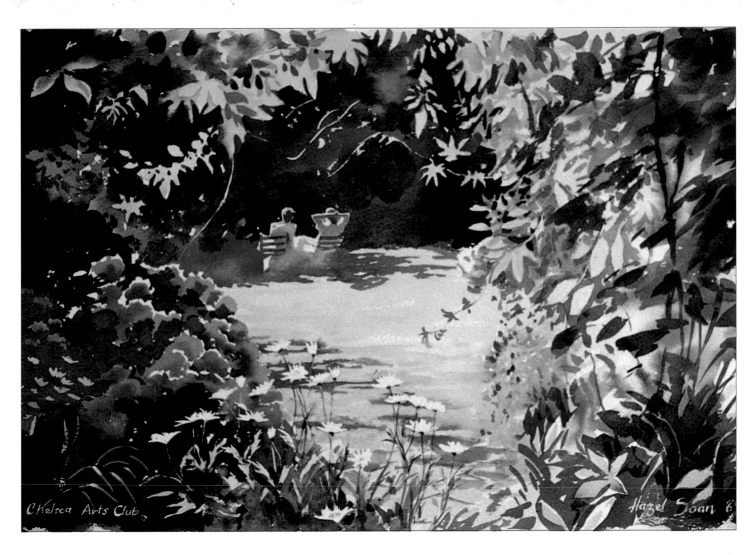

△ Relaxing

Hazel Soan • watercolor

Here the foreground flowers and foliage introduce and frame the figures, viewed across the lawns in the distance.

Sunrise, Sunset

Urania Christy Tarbet • pastel

The artist has focused on this backlit tree in the foreground. But the track leading past the tree to the left hints at the continuation of the landscape into an unseen middle distance.

strong compositional lines which act as signposts, literally directing the eye around the picture. This may seem a difficult, even impossible task when you are painting landscape, as you can't rearrange the flowers, trees, grass, and sky in front of you, but it is surprising what you can achieve by altering your viewpoint. You might move back so that you could frame the view with overhanging branches, for example, which will allow you to "introduce" the middle distance and background.

Sometimes the foreground appears to be playing no part at all in the painting. You may have seen landscapes in which the canvas is left bare, or only very lightly covered in the foreground. It is still playing its part, though, because its very unobtrusiveness directs you to more important and more highly finished areas.

Foreground as subject You have probably had the experience of choosing a view and then finding yourself so overwhelmed by what you can see that you don't know where to start.

This is a reaction that most artists have had, but with experience you will learn to be selective. You don't have to paint every tree, bush, flower, and blade of grass – you need to "edit" your view, or even restrict it by homing in on a smaller part of it.

So why not try focusing on the foreground alone? A landscape doesn't have to be a grand panorama of hills and valleys; you can view the world from much closer. The advantage is that you can concentrate on form and color without being distracted by the problem of creating space and distance. Concentrating on the foreground also allows you to treat it in more detail – though of course you don't have to paint flowers or leaves in the manner of a botanical artist, with every vein of every leaf included. The secret is to capture the basic form and color of your subject first, without allowing yourself to get bogged down in detail in the early stages, and to do this you will need to study your subject before you begin to paint.

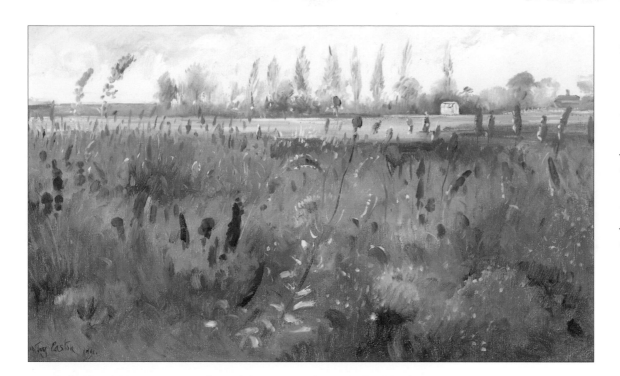

Delphiniums at Dusk

Timothy Easton • oil

By choosing a low viewpoint, the artist has focused attention on the foreground flowers. The eye lingers here before traveling on, encouraged by the tallest foreground flower, which acts as a signpost to the distant line of trees.

Choosing an Approach

ARRANGE YOUR VIEW SO THAT IT MAKES AN EYE-CATCHING PAINTING

ONCE YOU HAVE MADE one important decision – choosing your view – you must immediately make another, and consider how to make a composition of it. This means arranging your view so that it makes an eye-catching painting. Artists are constantly making decisions at each stage of a painting. When you are inexperienced, these can seem overwhelming; but if you explore different aspects of your subject before you start on the painting, you will be making decisions without realizing it.

First choose a viewpoint One of the first decisions is to choose where to view your subject from. You will discover the importance of this immediately if you look at your scene first standing up – as you will have seen it as you were walking around – and then sitting down. It may have altered almost beyond recognition – you find that a foreground hedge becomes the whole picture because you can no longer see over it. But a low viewpoint can be ideal; if you have decided to concentrate on the foreground, it will cut out inessentials.

Exploring by sketching Now you have to decide what to include in your landscape composition, and to decide how much space should be occupied by sky – if this is to be included. Exploring ideas by getting them down on paper in a sketchbook is a tried and tested way to get started on a painting. It helps you to see the options and will save you from making elementary mistakes.

Concentrate first on the foreground, and take time to consider the different ways in which the scene can be presented. Don't try to make elaborate drawings; a series of thumbnail sketches will help you investigate the interplay of shapes. Any strong lines in your view – for example, branches of trees, outlines of shadows – should be organized to direct the eye around the composition.

In a landscape you will find there is often a natural balance of vertical and horizontal elements. With trees and flowers, the emphasis is on the vertical, whereas clouds or a flat landscape with a patchwork of fields will accentuate the horizontal. A picture with nothing but horizontals can sometimes be dull. In a view of fields with hedges across them, for example, you may need something as a contrasting element, such as grasses and flowers, or a fence or gatepost, in the foreground. Checking that you have this natural balance ensures harmony.

Exploring light and dark The next thing to consider is tone, which means the lightness or darkness of color. Consider the way these light and dark areas are distributed in your view. For a harmonious painting, you should try for a balance of lights, darks, and mid-tones which complements the composition of directional lines. If on the other hand you want to induce a feeling of tension into your landscape, then you might emphasize small areas of extreme light and dark which jostle the eye and confuse the "reading" of your painting.

Exploring color You need to consider color before you begin to paint. You will probably have already done so in general terms, or you would not have decided on the particular subject, but now is the time for more detailed planning; careful use of color can be used to establish and emphasize the foreground. And if you intend to paint the scene back home later or are in any doubt that you will finish it before the light changes, then a color sketch or a few written color notes would be a good idea.

Using a viewframe If you find it difficult to choose a viewpoint or to imagine how your landscape view will look in your painting, you will find one of these gadgets helpful. They are easily made by cutting a picture-shaped hole in a piece of cardboard, or improvise with your hands. By moving the viewfinder around – holding it close to your eye and then further away – you can explore all the different options open to you, and you will be able to visualize the scene as a two-dimensional painting.

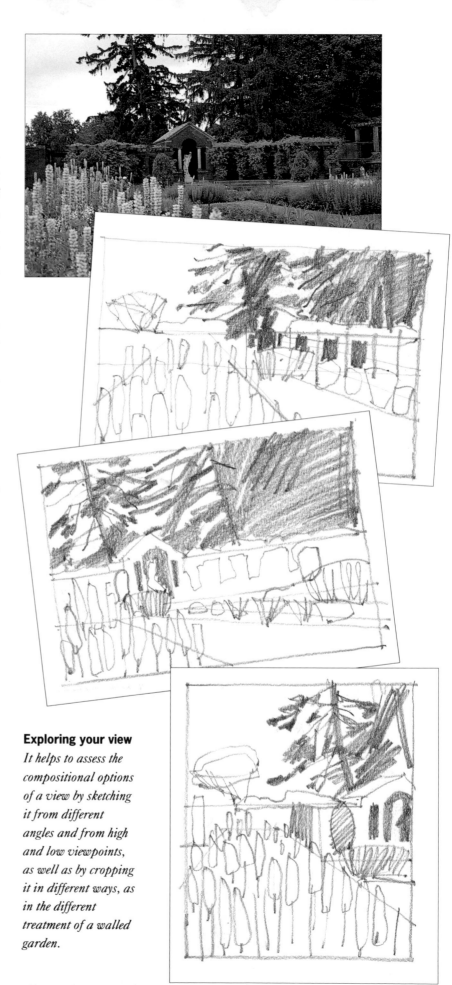

Exploring your view
It helps to assess the compositional options of a view by sketching it from different angles and from high and low viewpoints, as well as by cropping it in different ways, as in the different treatment of a walled garden.

Diana with Cedars and Columbine (detail)

Elsie Dinsmore Popkin • pastel

Each clump of flowers has individuality without too much detail, allowing the artist to portray the spirit of the garden, with its bold masses of color.

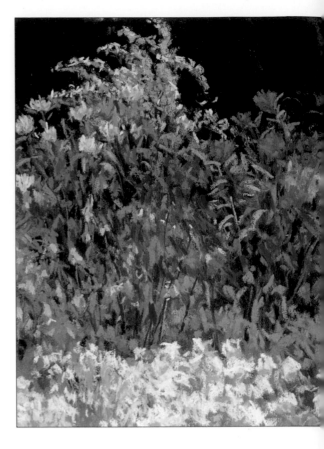

Detail and Edge Quality

LOOK FOR MAIN SHAPES AND COLORS, SUPPRESSING UNNECESSARY DETAIL

ONE OF THE BIGGEST problems encountered by landscape artists is that of detail – how much should or should not be included in the painting. On the whole, amateur artists tend to include too much, and the painting often becomes labored and dull. The aim should be to create an impression of the various elements of the landscape without too much over-literal description. Like everything else, this takes practice, but the key is to look first for the main shapes and colors.

You will be surprised how flowers, shrubs, and trees can be reduced to basics and still be perfectly recognizable. If you were painting a study of a single rose, for example, you might portray the spiral of petals unfolding, but when the flower is part of a landscape, you need to simplify the form. A tree usually has an intricate and complex pattern of branches, small twigs, and leaves, but it also has a characteristic overall shape. Color, too, is important. Rose bushes often have quite red stems and leaves,

Reducing the detail

A field full of buttercups can be created with no more than a yellow spatter across the foreground area without losing its impact. The emphasis is not on the forms of the flowers, but on the broad effect of the flower-strewn meadow.

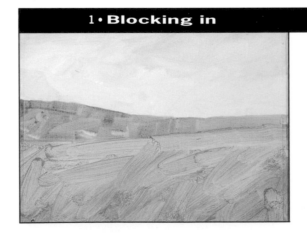

1 • Blocking in

2 • Spattering

▲ *Using diluted acrylic paint, the background is blocked in with broad strokes of the brush. This visible brushwork creates an impression of movement in the meadow grass.*

▲ *The area, to keep it free of spatter, is masked off with torn paper. A soft household paint brush is loaded with diluted yellow, and a finger pulled across the bristles to release droplets of paint.*

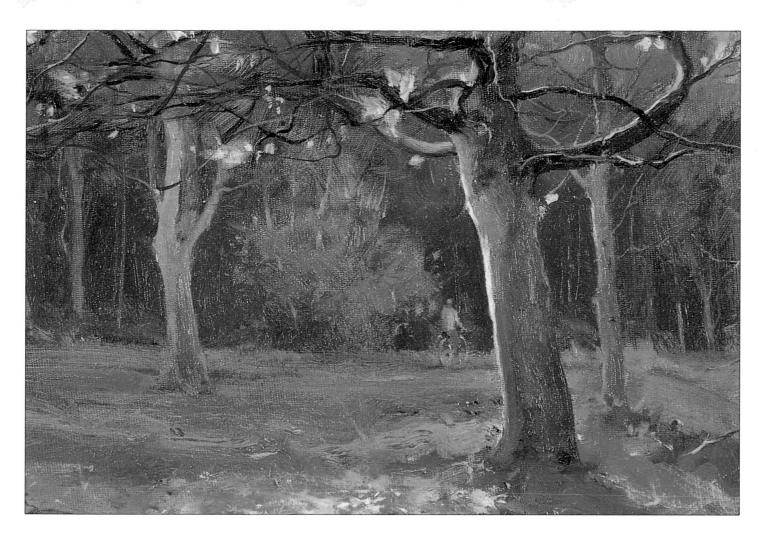

and the roses themselves change color as they bloom and die. So you may have different colored blooms on the same bush.

How much detail? Because the foreground is close to you – it may even be almost beneath your feet – you can see much more detail than

3 • Establishing foreground

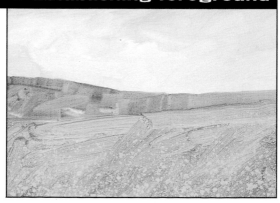

▲ *This band of spattered color creates contrast and interest, "pulling" the foreground forward to create the first step in the progressive journey into the picture space.*

in the distance or middle distance. But this doesn't mean you have to put everything in – you must decide how much to include on the basis of the rest of the painting. A foreground can be vague and generalized, but is perhaps often the most detailed part of the painting simply because you can see it in sharp focus. But if you make it too eventful, you will have to treat the rest of the painting in a similar way or the foreground will "steal the show." It can be a good idea to block in the main foreground shapes initially and come back to them after working on the rest of the painting. You can then see exactly how much you need in the way of precise definition. You may find that picking out one or two flowerheads or an occasional stem of grass is all that is required.

If you have chosen a scene entirely because of the foreground, however, you will want to gear the rest of the picture to it. You may be interested in different types of flowers, for example, and want to show the differences in shape and color, or you may be fascinated by a pattern of leaves on a nearby tree.

Late Autumn, Clumber Park

David Curtis • oil

Autumnal sunlight catches the fallen leaves and those few remaining on the tree, establishing the foreground planes of the picture through color and light.

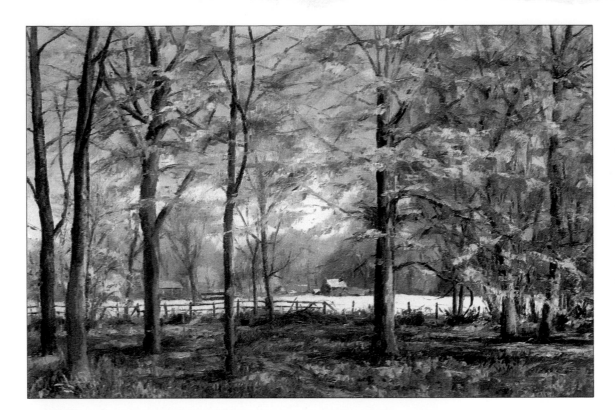

Bluebells in Ashridge

Brian Bennett • oil

You could not fail to recognize that this is a bluebell wood in springtime, yet no one flower is described literally. As long as enough clues are provided – in this case, the woods and the color and distribution of the flowers – the mind is very easily persuaded.

Detail and Edge Quality

PAINTING IS TRANSLATING, NOT COPYING. YOU ARE RENDERING NATURE IN TERMS OF PIGMENT

MANY OF THE BEAUTIFUL landscapes you see in art galleries, whether they are "old master" works or contemporary paintings, seem very simple, with the whole subject captured in a few deft strokes. The simplicity is deceptive in a way, because such paintings, although they may have been carried out quickly, are usually the end-product of years of experience. The artist has learned to be selective – to identify what is most important about the subject and to exclude anything that might detract from it.

Careful observation is the first step to acquiring this kind of skill – until you fully know your subject, you won't be able to translate it into paint. When you choose a landscape you want to paint, ask yourself what you like about it – is it the colors, the shapes, a particular lie of the land, or one dominant element such as an old tree? And then think about what you might exclude, or perhaps simplify.

Translating into paint Painting is not copying; it is translating. You are rendering organic materials – grass, trees, and flowers – into pigment colors, so consider how you can let your chosen medium help you. If you are using oils or acrylics, you can often build up shapes with brushstrokes, using sweeps of thick color to suggest a foreground plant or tree. In water color, too, you can "draw" with your brush, using different marks to suggest shapes.

If you want to indicate texture without overworking the picture, you might try a stippling method, dabbing paint on with a stiff brush, or use the dry-brush technique, in which your brush is loaded with just a little color and dragged over the surface to give a sketchy, broken-color effect. You can do this with watercolor as well as with any of the opaque media.

The power of suggestion For the more impressionistic type of painting, the foreground

Capturing a likeness *To translate a field of poppies into acrylic paint, the artist first isolates their basic color, shape, and distribution. He is careful not to place them too regularly across the picture, and to allow some to overlap for a natural effect. He adds more detail to flowerheads in the foreground so that we assume the same detail for those in the background.*

1 • Mapping out

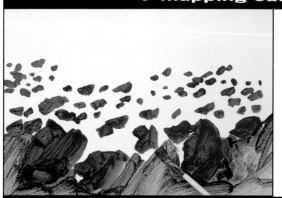

◀ *The basic shapes of the poppies are painted in first and the grass worked around them with broad brushstrokes suggesting the forms and textures.*

2 • Red over green

▶ *In the background, the red is painted over the green so that the colors mix slightly, reducing the intensity of the red. A smaller brush is used for the dot-like flowerheads.*

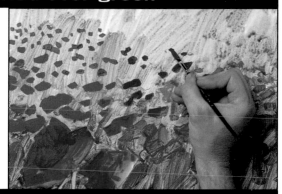

3 • Wet-on-dry

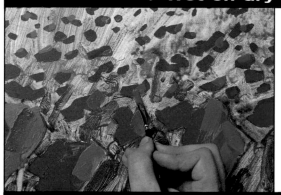

◀ *Simple three-dimensional form is given to the foreground poppies with the addition of highlights added to the now-dry paint.*

4 • Wet-in-wet

▶ *Now the centers are added to the foreground flowers, first black, then a touch of green painted wet-in-wet so that the colors merge softly.*

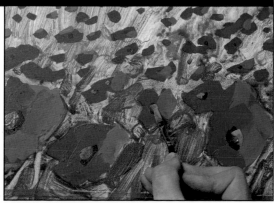

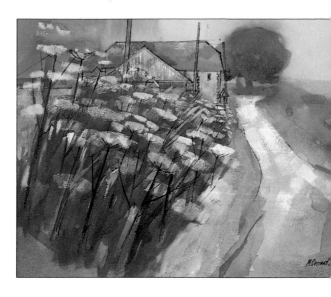

The Blue Tree

Michael Bernard • inks, acrylic and pastel

The bank of cow parsley is reduced to a stylized pattern of stem and flowerhead but nevertheless establishes the foreground.

needs to be treated fairly broadly. If you are painting a bluebell wood, you will be able to see individual flowers and leaves, but you don't have to put them all in. Try painting a sea of blue with bolder brushstrokes in the foreground, and the eye will read this as a carpet of bluebells. You will be amazed how easily the eye can be persuaded. Similarly, if you splatter red across the foreground of a summer field, you immediately have a field of poppies.

Capturing a likeness In the paintings opposite and above, color is the main key to the suggestion, but shape is equally important. One of the tricks of capturing the essence of plants, flowers, and trees in a few strokes is in working out what makes them individual. Take two yellow flowers, say, a sunflower and a primrose. You could hardly fail to see the differences in size and shape, so their outlines could never be confused, but there are more subtle differences, too, such as the proportion of flower to leaf and the way the flower grows from its stem. The sunflower stands out at a distance, begging for bold brushstrokes of thick paint (impasto), whereas the soft, delicate yellow of the primrose, closer in color and tone to its leaves, would benefit from a more subtle treatment, perhaps in watercolor or pastel.

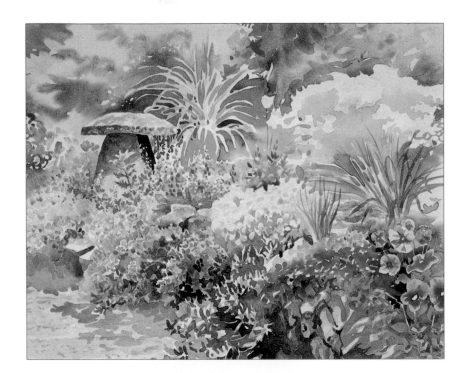

Wiltshire Garden

Hazel Soan • watercolor
A well-designed garden border contains contrasting hard- and soft-edged plants. The artist's job is to translate these variations into paint.

Detail and Edge Quality

ADD INTEREST TO YOUR PAINTING BY CONTRASTING HARD AND SOFT EDGES

IF YOU OBSERVE PLANTS and foliage carefully, you will notice that they vary in the quality of their edges. By "edges," we mean the boundaries of the form – the outline of a flower or leaf, or the contours of a tree. Gardeners, who are also artists in their way, will know not only about the colors of plants and flowers, but also about hard and soft edges, and will use such contrasts to advantage, juxtaposing hard-edged plants with the softer, more amorphous shapes of certain flowers. The artist can learn from the talented gardener. You don't need to know the names of the plants, as he or she certainly will, but you need to be aware of their characteristics in order both to describe them and to add interest to your painting.

Masking for crisp edges *Masking fluid is a useful aid in watercolor work, as you can keep certain areas white and clean. It is perfect for these hard-edged white clematis flowers. With the fluid removed, the edges are crisp and clear, and the darker tones used for the foliage enhance this clarity.*

1•Speeding up drying

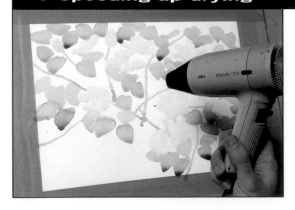

▲ *The masking fluid must be fully dry before the paint is applied. A hairdryer speeds up the drying process.*

2•Removal of masking fluid

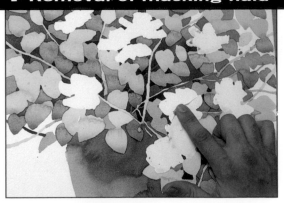

▲ *Once the background leaves are dry, the masking fluid is removed by rubbing it gently with a clean, dry finger.*

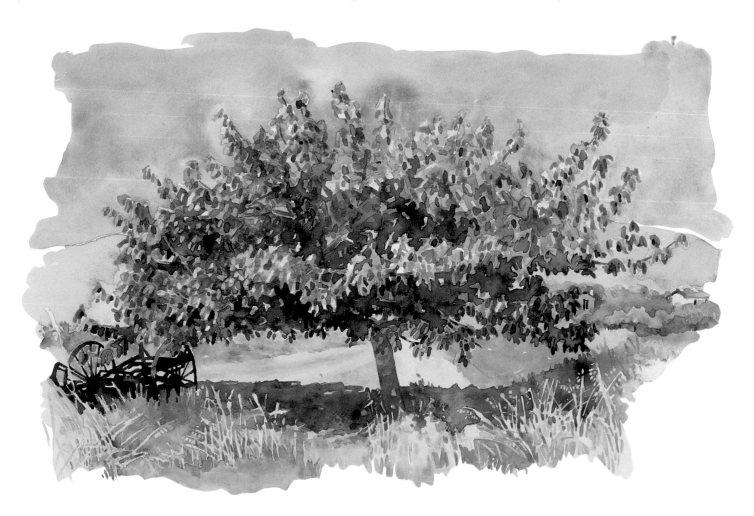

Using lost and found edges Judging edge quality has everything to do with observation. If you look carefully first at bushes, grasses or flowers in the foreground and then at those in the middle distance, you will notice immediately that the edges are sharpest and clearest where they are closest to you. As objects recede from you, the edges lose definition and become softer and more blurred.

But not everything in the foreground will have crisp edges; you will find there are dramatic variations caused not only by the differences in plant types but also by contrasts in color, the effect of light, and the background. Sometimes you will see that the boundary of a flower is not consistently hard or soft. One side of it may merge gently into shadow while the other stands out crisp and clear.

Peach Tree in the Rhône Valley

Moira Clinch • watercolor

Working wet-on-dry and from light to dark in watercolor allows you to create crisp edges by painting darker tones around lighter ones. You can see this effect in the foreground grasses and in the tree, where darker greens shape the yellowing leaves.

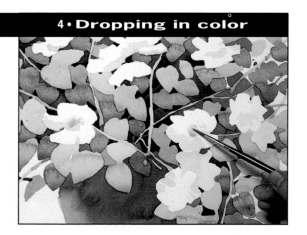

3 • "Finding" an edge	4 • Dropping in color

▲ *The artist "finds" the boundary between the two flowers by painting in the gray shadow on the flower behind.*

▲ *For the soft yellow centers, the area is dampened with clean water and the color dropped in with the tip of the brush.*

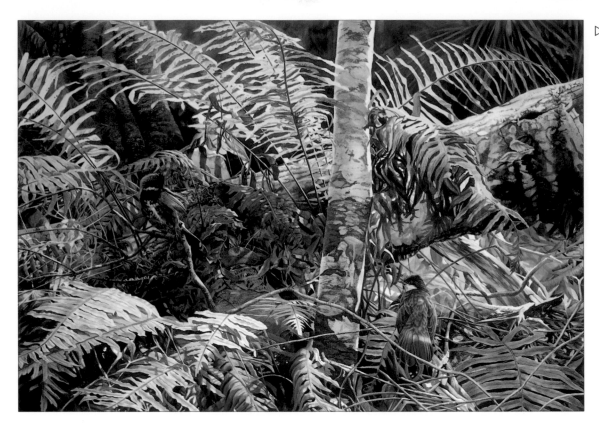

▷ **Path to Heligan, Mevagissey**

Don Austen • oil

This painting, done mainly with painting knives, shows how edge qualities can be built up with the medium itself. The crispness of the sunlit leaves in the center derives in part from strong tonal contrasts, but on the right and left of the painting, where there is almost no variation in tone, the forms of the leaves and tree trunks are created by the way the ridges of thick paint catch the light.

Coach Whips

James Luck • watercolor

Notice how the artist controls the edges of the ferns and undergrowth where the two birds hide. If you run your eye down the outline of the birch trunk, you can see how the edge is alternately lost and found through contrasts in tone and color between the trunk and the background.

These "lost" and "found" edges, as they are known, are important in painting, as they help to give your work variety as well as realism. In landscape painting, where there are often certain repeated features – trees, flowers expanses of grass, and so on, which can become monotonous – you can introduce an element of excitement by varying the outline. If you look at a single flower against darker foliage or a background wall, the outline will be clear and sharp where there is a strong contrast of tone – this is a found edge. If you look at a mass of pale flowers, many of the edges will merge into one another, and hence be lost. A painting of such a subject would rely on "finding" an edge here and there so that the eye registers this and "reads" the lost edges on the basis of that information.

How to describe edge quality Recognizing this illusive edge quality – whether it is soft or hard, lost or found – is an important step toward being able to capture the character of your subject with a few easy strokes of the brush. Some flowers and leaves are obviously hard-edged, and by describing these outlines you are at least halfway to describing the plant. An obvious example is a palm tree, which has leaves with sharp, linear edges. Garden plants with hard-edged leaves include daffodils, irises, rhododendrons, and waterlilies, while softer edges are found on leaves which are hairy, such as poppies. Flowers, too, vary in the quality of their outline. Waxy flowers like lilies have crisper edges than soft fluffy ones such as mimosa.

The size of the leaves or flowers also affects the way you perceive the edges. A box hedge, for instance, is made up of many tiny, hard-edged, waxy leaves; but because you can't see them individually, the hedge will have a stippled appearance. In the same way, tiny flowers on one stem may appear lacy or even as a vague mist of color spread over the greenery, even from quite close.

How to find lost edges There can be a problem when edges become altogether too lost, perhaps because there is not enough light-dark contrast or colors are too similar, so that the whole area becomes confused and difficult to read. Dark plants seen against a dark bank of trees, for example, will lose their contours and will read only as a deep green area.

There are various ways to overcome this problem. You could exaggerate the contrast between the tones, or you could introduce a subtle variation in the color if you want to

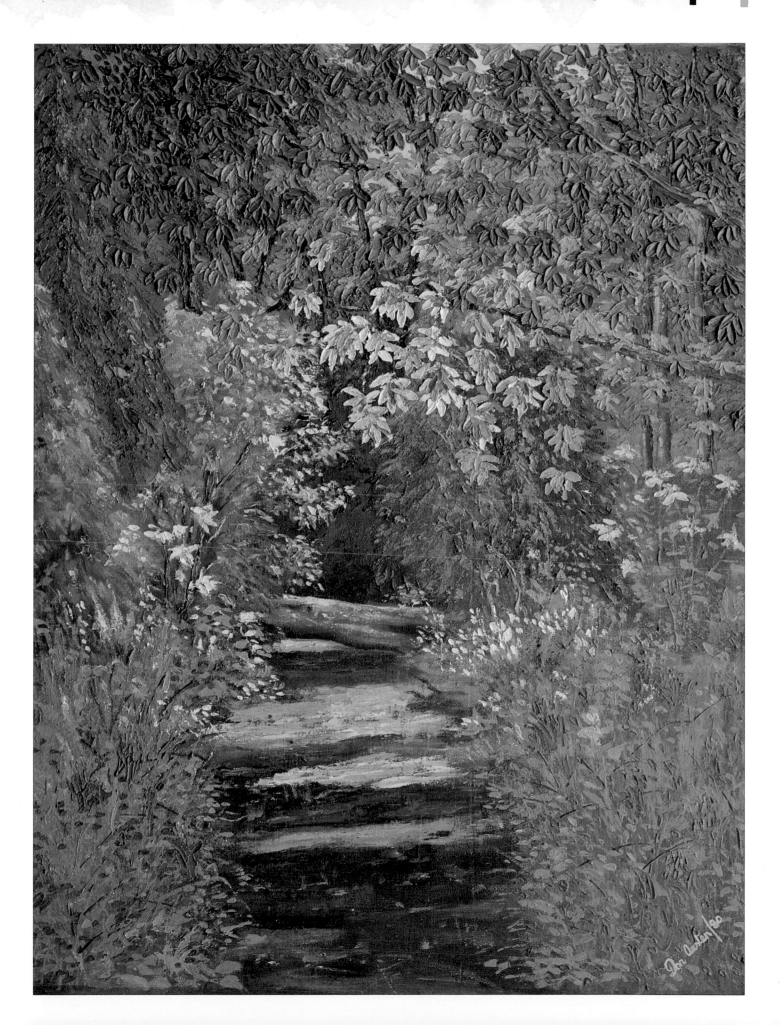

Impasto edges *These lilies are given three-dimensional form with thick impasto acrylic paint applied first with a brush and then with a small painting knife. The buildup of paint along the edges emphasizes the boundaries of the flowers and leaves.*

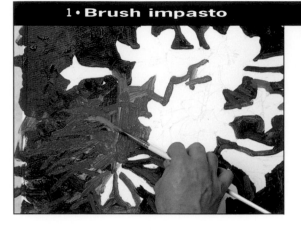

1•Brush impasto

2•Wet-in-wet impasto

▲ *Having sketched in the composition of lilies, the artist paints the dark background leaves with a round bristle brush. The contrast between the greens is very small, but the brushstrokes of thick paint define the forms.*

▲ *To create the flower buds, the brush is loaded with plenty of pink paint and the forms filled in, impressing the pink into the wet green below. The brushstrokes are bold, leaving an edge of pink which defines the form.*

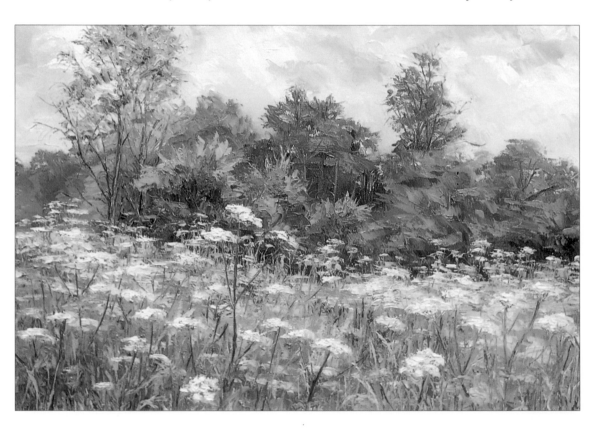

Hogweed

Brian Bennett • oil
The flowerheads are built up with a succession of tiny brushstrokes of thick paint in a semi-stippling technique to emphasize their texture. As it is not a bright day, tonal contrasts are not strong and the edges are soft except where the flowers are seen against the dark foliage of the middle ground.

keep the tones equal. Another method is to leave the ambiguous boundary unpainted, allowing some of the canvas or paper to show through along the edge of the plant or tree to give a subtle emphasis to the contours.

If you are using opaque paints such as oils or acrylics, which can be applied thickly, you can leave visible brushstrokes to sharpen and emphasize the contours, following the boundary with the brushstroke or building up the paint in an impasto "edge."

The effects of light Bright noontime summer sunlight will create very strong tonal contrasts – areas of dark shadow and bright highlights. This has the effect of making edges appear sharper. On a cloudy or overcast day, on the other hand, all the contrasts are reduced and edges appear softer.

You can experiment with the effects of such tonal contrasts by painting two blocks of black and white next to each other, then two blocks of gray. You will see that where the

3 • Knife impasto

4 • Emphasizing edges

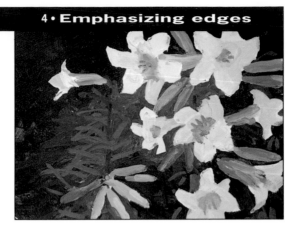

▲ *The waxy, hard-edged white parts of the petals are filled in with a small painting knife. The body of the knife has been used to cover the area, and the tip now guides the paint along the edge.*

▲ *The hard edges of the lilies are crisply defined by the impasto, while in the background, a more subtle buildup of paint hints at more ambiguous edges, with touches of thick paint catching the light.*

black meets the white, the edge will appear very sharp, while the boundary between the grays is softer – yet the edge itself is exactly the same. Sometimes you may have to increase tonal contrasts in a painting; for example, soft white mists of tiny baby's breath flowers will come into focus if painted against a dark holly hedge. On other occasions you may need to decrease them – very sharp-edged boundaries between a very light and very dark color can create a jumpy effect and may need to be softened a bit.

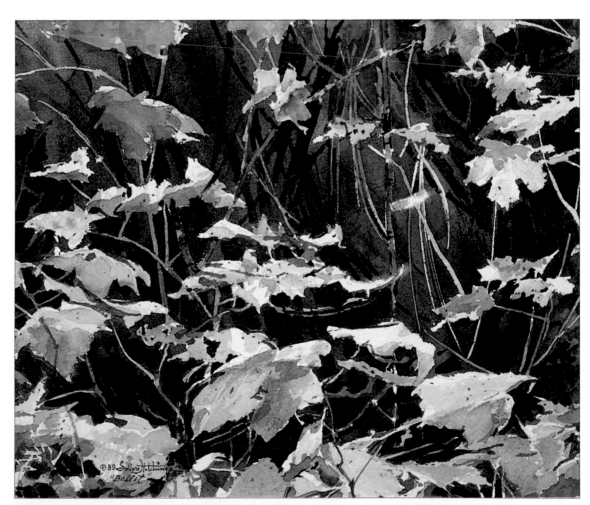

Ballet

LaVere Hutchings • watercolor
Catching the bright sunlight, these leaves contrast strongly with the dark background so that they appear almost to dance in mid-air – hence the title. Such extreme tonal contrasts make edges appear sharper.

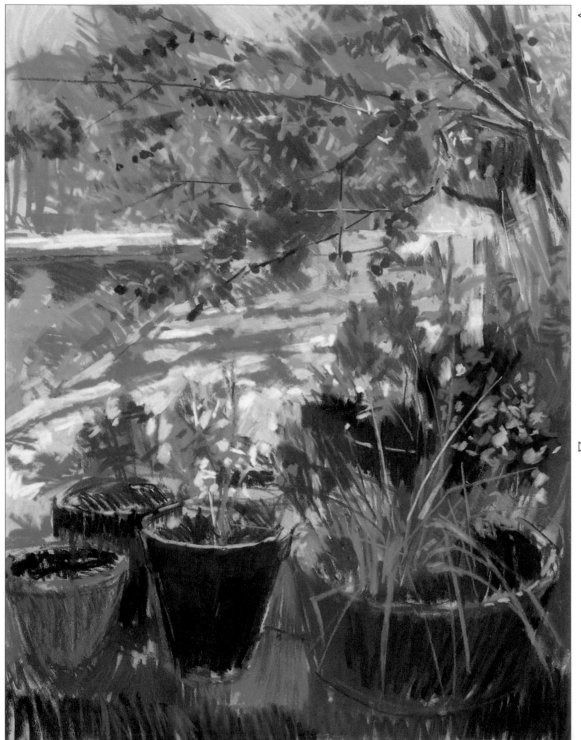

◁ **Flower Pots and Apricots**

David Napp • pastel

The definition of the grasses is surprisingly crisp and clear. Pastel is often thought of as a medium with which you can't achieve fine lines, but you can if you break a stick in half and draw with the broken edge. Alternatively, you can sharpen the end of the stick with a blade.

▷ **Sunflowers at Bonnieux, Provence**

Lionel Aggett • pastel

The foreground sunflowers form an interesting pattern of color and line, yet the boundaries of the flowers and leaves are not expressed through a linear outline but through a meeting of color and tone.

It is often tempting to use a small brush to "draw" in the outlines of the trees and flowers in your painting, but this is not usually a good idea. Uniform hard-edged outlines will give a flat and stilted impression, and exaggerating linear, two-dimensional qualities will prevent you from building up the impression of three-dimensional form – a hard line around anything immediately flattens it. Some artists do successfully exploit linearity as a style and carry this element right through their paintings, but as a beginner, you should try to avoid line as much as possible.

Make an underdrawing Most artists begin by making a drawing on their working surface, perhaps a careful pencil drawing in preparation for a watercolor painting, or a charcoal or brush-and-paint drawing on canvas for oil or acrylic. There is nothing wrong with drawing

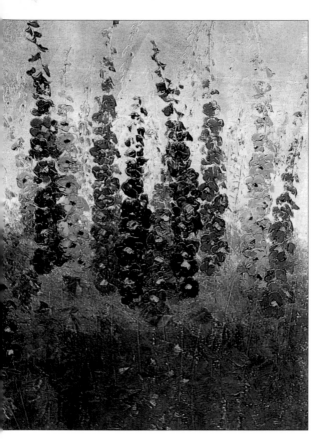

◁ **Delphiniums**

Sandra Johnson • oil on paper

In oil painting, it can be difficult to make very fine lines with a brush. A useful technique, which has been used for the foreground stems and edges of the flowers here, is to "etch" into the paint with the wooden end of your brush, the tip of a painting knife, or even your fingernail. This method, known as sgraffito, *can delineate forms and details either subtly or precisely.*

outlines at this stage – indeed you must. The underdrawing will give you confidence in the outlines, and once you have established the linear framework, you will be free to view these contours as a meeting of different colors and tones.

A potential problem One thing to remember is that you will have a problem painting sharp edges if you are working on a heavily textured surface such as coarse canvas or rough water color paper, because the weave will naturally break up the brushmarks and blur the edges. With oils and acrylics, you can overcome this problem by building up the earlier layers of paint to provide a smoother surface.

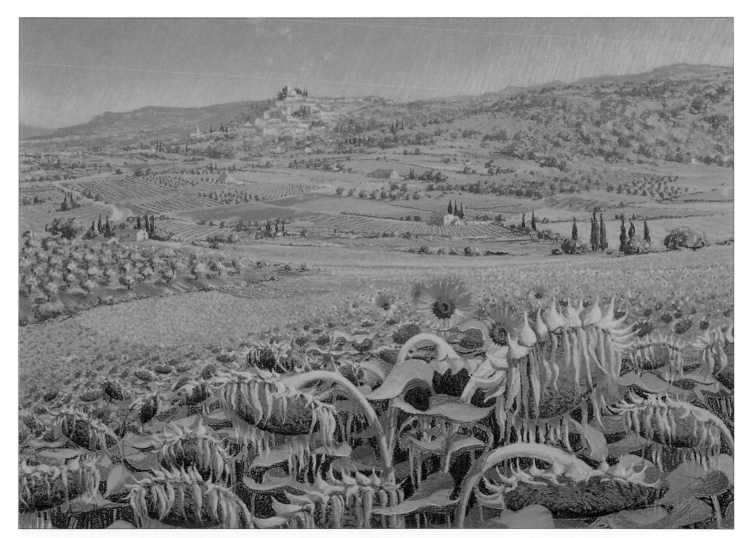

Fall in the North Woods
Doug Dawson • pastel

Pastel sticks can be broken to produce a variety of different marks and edge qualities. Notice the crisp directional strokes in the foreground.

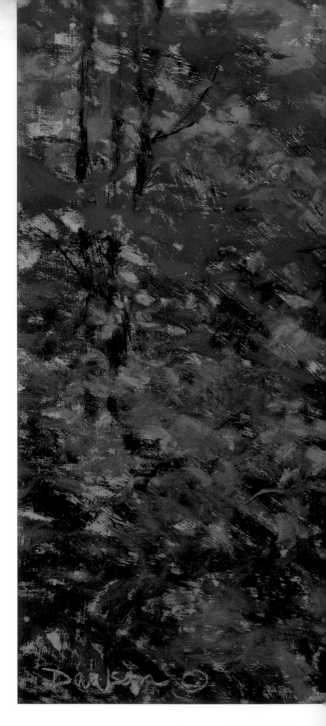

Detail and Edge Quality

LET THE SHAPE AND SIZE OF THE BRUSH MAKE DIFFERENT LEAF SHAPES

LEAVES, WHETHER THOSE OF trees, shrubs, plants, or flowers, are a dominant feature in most landscapes. In the foreground, leaf shapes are easily distinguishable one from another and play their part in identifying a tree, plant, or shrub, so it is not usually enough to paint in a formless mass of green and hope for the best. But, as has been seen earlier, it is seldom necessary to go to the other extreme and labor over reproducing each separate leaf. It is better to capture the shape and, most important, the color of the leaves with a few brushstrokes or pastel marks and perhaps pick out one or two for more detailed treatment.

Let your brushes help you So how can this be done? As far as leaf shape goes, your best allies are your paintbrushes. Whether you work in watercolor, oil, or acrylic, brushes come in different shapes and sizes, and each shape produces a different mark. If you find you paint mainly with one brush, it might be worth exploring a few others. Use a flat brush for hard-edged, long leaves such as irises and daffodils. You will find that dabbing with a round brush naturally produces the shape of many plant and shrub leaves. A filbert is especially useful, as it can be used both on the flat, mak-

Using the right brush
Picking the right brush for the job is often half the battle in painting, as you can sometimes describe a leaf with one brushstroke. In this watercolor, a long-haired round brush, soft and flexible, is just right for outlining and then filling in the large, heart-shaped leaves.

1•Outlining leaf shapes

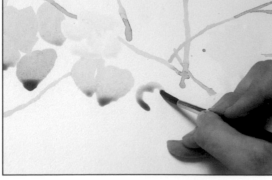

▲ *The artist first outlines the leaf, then fills in the center, allowing the paint to flood across.*

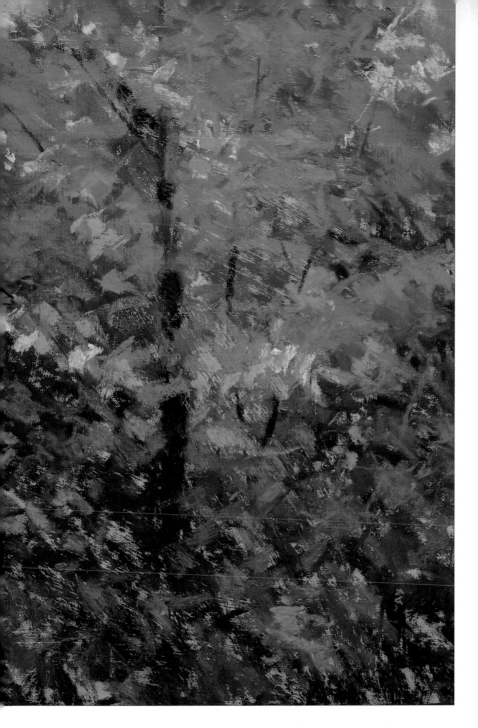

ing a slightly tapered blob, or on the side, which produces quite fine lines. Pastel marks, too, can be varied, by breaking the sticks into short lengths.

Analyze the shapes and colors There are so many different kinds of leaves, all with their own shapes and outlines, so don't be fooled into thinking you can generalize with an overall leaf shape. Variations in shape are probably the first thing you will notice, particularly in the foreground, where you can see everything clearly, but the color differences are equally dramatic. In the fall especially, they seem to borrow from most of the colors of the rainbow, but even in summer you will see colors ranging from purplish-red to blue-green and almost yellow. Leaves are rarely just green, and because of the natural fall of light, they are rarely all of one tone. Shrubs can often be painted with layers of similar dabs of paint, working from light to dark in watercolor, and vice versa with the opaque media (oils, acrylics, and gouache). Try building up a background wash of overlaid greens and then superimposing leaf shapes with dabs of the brush breaking through the outline in places.

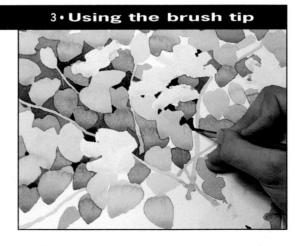

2 • **Building-up paint**	3 • **Using the brush tip**

▲ *Medium-toned leaves are added deftly around the dry lighter ones. Paint buildup adds color variation to the leaf.*

▲ *The tip of the brush is used for the small, complicated shapes of the darker leaves glimpsed behind.*

Adding an oil glaze

A canopy of leaves with the light shining through creates delicate colors for which glazing techniques are ideal. Here oil is glazed over acrylic, but you can create a similar effect by using acrylic for both underpainting and glazes.

1 • Acrylic underpainting

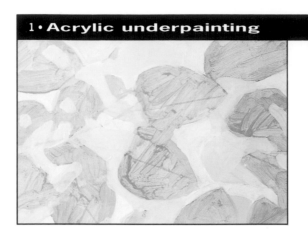

▲ *The leaves are reduced to two tones of green, with the paint used thinly and the brushstrokes suggesting the visible skeleton of the leaves.*

2 • Laying the oil glaze

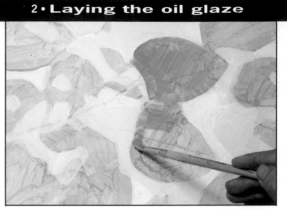

▲ *An oil glaze made from a mixture of sap green and cadmium yellow thinned with glazing medium is laid over the dry underpainting, modifying the darker tones.*

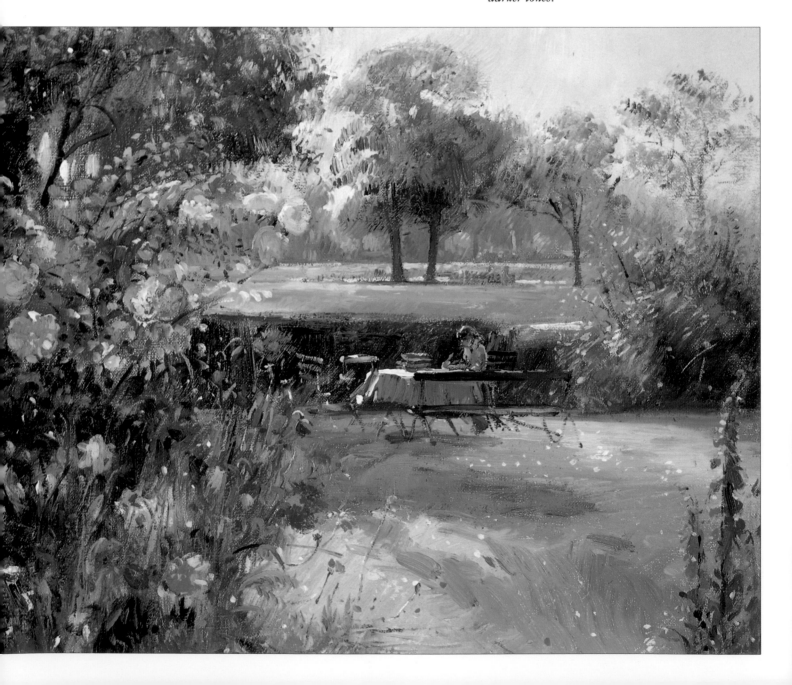

3 • Building up glazes

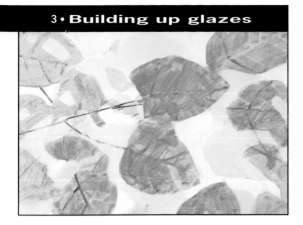

▲ *For richness and depth of color, you can build up layers of glazes, as soon as the previous one is dry to the touch.*

Light and movement The other thing you will notice once you start looking at leaves is how the light affects them. Some leaves, like those of the holly or laurel, are shiny and reflect the light, creating strong highlights. Others are matte and soft-edged, producing narrower contrasts. An example of this kind of leaf is the acer, which is also thin and veiny, allowing the light to shine through.

If you look up at a canopy of leaves in the woods, you will see many variations in color and tone, caused not only by the different tree types, but also by the relative density of the leaves and whether they are deeply layered or seen singly against the sky. You could try capturing the effect of sunlight shining through a canopy of leaves in layers of transparent watercolor washes. Similar effects can be achieved with transparent glazes of oil or acrylic color thinned down with a glazing medium (or plain water for acrylic).

Movement, too, affects leaf color. Some trees, like the eucalyptus and willow, have silvery undersides which, when blown by the wind, catch the light in a flurry of white flashes. Recording such characteristics will give your work authenticity.

The Morning Letter

Timothy Easton • oil

This painting pulsates with light and movement created by the energetic and varied brushwork and the dashes of pure color which lead the eye into and around the picture.

Glazing with watercolors *You can glaze with watercolors, too, using transparent colors such as earth colors and the cadmiums. Always start with the paler color and make sure the first color is dry before proceeding to the next.*

1 • From light to dark

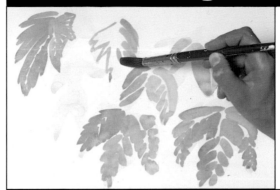

◀ *The maple leaves are first mapped out with a diluted wash of cadmium yellow. Once dry, further washes of diluted Venetian red are laid over the yellow.*

2 • Building up color

▶ *To give an impression of light shining through the leaf membrane, more concentrated combinations of Venetian red and burnt umber are glazed lightly on top.*

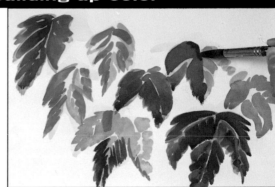

Capturing leaf movement *Only by close observation can you learn to recognize the shapes leaves can make as they are stirred by the wind and altered by the play of light. Capturing these shapes is the key to describing movement.*

Pattern and light

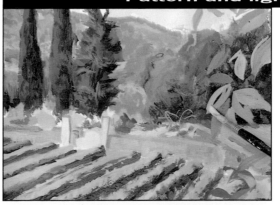

◀ *The shape and color of these olive leaves makes them instantly recognizable, but a more important element is the dancing pattern they make and the fall of light on their silvery undersides.*

Detail and Edge Quality

CAPTURING THE PLAY OF LIGHT ON FLOWERS IS AN IRRESISTIBLE CHALLENGE

IT IS EASY TO see why flowers are such a popular painting subject. A garden in full bloom, a field full of daisies and other wildflowers, or a single rose outlined against the sky lift the spirits of artists and non-artists alike. Painting flowers successfully, however, is not easy. When they are seen in the distance, they can be represented quite broadly, but when they are the foreground or main subject of a painting, you will need to think about how best to show them without losing the feeling of freshness which is the essence of flowers. On these pages we look at some useful techniques.

Watercolor The pure translucency of watercolors makes them ideal for flower painting, but you must plan before you paint. Start by mapping out the highlights that need to be "reserved" as white paper. If you need to reserve definite small shapes for flowerheads among greenery, you will find masking fluid helpful. First paint the shapes of the flower heads with masking fluid, let it dry, and then paint the foliage as you wish. Once the paint is dry, gently rub off the dried fluid with a plastic eraser or your finger, and you will have a clear, precise, white shape.

Capturing the play of light on flowers is a challenge for any artist. Delicate overlapping washes can produce the effects of light shining on and through petals, and so can working wet-in-wet, allowing one color to spread into another so that there are no hard edges.

This method is also very useful for multicolored flowers and those with a darker color at the center. In the latter case, paint the paler color, allow it to dry, and then re-wet the area where the darker color is to be, using a clean, wet brush. Quickly touch the center of the area with a brush loaded with the darker color, and it will spread out in the dampened area only.

Gouache The brilliance of gouache pigments combines with the velvety quality of these paints to make them particularly suitable for

Controlling wet-in-wet *Watercolor is hard to control when you are working wet-in-wet over a large area, but here it is confined to a small one. The first wash is allowed to dry and parts of it re-wetted before darker color is dropped in with a brush.*

1 • Finding medium tones	2 • Working wet-in-wet
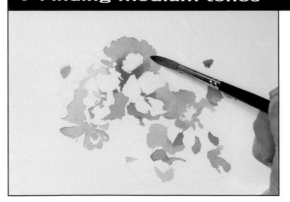	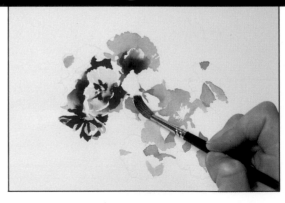
▲ Having carefully sketched the outlines of the geranium flowers, the artist fills in the medium tones with small, intricately shaped washes of diluted rose madder.	▲ Once the first layer is quite dry, a brush is dipped in clean water to wet the area that needs to be darkened by working wet-in-wet.

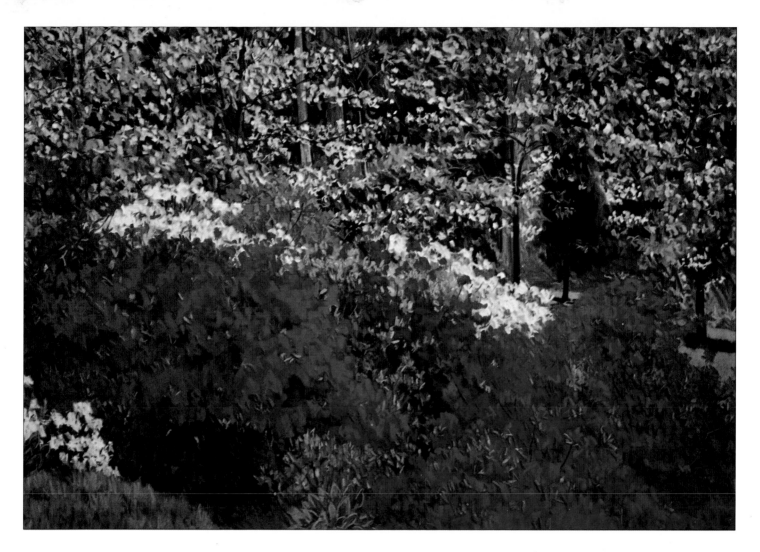

flower painting. Use the paint diluted for delicate passages and thicker where flowers catch the light and look more solid. Because gouache is opaque, you can add highlights last, but take care not to overwork, as each new layer of color can "melt" the one below.

3 • Dropping in the color

▲ *The tip of the brush is dipped into a darker mix of rose madder and alizarin crimson and touched into the wet center of the flower. The color radiates out from that point.*

Oils and acrylics Both these media can be used very thickly – the term for thick paint is impasto. This adds a new dimension to flower painting, as the edge of a petal can be described with an impasto edge of paint. Try adding touches of impasto either with your brush or a painting knife. More delicate effects can be built up with transparent glazes.

Pastels When you open a box of pastels, the range of temptingly brilliant colors and delicate pale tints immediately suggests flower painting. Pastels are highly versatile, as you can use them on their sides for broad areas of color and make fine, crisp lines with the tips. They can also produce all the variety of textures required, from smooth and velvety to soft and fuzzy. Try blending the colors together with your finger for the centers of flowers, and defining the edges with firm, linear strokes. You might also try oil pastels, which can be spread with mineral spirits or turpentine to form washes of color.

Azaleas and Dogwoods on Glen Echo Trail

Elsie Dinsmore Popkin • pastel

The vibrant colors of these azaleas are well expressed in pastel, which is a lovely medium for flowers. The different tones are integrated, yet kept fresh with clean, decisive marks.

Contrast and Color

EXPLORE THE EFFECTS OF BRIGHT AND DULL WEATHER, WORKING IN AS MANY LIGHTS AS POSSIBLE

Behind Closed Doors

Hazel Soan • watercolor

With medium-bright sunlight, the light/dark contrast is noticeable, but not extreme. The shadow cast across the doorway is important to the composition.

IF YOU ARE USED to painting outdoors, you will know how important light can be. When you are halfway through a landscape and the sun goes in, everything changes – the shadows disappear, the contrasts are diminished, and the colors lose their sparkle. But this doesn't mean you must always work in bright sunlight; although it sets up contrasts which produce extremes of color and tone, it also loses subtleties. Some artists find a narrower range of tones more interesting to paint and seek out overcast days to explore these particular effects.

When you first start painting, you need to try working in as many different lights as you can. The quality of the light varies not only according to whether it is sunny or overcast,

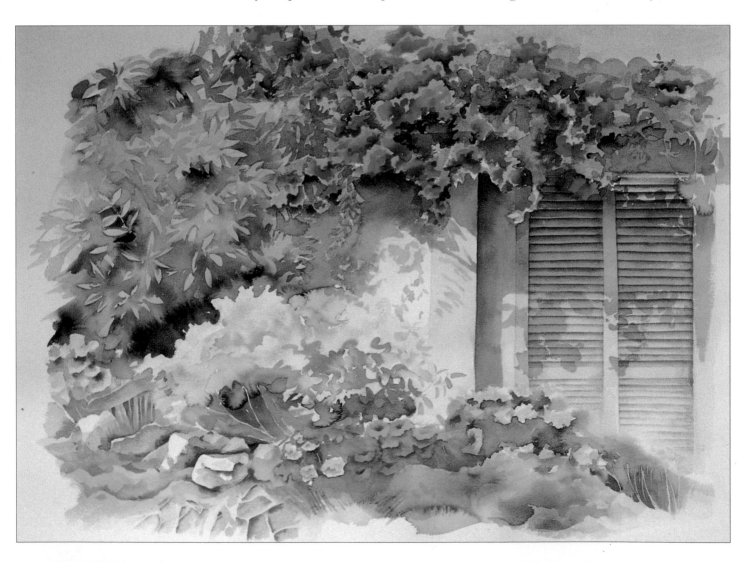

but also according to the time of day, the season, and where you are in the world. Try to capture the soft, yellow, raking light of a summer's evening or the pale pink, misty light of the early morning. It can be interesting also to paint the same landscape under different lights or even in different seasons.

Light and the composition Shapes, whether of trees and shrubs or fields and hills, are "modeled" by the way the light falls on them, creating dark and light areas. But light plays an equally important role in composition. You have probably noticed that as the sun moves around during the day, something that you saw very clearly when you began to work gradually disappears, and some other landscape feature comes into prominence.

When you first study a landscape scene, if the sun is out, establish its direction. This will help you plot the shadows and highlights. The strength of the light will determine whether the shadows are dark and well-defined or less intense and soft-edged. In the mornings and evenings, the sun is low in the sky and not so strong. Contrasts are in general narrower and shadows longer.

In the majority of landscapes the light comes from one side or the other, thus casting shadows on the opposite side and highlighting the near side of all forms. Such shadows can play an important part in composition, as they form an extra element. Light coming from behind you casts shadows away from you into the distance so that they play a less obvious part. If the light comes from in front of you, at the back of the composition, shadows are cast forward across the foreground, and if the light is strong, features such as trees will be silhouetted. Backlighting can create magical effects and is worth experimenting with.

Controlling shadows It is very easy to get carried away by painting shadows, making them too strong and dark. If you can, it is better to

Colorful shadows *Shadows are rarely just a single flat color, and even more rarely just gray. They are a mixture of the complementary color of the prevailing light and the color of the surface onto which the shadows are cast, sometimes with reflected color as well. Here, these subtle mixtures are created by means of superimposed washes of watercolor.*

1•The color of the light

◄ *The prevailing light is a golden yellow, and the composition is mapped out with diluted cadmium yellow, yellow ocher, Hooker's green, and cobalt blue.*

2•Colored shadows

▶ *The complementary of the golden light is a deep earthy purple, made by mixing Prussian blue and alizarin crimson. This color is modified by those beneath.*

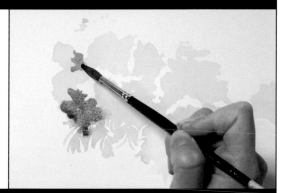

3•Paint accumulation

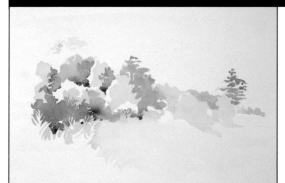

◄ *The board is propped up at a slight angle so that the paint runs down, creating an accumulation of color at the bottom of each area.*

4•Raking shadows

▶ *The purple mixture is again used for the long shadows created by the raking light, but the color appears different to the tree shadows, as it has been laid over yellow.*

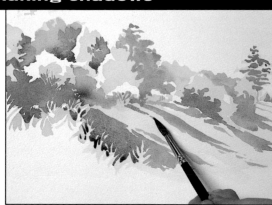

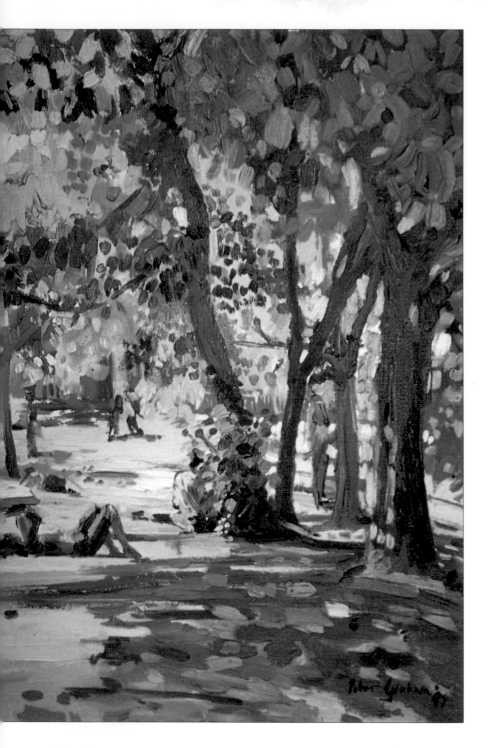

Indian Summer

Peter Graham • oil

Bold strokes of pure color combine optically to create the effect of these sun-dappled tree shadows.

▷ **Gubbio**

Jane Strother • acrylic

Bright sunlight creates sharp contrasts. Notice how the reflected color of the green leaves of the foreground tree has been worked into the shadow cast on the ground, as has its complementary color, red.

build them up gradually layer by layer, superimposing different-colored washes, brushstrokes, or pastel marks so that the shadows are a subtle mix of colors. If possible, work on all shadows in the same area of the painting at the same time so that they develop consistently.

Cast shadows are very rarely just gray; they will always contain some of the color of the ground or object onto which they are cast. Sometimes you will see touches of the color's complementary (its opposite) in either a cast shadow or the dark (shadowed) side of an object. If you are painting the shadow cast by a

tree onto grass, this will mean adding reds to darken greens (these two colors are complementaries). Try stippling them together or superimposing glazes of pure color, allowing the colors to mix optically. Dashes of reflected color from the object which casts the shadow will help to make your shadows sing.

Diminishing contrasts It has already been mentioned that the tone and color contrasts are stronger in the foreground than in the distance. This decrease is true whatever kind of light you are working in – it is just more noticeable when the sun is bright, so that the contrasts in the foreground are at their most extreme. The effect of diminishing contrasts is known as atmospheric, or aerial, perspective and is caused by particles of dust in the atmosphere which form a kind of ever-thickening veil over the distance, but do not affect the foreground. When the light is very bright and clear, you may find it hard to perceive this effect. However, it is always there to some degree, and you need to be aware of it because you will not be able to create a sense of space in your painting if you use uniformly strong tonal contrasts.

A monochrome overview Art teachers often encourage their students to make tonal (i.e. monochrome) sketches of a scene before painting. You may wonder why, and ask yourself whether it's worth the trouble, but in fact it is,

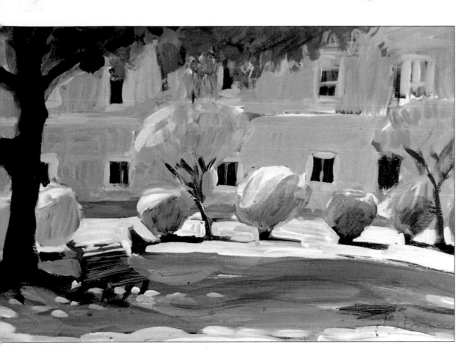

▽ **Honesty**

Brian Bennett • oil

The mist emphasizes the diminishing contrasts over distance, with the silhouetted tree and bee balm almost black and white in the foreground.

because it can provide you with a lot of constructive information.

For a start, you can study the fall of light and the consequent interplay of tonal values without worrying about color. This allows you to check in advance that the composition is tonally balanced – that there are no overbearing blocks of dark or light which upset the natural harmony of the painting. You can also check that your highlights are as bright as your shadows are dark, that there is tonal equality.

The tonal study is also useful if you find your colors getting muddled later on, and even more important, it can provide a visual reference to help you finish a painting which might otherwise have to be abandoned because of changing light.

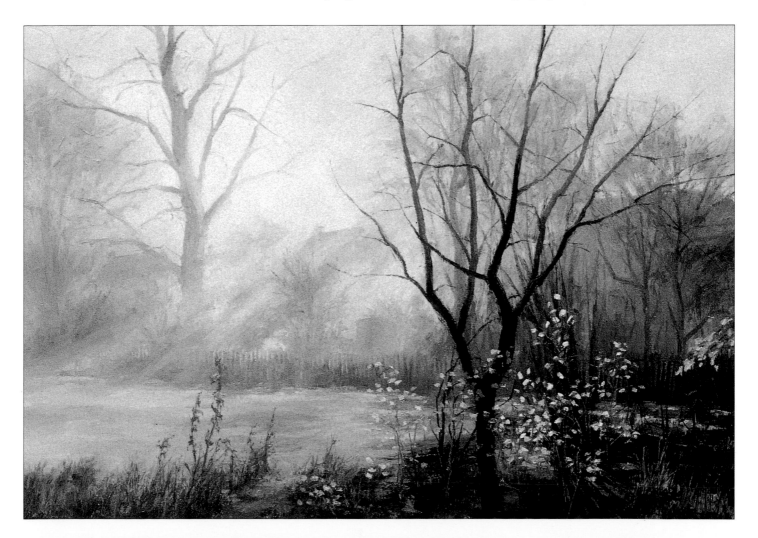

Contrast and Color

Colors are the "Words" in the Visual Language of Self-Expression

West Malvern Spring

Paul Powis • pastel

Be inventive in your choice of colors. At first sight, these colors appear quite simple and naturalistic, but there are also strategically placed dashes of pure color.

LEARNING ABOUT COLOR IS often compared to learning the vocabulary of a language. Colors, like words, will enable you to express yourself and describe objects either accurately or in a more personal way. The more you learn about colors and how they behave, the more assured your painting will be.

There are three separate aspects to learning about color, the first being the purely practical one of discovering the differences between pigments – how they handle, and how strong or weak they are. This is largely a matter of experience, but you will quickly find out that individual pigments have different properties – whether you are concerned with oils, acrylics, gouache, watercolor, or pastels. Some are more transparent than others; some are thick or grainy; some are very powerful; and some are relatively weak.

The second skill you must acquire is that of mixing the right colors for the subject, and this will only come with practice. There are so many colors in nature that it would not be possible to suggest mixtures for everything.

Finally, and perhaps most important of all, you will have to learn how colors react with each other, and how you can play on these relationships to create paintings which are more

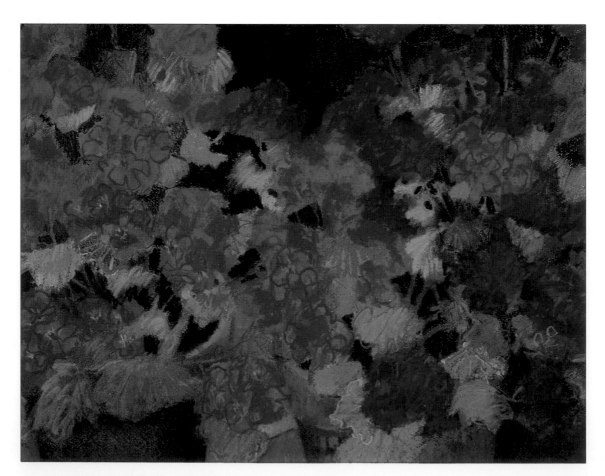

Full Bloom

Pat Pendleton • oil pastel

This pattern of glowing colors cannot fail to hold the attention. The pinks and reds of the geraniums are enhanced by the complementary greens, setting up a vibrant effect that makes the painting appear to pulsate with energy.

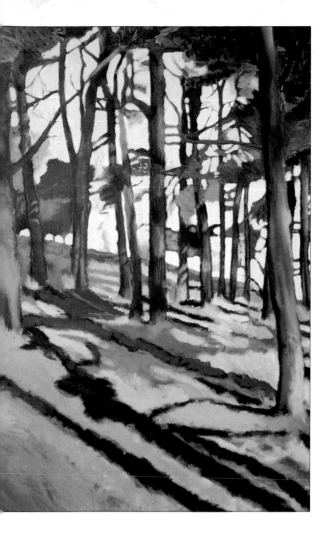

than just copies of nature. There are combinations of colors, for example, that are harmonious, and others that cause exciting or even disturbing effects.

Warm and cool colors We have already established that in general the colors in the foreground need to be stronger. They also need to be "warmer." Artists divide colors into two broad groups: the warm ones, which include the reds, oranges, and yellows and all colors leaning toward red, and the cool colors, which are those that lean toward blue. The warm colors tend to advance, that is, to come forward to the front of the picture, and the cool ones to recede, so if you use warmer colors in the foreground, you will "push" the middle ground and background away. The bias toward warmer colors can be very subtle; it may be simply a matter of yellowing a green or mixing a brown with a little red, but if you carry it through the foreground, it will both establish and unify this area.

If you find you have an ambiguous area in

Using warm and cool colors *If you can learn to be conscious of warm and cool colors as you paint, you will find it easier to define the different planes of your picture space. Warm colors – those which tend toward yellow and red – come forward, while cooler, bluer colors sink back. Here a good deal of blue has been used in the mixtures for the background greens.*

1 • Warmer foreground

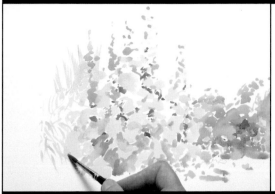

◀ *Using gouache, the artist begins with the foreground, building up the clumps of flowers with warm yellow-greens, oranges, and strong reds.*

2 • Middle-ground blue-greens

▶ *A cool, strong green made from a mixture of cobalt blue and viridian is "cut around" the lighter, warmer colors with the point of a Chinese brush.*

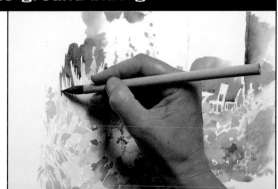

3 • Finding cooler versions

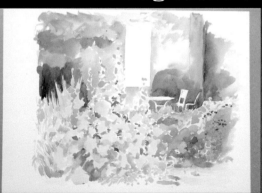

◀ *Rather than mixing to cool the colors, the artist has used a different version of yellow – yellow ocher – for the walls of the house.*

4 • Cooler background

▶ *The window provides a focus for the eye, but the colors are kept cool, as are those used for the foliage at the side of the house – pale mixes of lemon yellow and Prussian blue.*

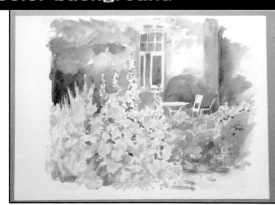

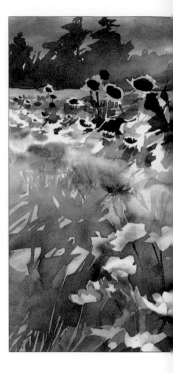

the picture, hovering between foreground and middle ground, you can anchor it in the foreground with color. Dot a grassy bank with yellow flowers, for example, and it will bring it into the foreground.

Keep your colors fresh Your foreground colors will appear brighter and more lively if you take care with your mixing. You can occasionally use colors "straight from the tube," but usually you will be mixing, tinting (making colors lighter) or shading (making them darker). But try not to overmix; a good rule is to restrict yourself to a maximum of three colors, particularly in watercolor. And don't push them around the paper or canvas too much after you have applied them, as they will soon lose their vibrancy.

Another way of keeping the colors fresh is to "mix" them optically on the painting surface by placing small dots or patches of colors side by side. Viewed from a distance, the two colors will read as a third color. This method is much used by pastel artists, but is equally suitable for oil and acrylic.

Using broken color Colors which are built up with layers of paint are always more interesting than those which are laid on as flat color. Try building up layers of transparent watercolor or glazes of acrylic or oil paint. If you are using opaque paint, try working one color lightly over another so that some of the first color shows through – you can do the same in pastel, using the side of the stick to make a delicate veil of color over another one. Such techniques are well suited to the deep purples or fluorescent pinks of some flowers, which are notoriously hard to mix – indeed sometimes impossible.

Make your colors sing You may feel that you don't need to learn how colors react together. After all, you might say, when you paint a landscape you are surely just painting what is there. Yet if you study the paintings of the Impressionists, whose avowed aim was not only to paint from nature but also to paint exactly what they saw, you will be amazed how carefully they controlled their colors. When Monet (1840–1926) painted his series of haystacks in different lights, he juxtaposed colors for maximum effect – you can see small touches of pure orange and blue separated by areas of slightly muted complementaries.

Complementary colors – those opposite one another on the color circle (red-green, yellow-purple, blue-orange) create a kind of

Title not known

Elizabeth Apgar Smith • watercolor

Watercolors need to be planned carefully to avoid overworking colors. These flowers retain a freshness because the colors have been laid down cleanly, with no hesitation.

Texture and broken color *Colors are usually more exciting if they are built up in layers, with one color allowed to show through another. Try painting in acrylic over a brilliant underpainting, using the* sgraffito *and dry-brush techniques to create both texture and color effects.*

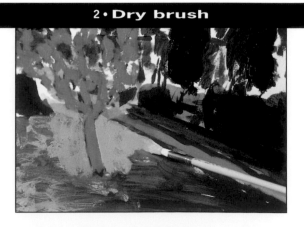

1•Sgraffito   2•Dry brush

▲ *The end of the brush has been used to scratch into the dark green paint. The bottom layer of paint must be dry, while the new color remains wet.*

▲ *Using a bristle brush dried on paper towels, a little undiluted green is scrubbed lightly over the red underpainting.*

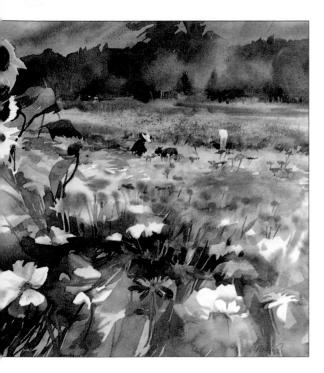

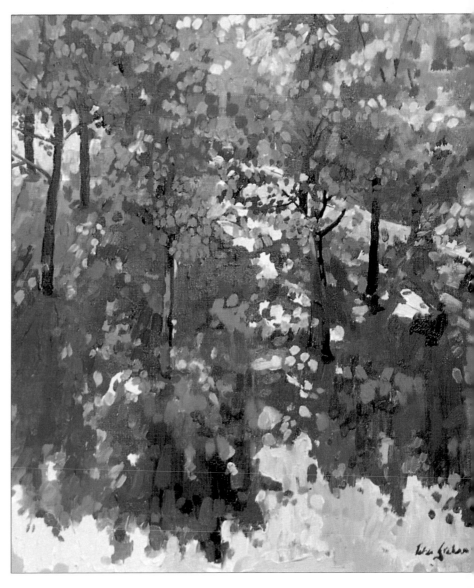

optical frisson when set against each other. This can be distracting and uncomfortable if the colors are full strength or if large areas are used, but if the complementaries are mixed with white, or if one is used at full strength against a toned-down version of its neutralized complementary, you can build up areas of wonderfully vibrant color.

You will probably have used complementaries without realizing it in landscape painting, as nature is rich in these contrasts. A field of poppies is one example, as are red geraniums and many other flowers – you may have noticed how some bright red flowers in strong sunlight appear to pulsate against their green leaves. When combining such complementaries in your painting, avoid overdoing it and spoiling the natural harmony – try placing patches of high-value red against a relatively neutral green.

Bluebell Wood

Peter Graham • oil

The pattern of light and color, and the wonderful rich blue of the flowers and shadows beneath the leaf canopy, have been built up with strokes of many different tones and colors of blue and yellow. Occasional touches of mauve – the complementary of yellow – are needed.

3 • Stippling

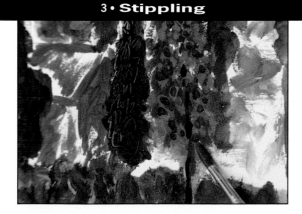

▲ *This small birch tree is created by a stippling method, with layers of colored dabs made with the tip of the brush, some applied wet-in-wet.*

4 • Building up shadows

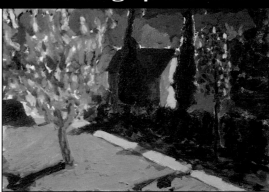

▲ *The shadows have been developed with touches of complementary colors – purples and yellows – giving a marvelous vibrancy.*

Scale and Proportion

REMEMBER THAT SCALE CAN AFFECT BOTH THE BALANCE AND MOOD OF THE PAINTING

not be very obvious, so neither will the divisions of your picture space. If, on the other hand, you include some flowers that dominate the foreground with their size, the contrast in scale between this and the background will be greater, and the effect more dramatic.

Cropping for effect It is well worth exploring the effects of cropping, which means allowing the top, bottom, or edges of your paper or can-

WHEN YOU ARE CONSIDERING a landscape view, it is not always easy to decide on the size you want to paint the major elements of the composition. If you have trees in the foreground, do you want them large and domineering, or small, giving a sense of infinite space? Perspective (see pages 86–87) can help you order the elements of the landscape – trees, hedges, flowers – in the picture space, but choosing the scale can be tricky. It is an important decision, however, affecting both balance and mood.

It is in the foreground plane that the scale of the painting is set. You could fill your foreground with a large-scale row of tall flowers, for example, and cut off the picture space at that point, making the foreground virtually the whole picture. But if you want to depict an illusion of space, you will need to consider the contrast between those elements in the foreground (which will be bigger) with those in the distance (which will be smaller). If you push the foreground away from you (it doesn't have to be physically close) and depict the nearest flowers as tiny specks, they will be even smaller in the middle ground and background, but the contrast between them will

Reynolds Gardens – Pink Cannas and Mexican Sage

Elsie Dinsmore Popkin • pastel

Painting these lilies so large has helped to express their voluptuous nature. Cropping them keeps them in the foreground and makes those in the center appear to burst forward.

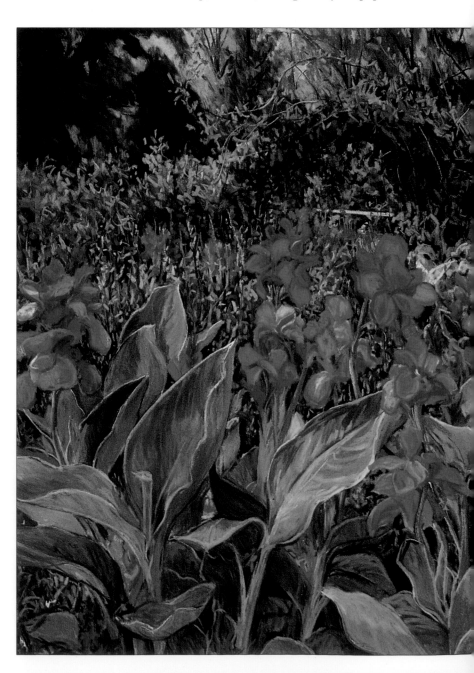

vas to cut across some foreground object, such as a tree or bush. This has the effect of exaggerating the size of this element by suggesting it is too large to fit into the painting. You will be able to see the effects of cropping if you use a viewing frame (see page 17).

Cropping with the frame is also a useful device for anchoring an element at the front of the picture plane. If you cut off a tree at the top, it will come forward into the same plane as the frame, effectively pushing back any uncropped landscape elements such as bushes in the middle distance. It is worth sketching your view before you paint it to discover the best way to do this, as cropping needs to be carefully handled – it can look as though you were just careless with your drawing and couldn't fit the whole tree in.

Another effect of cropping is that trees and flowers treated in this way can be reduced to semi-abstract shapes. If you crop a group of trees in the foreground top and bottom, these almost abstract shapes will frame the view visible between them. The eye tends to focus on what can be seen through these shapes – the view beyond.

Overlapping subjects By overlapping things, you immediately explain in visual terms that one object is behind another, and you also establish their relative scale. Place one clump of flowers in front of another, for example, and you are stating which are in the foreground. This is such an obvious device in establishing the foreground planes that its importance is often overlooked.

Sometimes you will have ambiguous situations where a tree in the foreground appears to be the same size as one in the middle ground, but if you overlap them, their positions will be clear. This may mean moving your viewpoint so that they overlap or extending the foliage for the same effect. You may need to exaggerate the overlapping edges, turning lost edges into found ones (see pages 23–27).

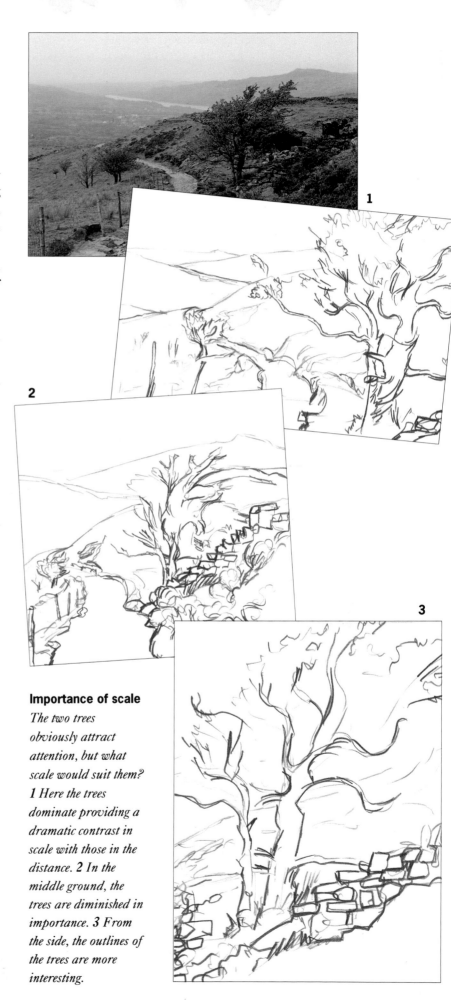

Importance of scale
The two trees obviously attract attention, but what scale would suit them? 1 Here the trees dominate providing a dramatic contrast in scale with those in the distance. 2 In the middle ground, the trees are diminished in importance. 3 From the side, the outlines of the trees are more interesting.

In the Field

FOREGROUND FLOWERS

BRIAN BENNETT HAS CHOSEN A high viewpoint for this landscape – he is looking over a valley from the vantage point of a hillside. This allows him to make the most of the foreground flowers, but his careful and sensitive treatment of the distant view and the middle ground (see pages 111 and 56–57) show that he sees these parts of the painting as equally important. Working fast in oils, he builds up the paint with various customized painting knives, creating a thick impasto relief on the surface. As you can see, these knives are capable of achieving considerable detail, but they nevertheless encourage an impressionistic treatment – a telling combination of edge, color, and texture.

Materials: canvas 24 x 18 in. (61 x 45.7cm); painting knives; oil paints; wooden palette. **Colors**: white, Mars yellow, chrome yellow, cadmium yellow, yellow ocher, burnt umber, indigo, cobalt blue, ultramarine, Winsor green, alizarin crimson, flesh tint (for clouds).

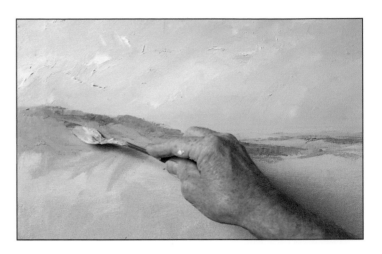

❶ *Having mapped out the painting, the artist starts from the top (see page 111), touching down the mix of color with the edge of the knife and then smoothing it out.*

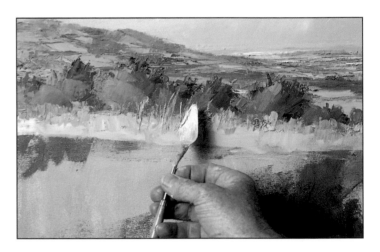

❷ *Now the middle-ground area is developed carefully (see pages 56–57), although much of it will be hidden by the foreground. The edge of the knife is used to create fine lines suggesting grasses.*

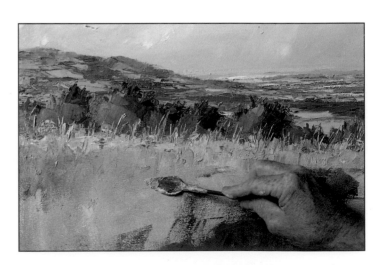

❸ *The foreground tones are now established, using greens mixed with indigo and chrome yellow. Touches of yellow ocher are added to lighten the mixture, and Winsor green to sharpen it.*

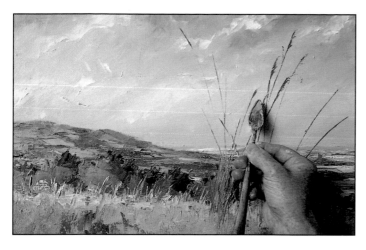

4 *With a clean stroke, the artist "draws" the blade of grass with the edge of the knife, creating a varied line by altering the pressure along the edge as he proceeds.*

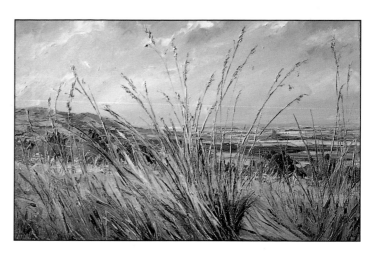

7 *At the end of each "stage," the artist stands back and assesses the painting. A break in the grass has now been developed to form a "tunnel" in the foreground, leading the eye into the distance.*

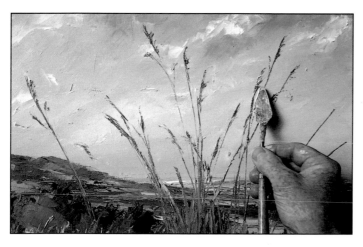

5 *Seed heads are added with delicate sideways strokes made with the tip of the knife, using superimposed mixes of yellow ocher, white, and burnt umber.*

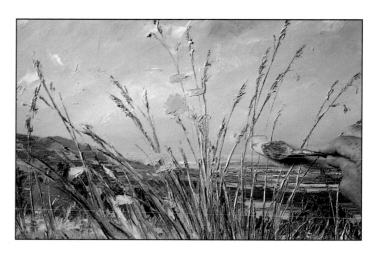

8 *A loose mix of chrome and cadmium yellow is used for the flowerheads. Some of the underlying paint has been scraped away so that the yellow does not mix into the blue and become diluted.*

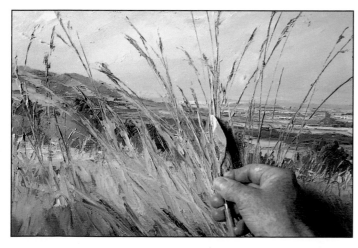

6 *A sense of depth and movement in the foreground grass is created by strong directional knifemarks and a thick buildup of paint.*

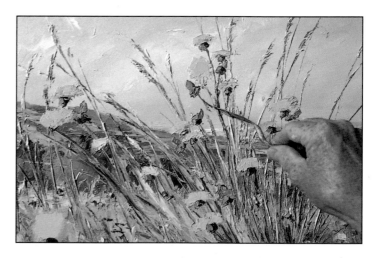

9 *The yellow flowerheads are built up further and a few buds added with pure Mars yellow.*

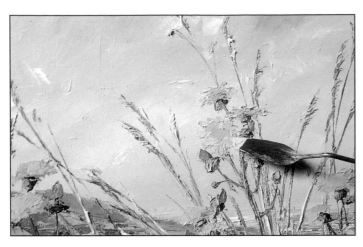

10 *The thick paint and tonal contrasts in the flowers make them stand out against the bright sky. Although yellow is a naturally light-toned color, the flowers are darker than the pale blue.*

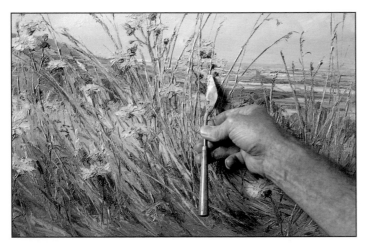

11 *To increase the sense of space, some grasses are painted over and in front of the flowerheads. Notice that the light sides of the grasses are lighter than the sky and the shadowed sides darker.*

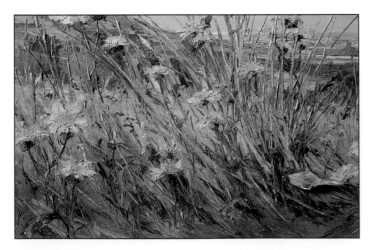

12 *The blue flowers are painted with a mix of indigo, alizarin crimson, ultramarine, and white, with texture created by using the tip of the knife and lifting off.*

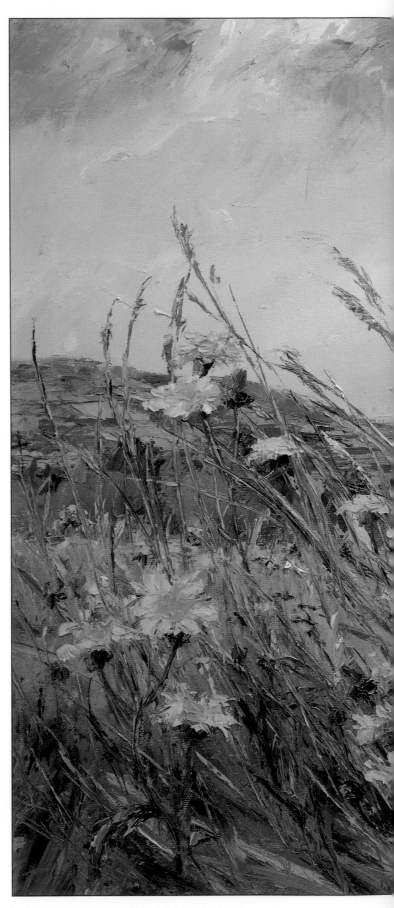

13 *The painting was completed in one sitting. Final touches were to dot white seedheads around the foreground and build the light grasses up further over the top, lighter against the darker greens.*

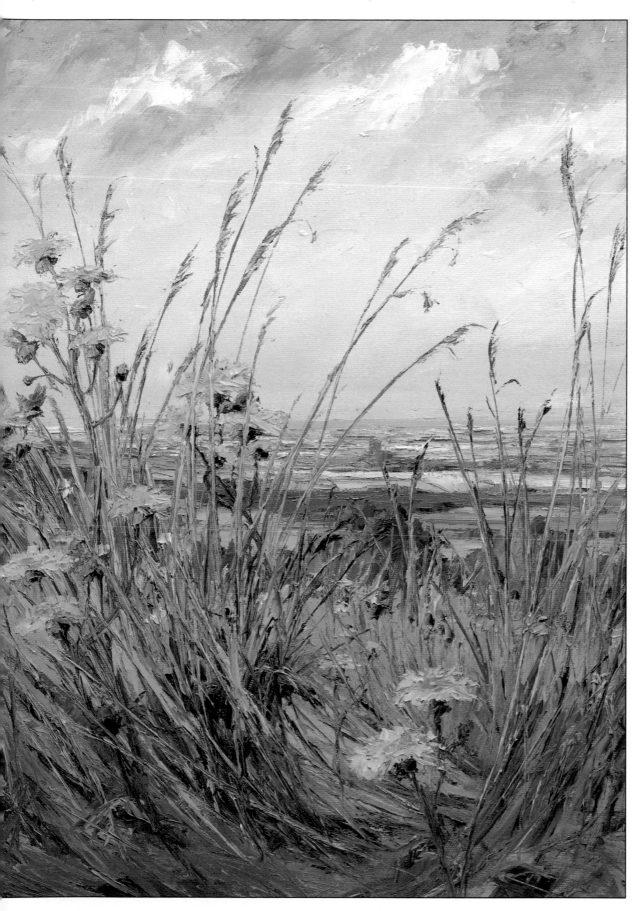

The sense of space is very powerful in this painting, and it also gives the impression of intricate detail, although in fact only a few of the flowers and grasses have been literally described.

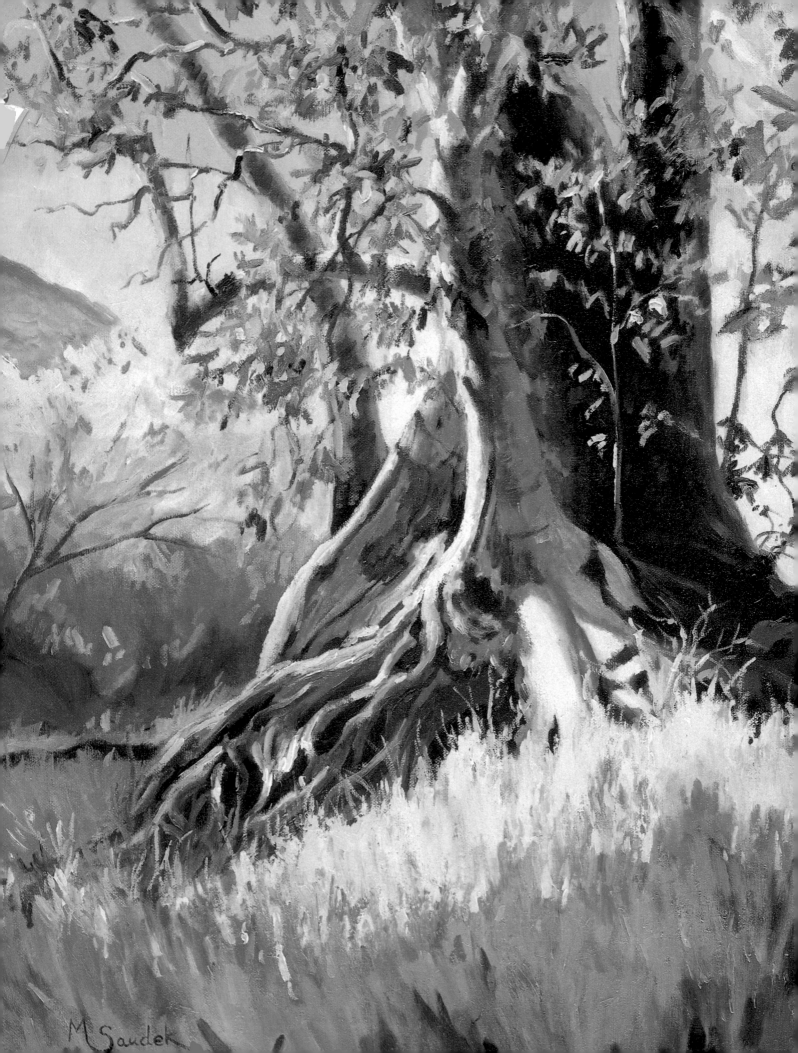
M Saudek

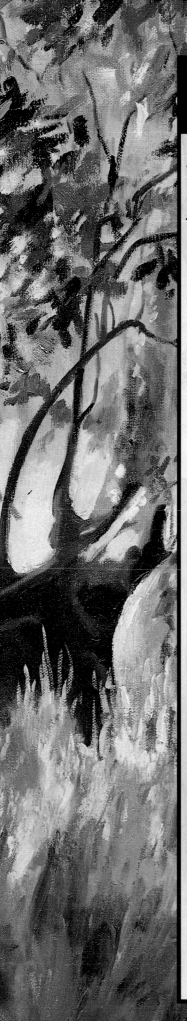

Chapter Two

MIDDLE GROUND

ABOUT LOOKING   52

CHOOSING AN APPROACH   54

DETAIL AND EDGE QUALITY   62

CONTRAST AND COLOR   76

SCALE AND PROPORTION   86

IN THE FIELD   92

HAVING DEALT WITH THE foreground, we now move further into the picture space and focus on the middle ground. This area can sometimes become rather lost – a kind of no-man's-land between foreground and background, but it can also be the most important part of the picture, as it is often here that the focal point, or center of interest, is located. How the middle ground is treated depends very much on the kind of landscape view you have chosen, but it should always be viewed as an area of potential interest which gives you an opportunity to create the series of visual links that carry the viewer's eye through and around the picture. In this chapter you will discover how to achieve this aim through careful composition and the control of color, light and shade, and perspective.

El Viejo

Martha Saudek • oil

SEEING THE MIDDLE VIEW

THE SCENE VIEWED in the first chapter is now explored again, this time in relation to the middle ground. In the main picture, the middle ground is neatly defined by the dry-stone wall, which is interrupted by the gate on the right and "introduced" by the large tree. The middle ground here could be said to stretch as far as the background trees, with the hill constituting the distance. You can see, however, that by moving around the area, you can change these boundaries.

On these two pages the focus is on the middleground.

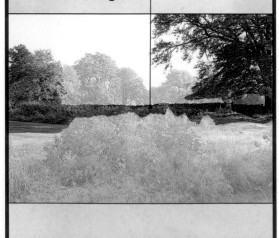

▶ *With a low viewpoint, and misty weather reducing color and detail, the horizontal element of the picture space is stressed, with bands of foreground shrubs, middle-ground wall and tree, and distant treetops.*

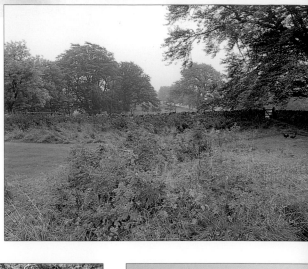

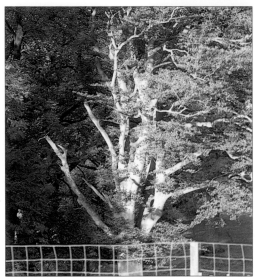

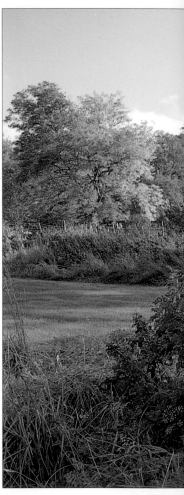

▲ *Focusing right in on the view, more abstract pattern of branches and patches of light and dark emerges in the middleground trees. The distance here is merely hinted at in the spaces between the branches.*

▼ *Looking now to the left, the wall and fence become the foreground, with the trees forming the middle ground and the distant hill the background.*

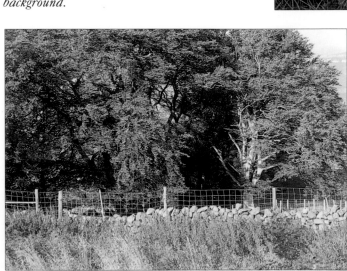

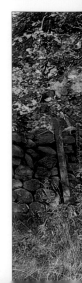

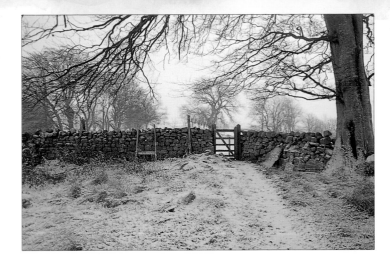

◀ *With the viewpoint again low, but now closer to the gate, the middle ground in this almost monochromatic winter scene is marked by the wall and the tree on the right.*

▼ *Moving closer still to the gate gives a view over the wall, thus increasing the sense of space and distance. The middle ground now is the snow-covered field.*

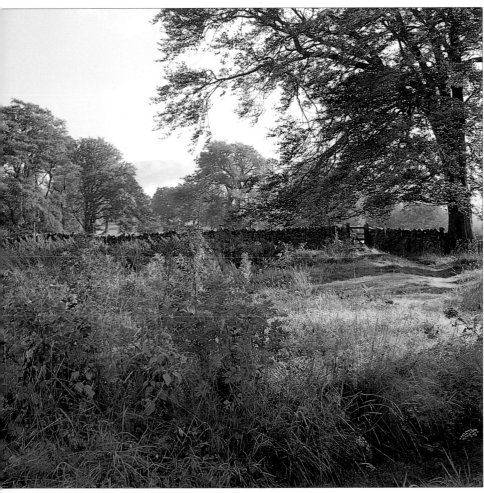

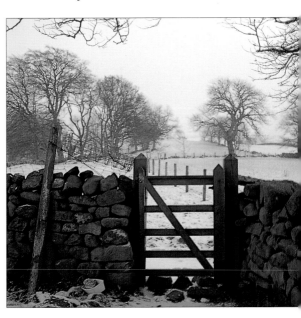

▼ *The same scene in summer provides a challenge in handling colors, particularly greens, and in creating recession through the effects of aerial perspective.*

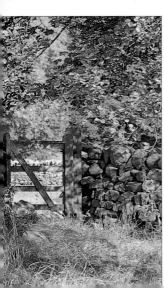

◀ *Again, altering the viewpoint makes a surprisingly picturesque subject. In this lower view, the wall and gate still constitute the middle ground, with foreground grasses and the distance seen through the gate.*

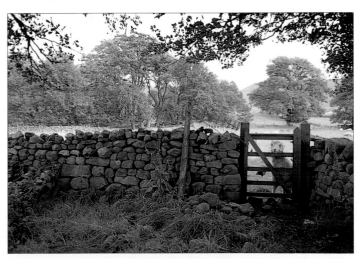

Choosing an Approach

THE MIDDLE GROUND CAN BE THE MOST IMPORTANT PART OF A LANDSCAPE

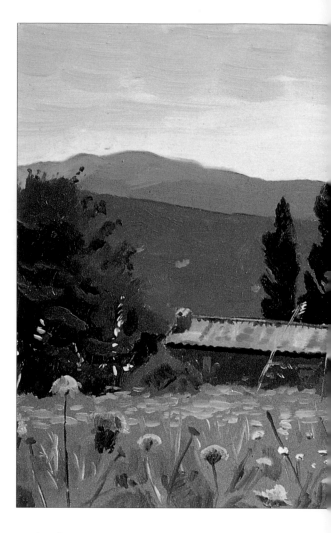

My Parents' Garden in Winter

Paul Bartlett • watercolor

The hedge and the façade of the house delineate the middle ground, with roofs and trees visible beyond.

IN ORDER TO BUILD up a sense of space in your landscape painting, you must encourage the eye to progress into the picture in stages so that the viewer has the feeling almost of walking into and around the painted landscape. Inexperienced artists often make the mistake of creating a strong foreground and background while ignoring the importance of everything that lies between. Or sometimes the middle ground is treated over-zealously, with too much attention to detail, so that it overwhelms the foreground.

One of the problems with the middle ground is identifying it. It may be a very large area, made up of any number of planes, or quite a small one. And it may merge into the distance – the third area of the picture space – with no definite division between the two. Sometimes there are natural elements in your view which will suggest the division of the picture space. These might include a hedge, a line of trees, a group of houses, or the brow of a hill, any of which might give you a naturally delineated middle ground which can be treated in a different way. These dividing lines may not necessarily run horizontally across the composition; indeed, they are unlikely to do so unless you are painting a very flat landscape.

Looking out of my window, I can see my backyard with a wall at the end of it and my neighbor's yard beyond. How would I divide this, and how much of it would I allocate as the middle ground? I can see that there is a tree that will establish the foreground plane, then there is a stretch from a flowerbed to the end

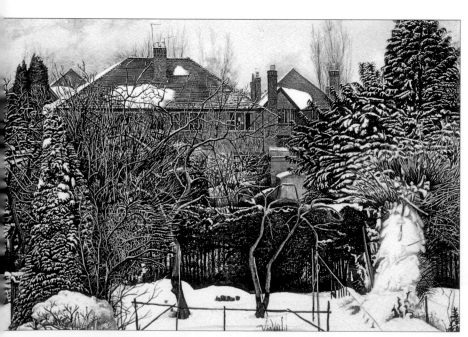

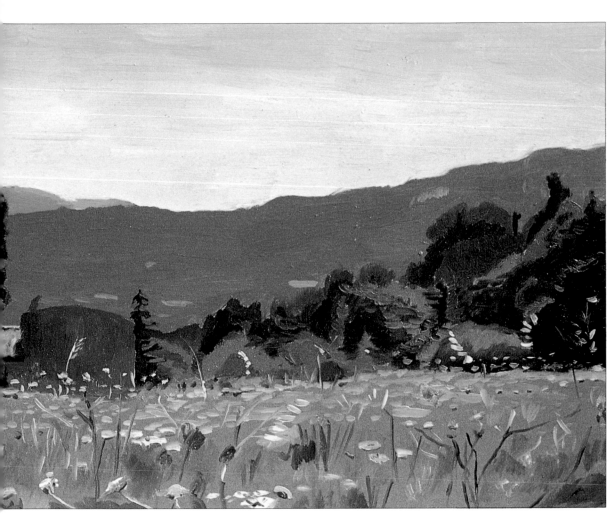

Provençal Meadow

Jeremy Galton • oil

The focus here is very much on the terracotta-tiled roof and band of trees in the middle ground, but the flower-strewn meadow creates distance and interest in the foreground.

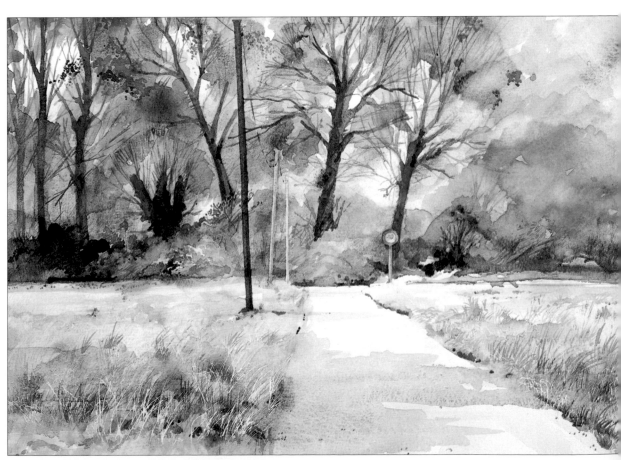

Road and Trees, Northam

John Lidzey • watercolor

The foreground, made up of many planes, leads you to the middle-ground line of trees. Space beyond and through the trees is hinted at with atmospheric washes applied wet-in-wet.

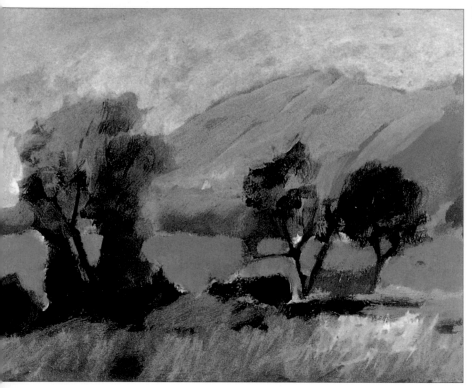

Montadon

Paul Powis • acrylic

There is a natural division of space here – a foreground stretch of grass, a middle ground bordered with trees and hedges, and distant mountains.

wall, which is the natural middle ground, with more trees and a building forming the distance. The flowerbed and wall act as boundaries at the front and back of the middle ground, helping to establish this area.

Once you have worked out a natural division, it is easier to decide how to approach the painting, but at this stage a few thumbnail sketches would be wise. These will help you to explore your initial observations and to try out a few different ideas.

▷ **Autumn Shadows**

LaVere Hutchings • watercolor

There are divisions in the picture space here, even though they are very subtle, relying on strong vertical tree trunks and patches of horizontal light and shade.

A center of interest As we have seen in the previous chapter, the foreground can be the dominant area of a painting, but it is perhaps more common to see the foreground used as a "pointer" toward the middle ground. A typical category of view contains a stretch of grassland, marsh, water, or sand in the foreground and a line or group of trees in the middle distance. This formula, in different variations, has been used by landscape artists for centuries, and the reason for its success is that it has a natural sense of distance – the eye is led into the painting, traveling over the foreground space to focus on the middle distance and then passing on beyond to the far distance.

One of the problems of this type of painting is keeping the balance of interest. The foreground may be uneventful in terms of objects or detail, but it must still hold enough interest to "carry its weight" and introduce the middle ground. The composition of the middle ground, which is the focus of the landscape, has to be strong enough to draw the eye, but it also has to remain in its proper position in space, and so must be carefully controlled in terms of color, tone, and detail.

Focus on middle ground *The distance and middle ground of this painting are carefully built up, although much of the latter will be subsequently covered by the foreground (see pages 46–49). To keep a balance of interest, some detail is included, but not too much.*

1 • Laying medium tones

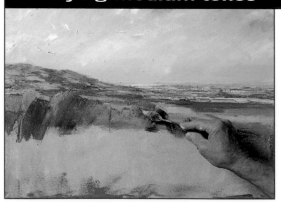

▲ *A bank of hawthorns is mapped out across the middle ground in a medium-tone mix of indigo, chrome yellow, and white. The paint is applied fairly thinly, with slanted "strokes" of the knife.*

2 • Building up tone

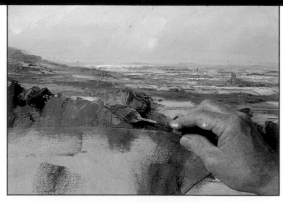

▲ *The tones are built up further, using the same mixes as before but in different proportions. The color is applied thickly, with the knife following the forms of the trees.*

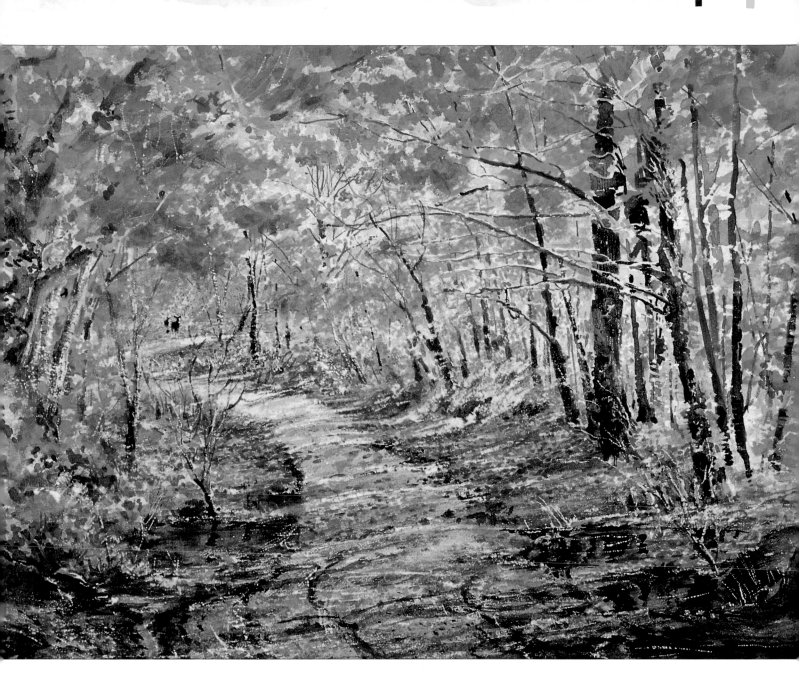

3 • Adding detail

4 • Final touches

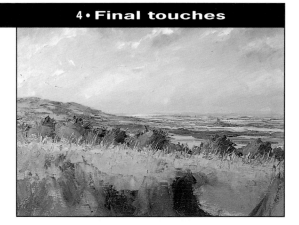

▲ Again, the artist works from the general to the particular; having mapped out the area of grass with pale ochers, he now touches in individual clumps of grass using the side of the knife.

▲ The yellow and blue flowers have also been touched in with the tip of the knife, but with enough pressure to push and blend the new colors into those below.

Choosing an Approach

TRY TO ORGANIZE "SIGNPOSTS" TO GUIDE THE EYE AROUND THE COMPOSITION

YOU MAY WONDER HOW you can "compose" your middle ground when nature has already done so for you – the trees, shrubs, and flowers are already there, and you can't move these elements of the landscape around. But you yourself can move around to find the best viewpoint and thus manipulate what you see. You might, for example, like the shape of a particular tree, but find that from your first viewpoint it is lost among other trees. By moving ten yards, you could find it separated from its neighbors and now silhouetted against the sky.

There are also steps you can take to improve on nature once you have decided on your view. You can't invent trees and other features, but you can omit things that don't help

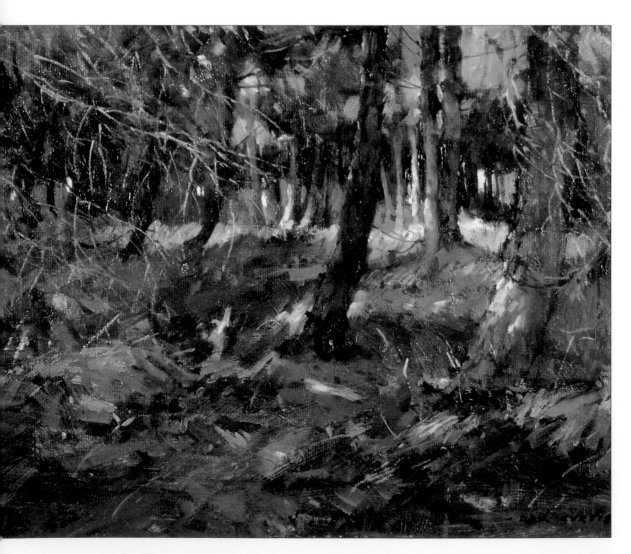

Pinewood in the Peak

David Curtis • oil

Patches of light and color – dappled light on the ground and touches of sun on the tree trunks – guide the eye through and around this composition. But attention is drawn to the middle-ground area bathed in pale sunlight.

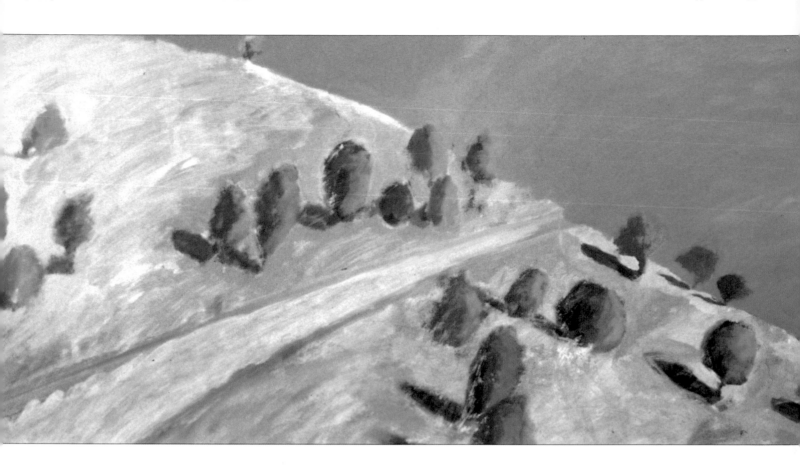

the picture. And you can also influence the composition by emphasizing certain lines which will help to direct the eye.

Extending the middle ground Sometimes you will find that your landscape doesn't appear to have a middle ground as such. This is often a viewpoint problem, too, and can sometimes be rectified. The window view of my yard, which I described in the previous pages, was from the first floor, allowing me to see over the boundary wall. Had I been viewing from ground level, the overall depth would have been much reduced, with the middle ground less important. So a higher viewpoint will extend the middle distance, giving you more to play with.

You can't, of course, take a stepladder out with you, but you will find there is a marked difference even between sitting and standing, so it is worth experimenting to see if you can improve the subject in this way.

Guiding the eye Have you ever wondered why you find some landscape paintings fascinating and want to linger over them, while with others one brief look is enough? It may be, of course, that the subject or style doesn't interest you, but it is often simply that the

artist has failed to structure the painting.

In a good landscape – or indeed any painting – the artist will have arranged a series of "signposts," or guiding lines taking the eye from one area of the picture to another. The eye travels naturally along a curve or diagonal line, so you will often see landscapes in which a curving path or river has been used to introduce the middle distance and form a link between it and the foreground. Remember, though, that because the eye obediently travels along a curve or line, you may – if you are not careful – lead the viewer out of the picture. If one of your guiding lines goes "out of the frame," try to arrange another one that points back into the picture. And if you are using a path as a natural introduction to the middle distance, don't give the impression that the end of it is the end of the journey; break across it with shadows, branches of trees, swathes of grass, and so on to lead the eye away into the surrounding landscape and then back.

Trees are particularly useful in guiding the eye. Branches emphasized by a patch of sunlight or with strong directional brushwork make ideal "signposts," and edges of trees can be "lost" or "found" (see pages 23–27) to make compositional lines to suit the composition.

Northhill

Paul Powis • oil

With a high viewpoint, the "ground plan" is extended, often finding a potentially lost middle ground. The artist creates a sense of space, but is more concerned with pattern and color.

Choosing an Approach

LOOK FOR VARIETY IN TREES, EMPHASIZING SMALL DIFFERENCES IN SHAPE, TEXTURE, COLOR, AND TONE

IN THE COURSE OF this chapter we will look at the way trees differ in shape, size, outline, and color, thus giving the artist scope for composition – a line of trees can become a subtle essay in progressions and transitions of color, tone, and texture. But what is meant by "composing"? In many cases this will take the form of minor manipulations of the scene through emphasis, slightly exaggerated color contrasts, or by finding or losing an edge. It can also involve using your artistic license to edit out a tree or other feature which weakens or is extra-

neous to your composition. But composing can take a more extreme form, with "ideal" land-scapes being composed in the studio from sketches and drawings made on the spot.

Seeking out contrasts Nature, on the whole, provides a greater wealth of variety than the human imagination can come up with, but sometimes needs a helping hand in terms of composition. A good landscape needs contrasts, so if trees are the theme, you need to look for variations on it, balancing tall with small, light with dark, soft textures with hard, and so on. Usually you will find these contrasts already exist, and you can draw attention to them. You could make a pale birch tree and a dark fir the painting's center of interest, playing up the differences in size, color, outline, and texture.

Introducing contrasts Sometimes you will be painting a group of trees of the same species, so how can you introduce contrasts in this case? Once again, they will be there if you look for

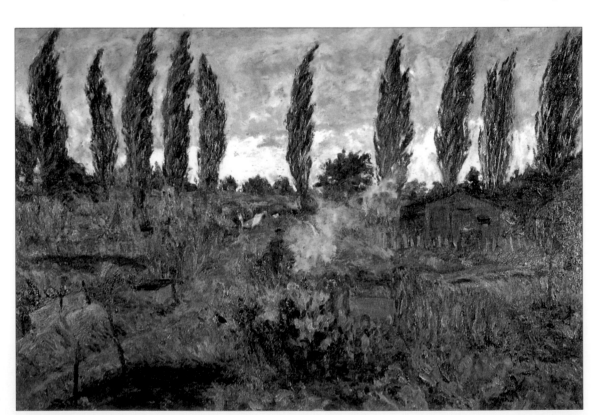

Row of Poplars, Stormy Day

Patrick Cullen • oil

Each tree is treated as an individual in this carefully observed painting. The most obvious differences are in outline, but there are more subtle variations also, such as the contrasts in color and tone caused by the brighter light in the sky on the right.

Composing with trees *In an oil sketch painted alla prima, or in one session, you won't have time to make major changes, so first seek out a happy arrangement of the trees and then emphasize subtle differences in shape, color and tone. Painting alla prima involves working mainly wet-in-wet so, to avoid too great a buildup of paint, thin it with turpentine alone in the early stages.*

them; trees are never exactly the same. They will vary in small ways in shape, size, and even color. Such differences can be emphasized – perhaps by making much of a scarred trunk or a bent bough, and using patches of sunlight or touches of color to draw attention to it.

You can also manipulate your tones by setting light against dark and dark against light. Changes in weather will often inspire this kind of counterchange. A sudden shaft of sunlight will illuminate one tree in a group, or a stormy sky throw foliage or blossom into high relief. Similarly, a fall of snow on hills or mountains will form a brilliant backdrop for a forest of dark green firs. For a line of trees in the middle ground, encourage counterchange by devising areas of contrasting highlights and shadows.

Studio landscapes The large landscapes of the great British artist John Constable (1776–1837) were not painted on site, but carefully composed in the studio from elements recorded in sketches. Many of today's artists work in the same way, making line, tone, and color notes in sketchbooks, and often using a camera as well to provide visual information for paintings to be composed and painted indoors.

This method has many advantages, particularly for large paintings. You don't have to race against time, recording impressions before the sun moves or the snow melts. You can take as long as you like to organize your composition, and you can work slowly and methodically. The traditional oil painting technique, for example, was to build up the paint in layers which may have taken days to dry, and some artists still like to paint in this way. Large watercolors, too, can take a long time, as unless you are working wet-in-wet, each wash must dry before the next is applied. The "down side" of studio landscape painting is that you may sacrifice spontaneity – the majority of today's landscape painters do work direct from the subject for this reason.

1•Brush drawing

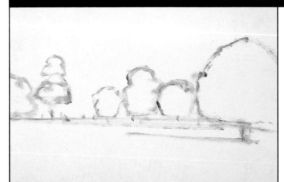

◄ *The shapes of the trees are established with a medium-green brush drawing. Any incorrect lines can be erased with a rag dipped in mineral spirits.*

2•Building up tones

► *The artist has begun with the lighter tones and then put in the medium tones. The greens are all mixes of sap and chrome green, cadmium yellow, and white.*

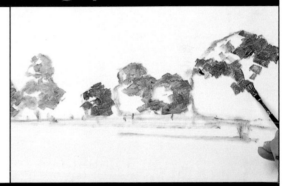

3•Working wet-in-wet

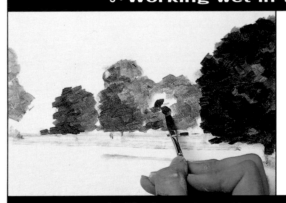

◄ *He now adds blue and black, and works in the darker tones wet-in-wet to create soft blends. Note how the shadows here "find" the edge between the two trees.*

4•Balancing the tones

► *Even in a composition as simple as this, it pays to work across the whole painting at the same time, building up all the tones of the trees together to achieve a good balance.*

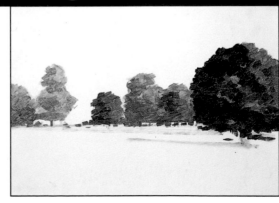

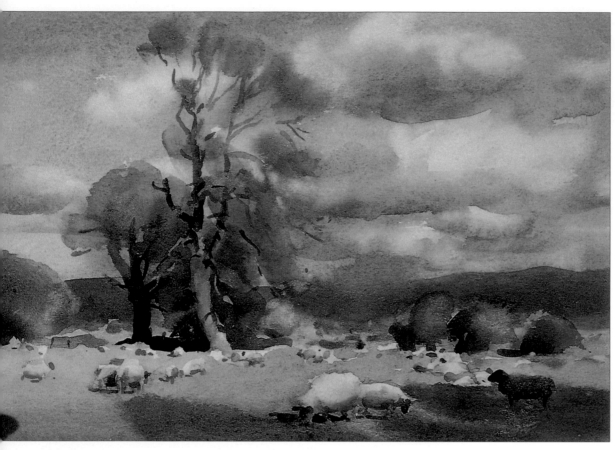

◁ **Sheep on the Meads, Hertford**

Trevor Chamberlain • watercolor

Delicate wet-in-wet washes form the soft edges of the middle-ground foliage. You can see the trunks and branches of the larger trees, but not each leaf.

Detail and Edge Quality

DISTANCE CREATES A GRADUAL DECREASE IN DETAIL AND A SOFTENING OF EDGES

AS WE HAVE ALREADY seen, one of the major problems facing the landscape painter is deciding how much detail to put in, whether you are dealing with foreground, middle ground, or distance. You may be able to distinguish a good deal of detail in the middle ground – depending on the size of the "piece of space" you have decided to paint – but you don't have to put it all in. If the middle ground is too carefully described with clear, sharp edges, there will be no contrast between it and the foreground.

Remember that over distance there will always be a gradual decrease in detail, and edges will become softer. Leaves will not be seen individually; they will "melt" into the overall green mass, and flowers will be distinguishable only by their general shape and color. Learn to trust your eyes – unless you can see details clearly, don't try to invent them.

Softer edges In general, although there are differences between edge qualities in foreground objects, the overall focus is relatively sharp and clear. In the middle ground, there is still definition, but the edge quality is less pronounced. A line of trees against the sky may seem blurred, merging into the sky. Inexperienced painters often make the mistake of painting trees with hard outlines, but this not only makes the tree look like a flat

▷ **Mid-day in the Lane**

Timothy Easton • oil

Small dabs of color over flatter layers of paint give the impression of dancing foliage. In the middle ground, the detail and tonal range are reduced.

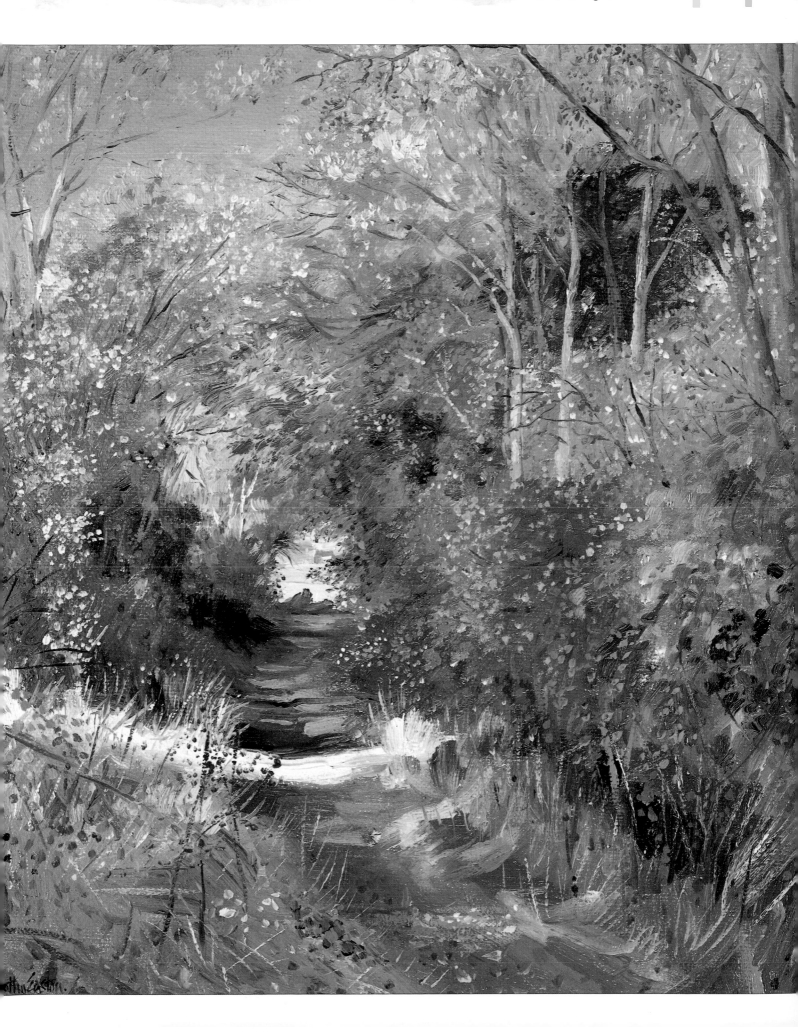

Softening edges

As your painting develops, stand back now and again to assess your progress. Look at it in a mirror for added objectivity. Check that all the elements appear to be in their proper place in the picture space. If not, minor adjustments are needed. Here, softening an edge did the trick.

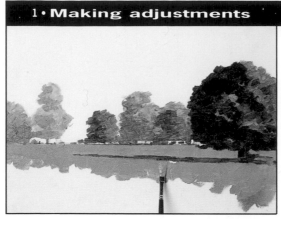

1 • Making adjustments

▲ Once the foreground area has been added to the trees (see page 61), it is time to assess the overall effect. The contrast between the tree and the grass brings it forward, and the edge is too stark.

2 • Softening the edge

▲ Oil paint remains workable for some time, so it is easy to soften this edge and to break down the contrast in tones simply by blending the two edges together.

Soft edges in pastel

A middle-ground blossom tree is captured with soft-edged pastel techniques. The pink cherry blossom is built up with repeated "dibbled" marks to soften the edge.

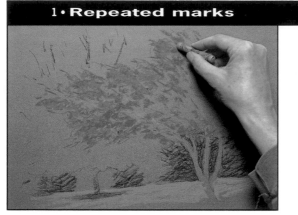

1 • Repeated marks

▲ The color and character of the blossom are established with bright pink over a dull brownish-red, using repeated marks made with the pastel tip.

2 • Softening the outline

▲ The stick is then held at an angle to the paper and pushed away so that it vibrates, making a broken line of irregular dots.

Soft edges in acrylic

Here the underpainting is used as a way of softening edges. The trees are built up on top of thinly painted cobalt blue, which is allowed to show at the edges to soften the outline.

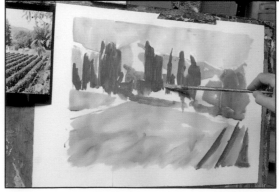

1 • The underpainting

▲ The pure cobalt blue of the trees and the paler blue used for the mountains sets the color and tone for this area of the painting. The brush is held near the end to give loose, generalized strokes.

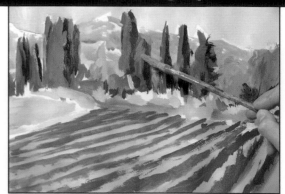

2 • Building up

▲ With the underpainting now dry, thicker paint is used to build up first the darks and then the lights. Note the green is not taken right up to the edge.

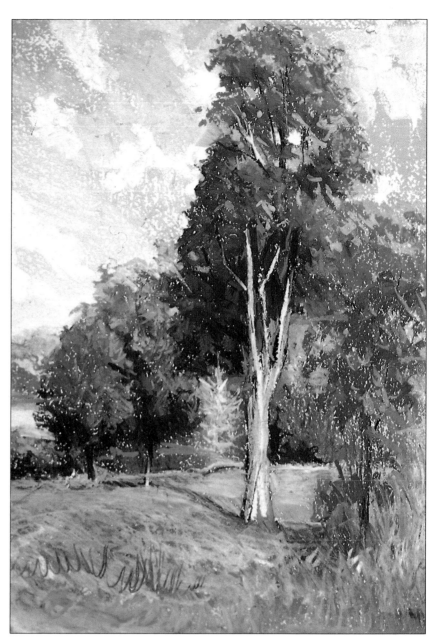

▷ **Queechee Trees**

John Elliot • pastel

By means of sharp edges and strong tonal contrasts, the artist places the focus of the picture is on the middle-ground tree. Notice how lightly the foreground has been treated in comparison. Having worked the foliage color onto the sky first, the sky color has then been used to adjust the edge, softening it in places.

3 • Creating movement

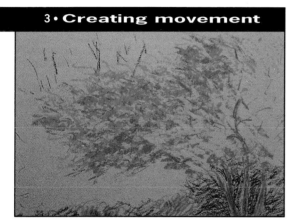

▲ *The "dibbled" lines have given a sense of movement as well as softening the outline of the tree.*

3 • "Cutting in" the sky

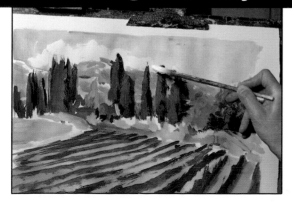

▲ *The ocher sky is now overpainted loosely with near-white, cutting around the tree tops. Touches of the underpainting soften the edges.*

4 • Avoiding too much detail

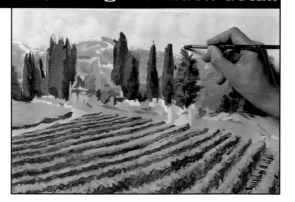

▲ *With a smaller brush, held at the ferrule for more control, a little more detail is added to the trees, which in places break over the edge into the sky.*

▷ **Descanso's Woodlands**

Martha Saudek • oil

Strokes of yellow in the dark green mass capture the sunlight and model the shape of the tree canopy, the edge of which is almost "lost."

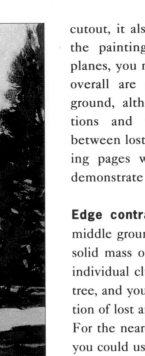

cutout, it also destroys the sense of space in the painting. To establish middle ground planes, you need to make sure that the edges overall are softer than those in the foreground, although of course there are variations and you will still need contrasts between lost and found edges. On the following pages we look at some techniques to demonstrate ways of creating softer edges.

Edge contrasts If you look at a tree in the middle ground, you will see that it isn't just a solid mass of greens. You can distinguish the individual clumps of foliage that make up the tree, and you can describe these by a combination of lost and found edges (see pages 23–27). For the nearer patches of foliage, for example, you could use a found edge on one side where the clump catches the light, and let the shadowed side merge into the green mass. The top of the tree might be a found edge, contrasted with a bright sky, or lost in parts and found in others to avoid the outlining effect. Parts of one tree can be lost in the foliage of its neighbor and then found again with a subtle color or tonal change, or decisive brushwork to emphasize the boundaries.

Autumn Shadows, Hampstead Heath

Jeremy Galton • gouache

The shaping of the foliage of the individual trees has been simplified into areas of light and dark to make a pattern of greens in the background.

Sponging foliage

Many different types of sponge are available, from natural sponges to closely textured synthetic materials, all creating different effects. The medium you use and the dilution of the paint also varies the result. Watercolor and a small natural makeup sponge are used here.

1 • Setting the scene	2 • The foliage
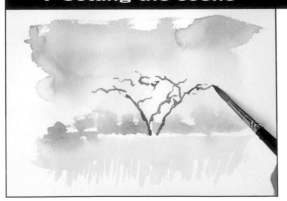	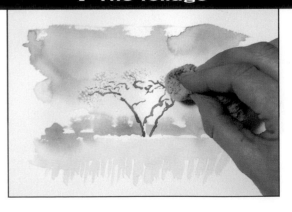

▲ *The painting is initially established with wet-in-wet washes, which are allowed to dry before the tree trunk is painted with a round sable brush.*

▲ *The sponge was dampened and then touched into a fairly dry mix of yellow ocher and cobalt blue, which is sponged delicately onto the paper.*

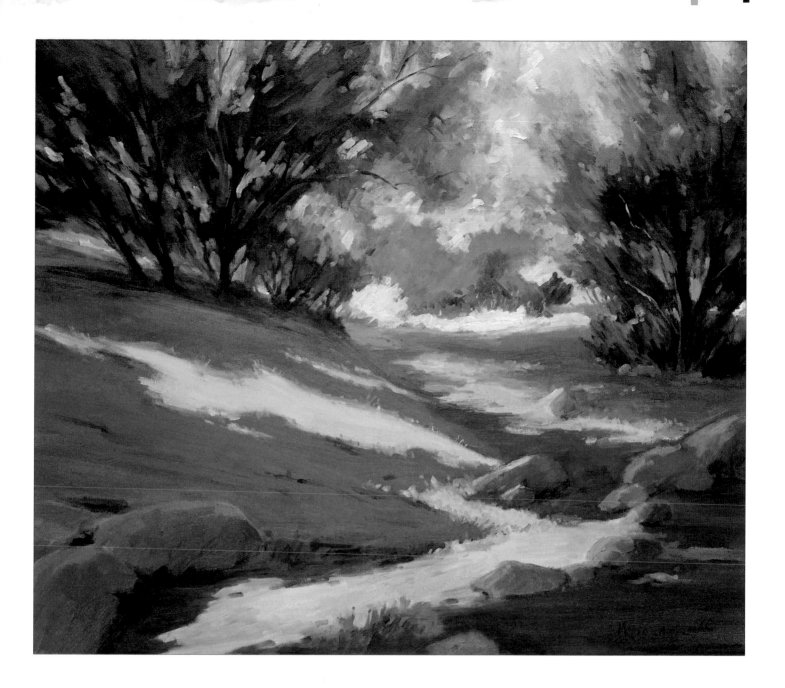

3 • Building up layers

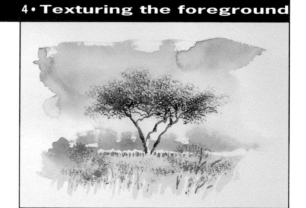

▲ Two further layers of color are now superimposed over the first – alizarin crimson and then cobalt blue. The sponge is washed clean between colors and the paint kept as dry as possible.

4 • Texturing the foreground

▲ To preserve a unity of technique, the same method is used for the foreground grasses, with a touch of the sponge suggesting texture. Notice how the color on the tree varies in density, creating a soft edge.

Detail and Edge Quality

Get to know your brushes and understand how they can help you describe edges

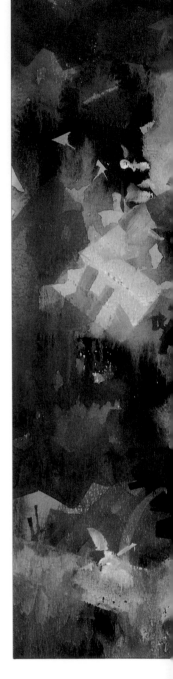

River at Lanhydrock, Cornwall

Don Austen • watercolor

Using a crisp square brush, the artist has reduced the foliage to blocks of tone, superimposed wet-on-dry so that they retain the geometric shape of the brushstroke.

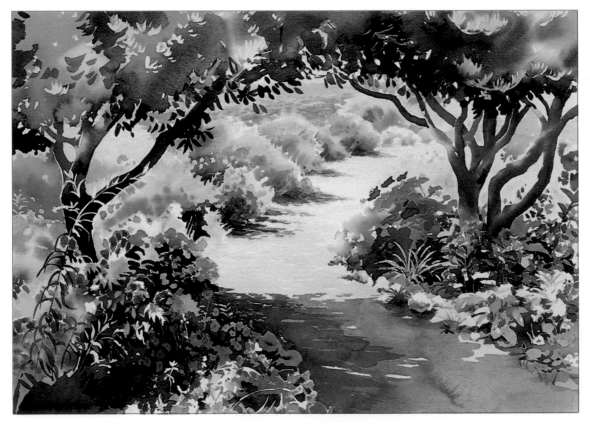

Pathway to the Sea

Hazel Soan • watercolor

For the foliage, patches of light were "reserved" with masking fluid before washes of medium-tonal greens were laid wet-in-wet over the canopy area.

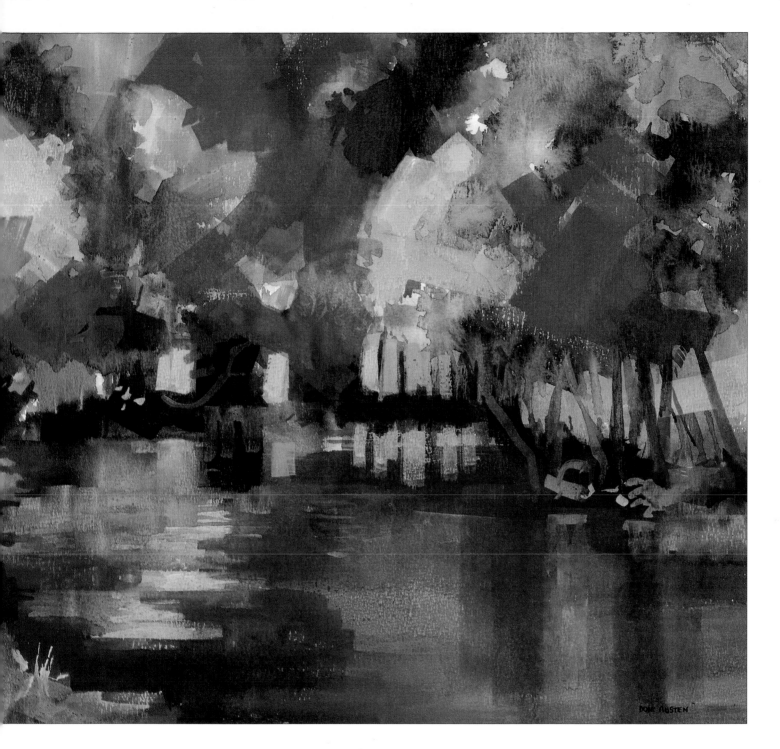

ARTISTS GET TO KNOW their brushes like old friends – in oil painting these might include a worn-out round bristle which produces a good grass texture and a crisp flat brush or filbert which paints a crisp edge. In watercolor it might be a soft squirrel-hair brush, perfect for loose washes, and a springy sable for more detailed work. But it is not only the texture and shape of a brush which concerns us, but its size, and it can be instructive to try larger brushes than you would normally use. This strategy helps you to restrict the amount of detail you put in and to go for a broad general-

ization. It also encourages you to use brush-work in a suggestive rather than literal way.

Experiment for yourself. Try painting an apple tree in blossom, using your normal brushes plus a small one for finishing touches, then repeat the exercise using larger brushes. You will find the latter will force you to paint in a looser way and make it impossible to become bogged down in small details.

A similar exercise can be carried out in pastel. If you normally work with the tips, try using side strokes only, breaking the sticks into short lengths.

Detail and Edge Quality

LOOK FOR THE MAIN CHARACTERISTICS OF TREES – OUTLINE, SIZE, COLOR, AND DENSITY

contemporary Turner (1775–1851).

Although formulas are generally best avoided, as they can lead to rather dead and unconvincing paintings, there are certain general characteristics of trees that it is worth bearing in mind – in conjunction with your own observation. The artist must always consider how best to hint at the rich variety of the arboreal world while avoiding too much detail, which can give a labored impression.

LANDSCAPE PAINTERS OF THE 17th century, notably Claude Lorrain (1600–82), who painted highly idealized landscapes, devised certain formulas for painting trees. Although these landscapes are beautiful and full of poetry, they lack the kind of realism we usually seek today and were criticized by the 19th-century artist and writer John Ruskin, who much admired the more naturalistic approach of his own great

Recognizing tree shapes Trees can be easily recognized by their general outline, size, color, and the density of their canopy. Even at a distance, you will only need to give a few clues in your painting to make your trees recognizable as a particular species.

Many of the problems encountered in painting trees can be put down to poor observation. A common mistake is misjudging the size

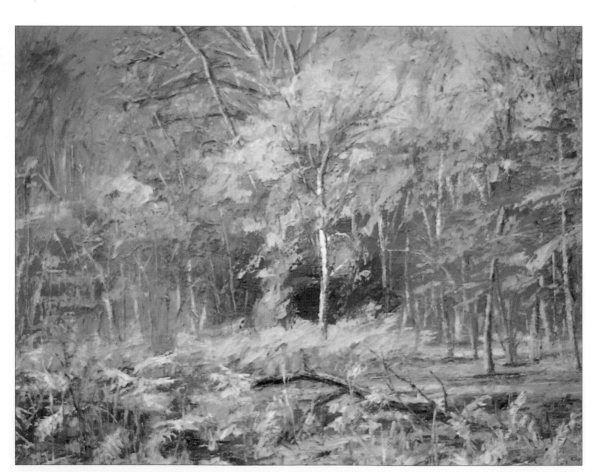

Ashridge Beeches

Brian Bennett • oil

A combination of the trees' shapes defined by the trunks and branches, and the color of the autumn leaves makes this a completely convincing "group portrait." The leaves have been created with deft touches of the tip of a painting knife.

Silver Birches

Daniel Stedman • acrylic

Even though only part of the tree is visible, it is immediately recognizable by its "silver" trunk and by the way the small, sparse, leaves hang off the branches and catch the light. Note how the artist focuses on the lower branch, so keeping the eye in the center of the painting.

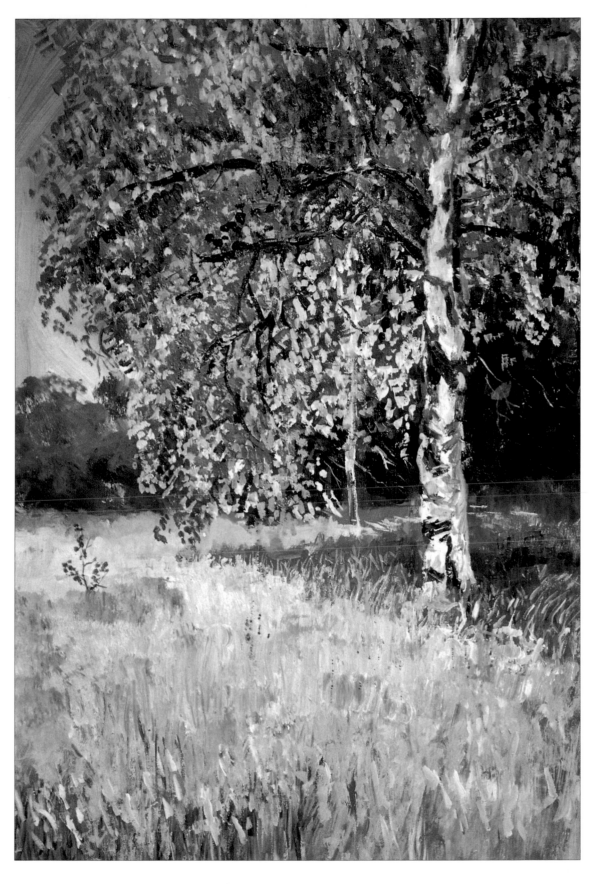

of the leaf canopy in relation to the tree's trunk. Often it is painted too small, making the trees look like lollipops. The ratio of leaf to trunk varies enormously. A cypress tree, for example, is tall and narrow, while beech trees have widely spreading branches, and hence broad canopies. Some trees are even broader than they are tall. The density of the leaf canopy, of course, changes depending on the time of year. In spring, the bare branches are

Sky holes *Trees are seldom solid masses of unbroken color — little patches of light are usually visible through the foliage and between the trunk and branches. With opaque paints or pastels, which are also opaque, add these "sky holes" in the final stages of the painting. With watercolor you have to think ahead and reserve these areas at the outset.*

1 • Further assessment

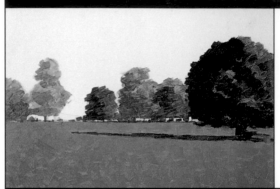

◀ *Having reached this stage, see pages 61 and 64, the painting is again assessed. The large middle-ground tree is still too overbearing and looks unrealistically solid.*

2 • "Cutting in" with sky color

▶ *The painting is turned upside down, and a good square brush, which produces a clean edge, is used to work the sky blue in and around the tree shapes.*

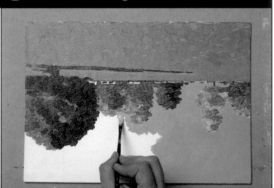

3 • Adding sky holes

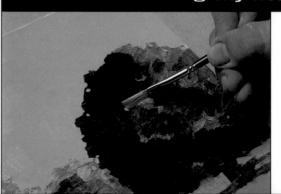

◀ *Using the same sky blue, the corner of the brush is touched lightly down onto the green canopy and along the edge — a dot here and there to break up the density of the leaves.*

4 • Unifying trees and sky

▶ *The sky holes have reduced the solid appearance of the middle-ground tree, linking it better with those in the background and also helping to unify the trees with the sky.*

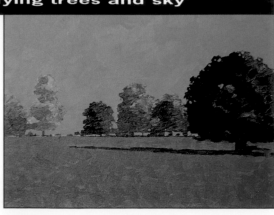

lightly colored with a yellowish-green tinge as the buds break through, and as the season progresses, the leaves grow thicker and darker. In full summer, when the canopy is thick and lush, the tree may appear top heavy, often with very little trunk visible.

"Sky holes" An important thing to remember when painting a tree seen against the sky is that it is seldom, if ever, a solid green shape. The leaves grow in clumps at the ends of the branches, so that near the trunk there are nearly always little light patches where the sky shows through. Points of light sky will also

Exploiting your painting medium *One of the first steps in painting is discovering the capabilities of your chosen painting medium and learning which colors make the best mixtures. The pictures below provide some hints, but there are always several different ways of doing things, so get into the habit of thinking about suitable colors and mixtures.*

Pastel: red and yellow-browns, dark and bright greens. From dark to light, work into and around colors beneath.

Gouache: ultramarine blue, carmine, viridian, white.

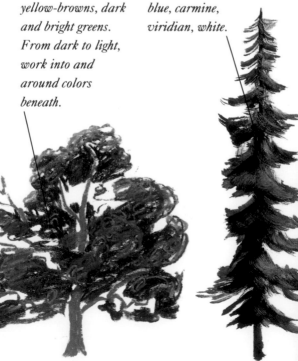

Oak   **Fir**

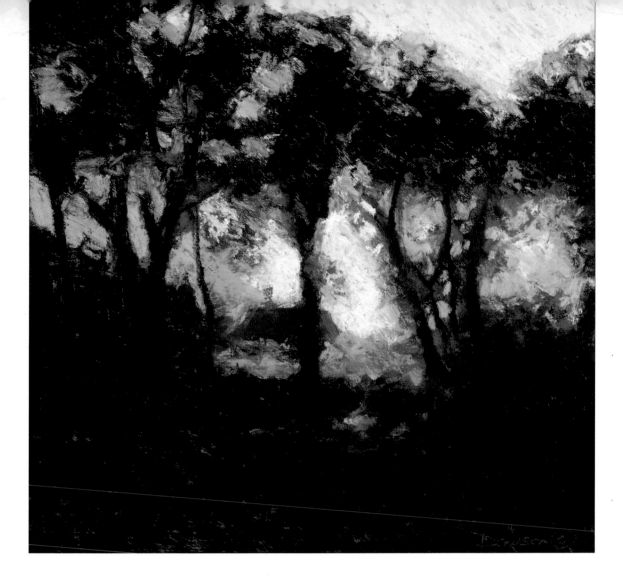

Kipling Woods

Doug Dawson • pastel

This dramatic line of trees, towering over the distant house, have an awesome presence. Small dots of the pale tinted paper are visible through the dark canopy of leaves, which is further broken with patches of superimposed sky color.

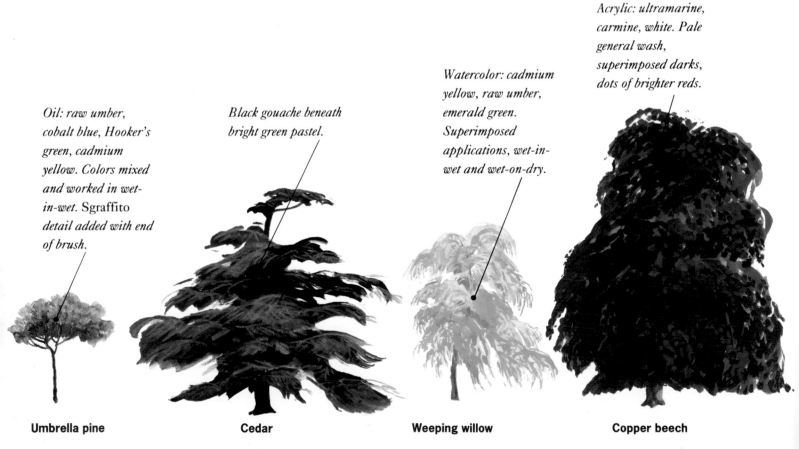

Oil: raw umber, cobalt blue, Hooker's green, cadmium yellow. Colors mixed and worked in wet-in-wet. Sgraffito detail added with end of brush.

Black gouache beneath bright green pastel.

Watercolor: cadmium yellow, raw umber, emerald green. Superimposed applications, wet-in-wet and wet-on-dry.

Acrylic: ultramarine, carmine, white. Pale general wash, superimposed darks, dots of brighter reds.

Umbrella pine

Cedar

Weeping willow

Copper beech

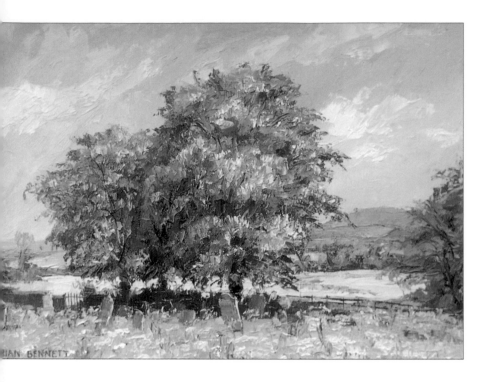

Wild Parsley and Chestnuts

Brian Bennett • oil

Even through the heavy foliage of the chestnut tree, small patches of sky are visible. Notice how at the edge of the canopy more patches of light sky show through the thinning leaves.

show through the foliage at the ends of branches, where there are fewer of the tiny leaf-bearing twigs. With opaque paints or pastels, these sky holes can be painted in last, which gives you a chance to redefine the shapes of the clumps of foliage. They are trickier in watercolor: you can usually paint foliage over a pale wash for the sky, but you must then remember to "reserve" small light areas for the sky holes which means you must be sure about the shapes from the outset.

Even when a tree is not seen against the sky, it is a mistake to make the foliage too dense.

Painting tree trunks It is often jokingly said that artists have trouble painting horses' hooves and therefore like to "lose" them in long grass. Hooves – and people's feet – are certainly difficult, and so is the area at the bottom of a tree, where the trunk grows into the earth. If there is long grass, the problem is disguised, but often the roots may be growing into bare earth, so you will have to cope with it.

Once you start concentrating on this problem area, you will notice how many differences there are in the roots of trees and how they grow. Getting this right is another important clue to the tree's species. Large deciduous trees such as the oak, ash, beech, and maple fan out at their bases, spreading their roots above ground. Birches, palms, and some species of fir grow out of the ground almost as parallel lines, tapering off toward the top.

Seen close to, tree trunks are full of fascinating colors, textures, and irregularities, with signs of broken limbs, scars, bumps, and twists in the bark hinting at the passage of time. The bark of some trees are as inventive as animal markings, so don't make the mistake of painting them all-over brown. Silver birches are literally silver as well as pink and many other

Tree-trunk texture

Pastel artists nearly always work on textured and tinted paper. The texture, or "tooth," helps to hold the soft pigment in place, but it also creates a broken-color effect, as the pastel catches on the top of the grain, letting glimpses of the paper show through.

Scumbling

Hinting at details

▲ *The texture of the bark is suggested by scumbling dark brown oil pastel over the gray-brown paper. The pastel stick is held on its side, and the area lightly covered with downward strokes.*

▲ *You probably could not see very much detail in these dark woods, but you need to be able to hint at detail, as the artist has done here with occasional light strokes and fine lines.*

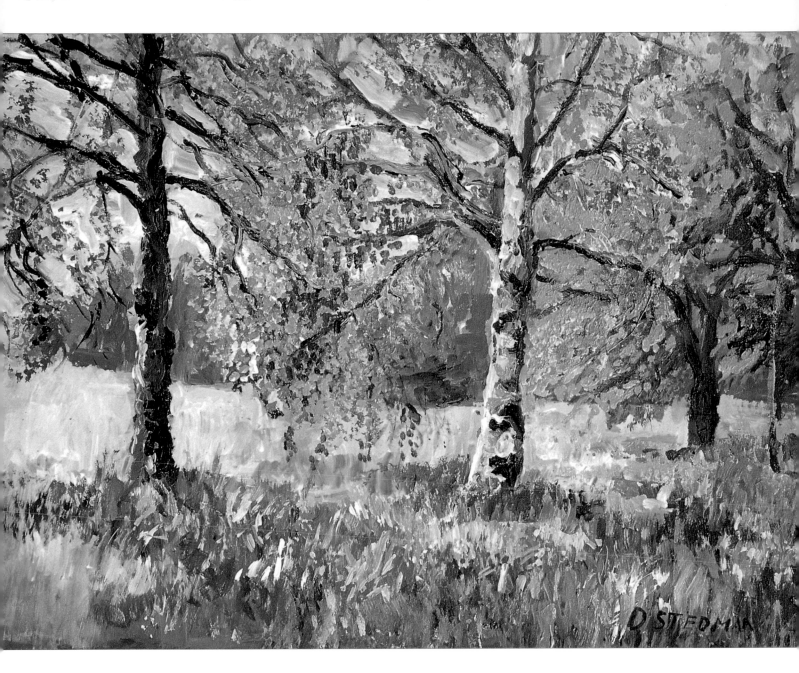

unexpected colors, with markings going around the trunk rather than up and down. It is worth making studies of tree trunks to help you incorporate such detail into your paintings.

In oils and acrylics, brushwork can be used to suggest textures and the direction of markings, as well as the flowing, sinuous curves of trunks and branches. You can vary the consistency of the paint also, using it more thickly for rougher textures.

Winter trees Trees devoid of their summer foliage can be hard to deal with, yet here too the problem usually stems from lack of observation. Even without their leaf canopies, there are recognizable basic characteristics; different species of trees have individual patterns of

branches which make up a definite shape.

There are technical problems, too, though. How, for instance, can you give the impression of the overall shape of the tree and the network of tiny twigs at the ends of branches without painting every detail? The answer is to generalize and suggest these intricacies by the way you use your paint. Having outlined the main structure of the tree, the smaller branches, which in the middle distance create a delicate haze of color, could be indicated with the drybrush method, or with pale brushstrokes or washes of paint. With pastel, light side strokes can be used, with perhaps one or two small branches picked out with a delicate linear mark.

Summer Winterbourne

Daniel Stedman • acrylic

Built up with small dabs of colored grays over darker paint, this central birch trunk looks very convincing. Touches of pink show through in places from the underpainting.

Contrast and Color

Keep the middle ground in its place by carefully controlling the tones

WE HAVE ALREADY SEEN how landscape features become less clearly defined as they recede into the middle distance. But this is not the only effect of the so-called aerial perspective (see page 38). It also changes the tonal values and colors: the tones become lighter, with less contrast, and colors paler and cooler – that is, bluer. If you look at a distant tree-clad hill, you will see a predominance of blue with just a hint of green, while in the middle distance these changes are more subtle.

Recognizing and using the effects of aerial perspective is one of the main ways in which artists create the illusion of distance in their paintings, so here we will look at its effect on tonal contrast and the strength of color.

Diminishing contrasts Having decided roughly what constitutes your middle ground and how you will deal with your foreground, you can begin to plot the tonal "map" of your painting. In the middle ground, the tones will be lighter than those in the foreground, but they will also be darker and with more contrast than those in the distance, where you can often see almost no variation in tone.

To help you to understand the concept of diminishing contrasts, think of a band of nine tones going from white (1) to black (9), with graduated grays in the middle. In the foreground the tones might vary from the lightest gray to the darkest, that is, from near-white (2) to almost black (8). In the middle ground the contrasts will be reduced, varying from about 3 to 7, and in the distance, with further reduction in contrast, the tonal range may be from 4 to 5. Even if you can see snow-covered mountains in the distance, they will seldom be pure white, as atmospheric perspective will have dulled and blued any white highlights.

It takes practice to judge tonal values and relate them to colors. Although some colors straight from the tube are lighter than others – yellows are always light, and grays and browns

Diminishing contrasts *One way of dealing with diminishing contrasts is to map out the painting in medium tones and then step up the contrasts of the foreground elements to bring them forward. The background can be "knocked back" at the same time.*

1 • Blocking in the shapes

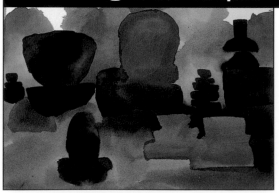

▲ *Working in gouache used fairly thinly, the shapes are painted in the medium tone of each particular tree or bush.*

2 • Building up the lights

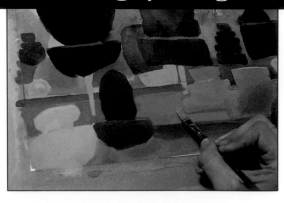

▲ *Starting with the lights, the contrasts are increased on the nearer features. The gouache is now used more thickly, but you should always build up from thin to thick.*

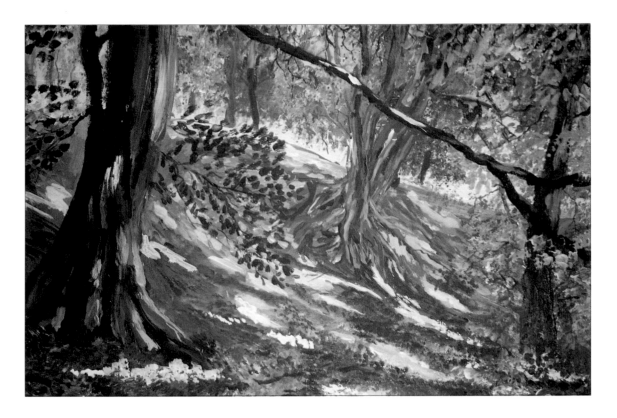

dark – you will always find you have to do some careful color mixing. Lemon yellow may be pale in tone, but it is also a very vivid color, so if you were to use it undiluted in the middle distance, it would need to be balanced by a very strong foreground or it would "advance" out of its proper position in space.

Reducing tonal values Artists don't usually work on one area of a picture in isolation; they build it all up at the same time, constantly relating one tone and color to another. With

opaque paints, it is seldom wise to start with the lightest areas – the usual practice is to work up to them so that you are gradually reducing the tonal value of your mixes. So how do you do this? Adding white, of course, is the obvious way of making a color lighter, but it can also change its nature and sometimes deaden it.

There are other ways to lighten colors, one being to use them more thinly. This is the watercolor method, but it can also be adapted to oils and acrylics, which can be diluted with turpentine or water respectively. You can't, of

Summer Shadows

Daniel Stedman • acrylic

In these beech woods, the distance between the trees in the foreground and those in the middle ground is conveyed by reducing the contrasts in tone, making the range narrower and generally lighter. The foreground branch which breaks across the middle ground tree trunks makes this very clear.

3 • Building up the darks

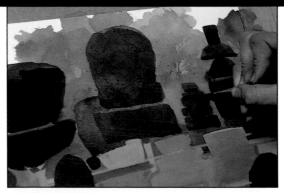

▲ *Darker green is now added where the shadows fall on the small tree. Tone is built up in gouache by adding layers of paint cleanly so that new colors do not interefere with those beneath.*

4 • Spattering texture

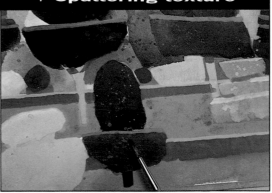

▲ *The trees closer to the foreground will be more textured. Clean water flicked onto gouache lifts off small specks of color, creating an interesting mottled effect.*

Capturing middle-ground poppies

Here the foreground poppies are pure red, while in the middle ground and distance, they are neutralized with their complementary, green. For variation, some of the middle ground flowerheads are painted over the green, while others are neutralized by painting green over the red.

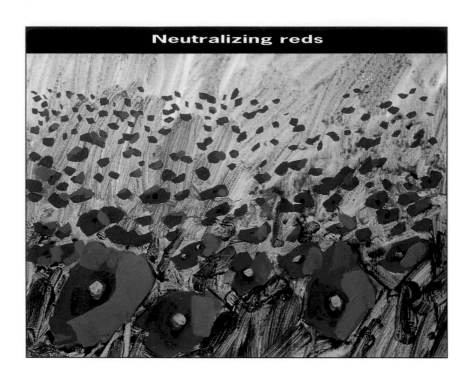

Neutralizing reds

course, put thin paint over thick, so in this case you would have to work light to dark. If you want to keep the paints opaque, try using one of the naturally lighter colors in your mixture, adding lemon yellow or cerulean blue to a green mix. With mixes you can alter the proportions, so a green made from lemon yellow and Winsor blue can be made lighter by adding more yellow.

You can also trick the eye and lighten colors by contrast; don't forget that colors are radically affected by the colors and tones around them. A particular green in the foreground will appear lighter if set against a darker color in the middle ground.

Increasing tonal values With watercolors you must work from light to dark, building up strong colors and tones gradually. Because the buildup of darker color will be most intense in the foreground, a common method is to start with the sky and distance and work forward to the foreground.

So with watercolor you will have to consider how to darken colors. Black can be useful, but like white it often changes the character of a color. For example, black and yellow make green, and black and red make brown (incidentally, a black and cadmium yellow mix is very useful for foliage). Most colors have a bias which will suggest how to darken or lighten them. Cadmium yellow is a rich, warm

yellow with a bias toward red, so to darken it, you will need to add a red or orange.

But physically mixing colors on the palette is not the whole story in watercolor, because you can also mix on the paper surface by laying one wash over another. If you find a color looks too light when it is dry (watercolors dry much lighter), you can increase the tonal value by repeating a wash once the first one is dry. You can also build up the depth of color and tone with superimposed washes of a different color of the same tone.

Gardener's Yard in Summer

Simie Maryles • pastel

A wide variety of foliage greens are built up with pastel strokes in many different colors.

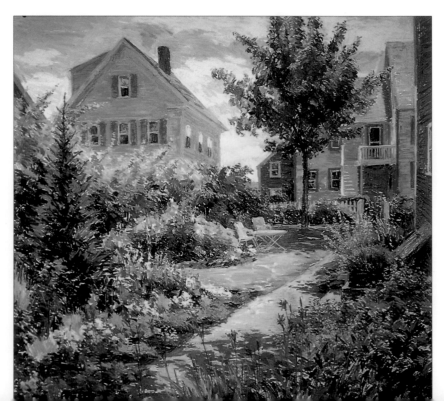

Neutralizing colors

Colors in the distance are paler and less vivid – or "saturated." Distance appears to neutralize colors, taking them toward gray. To neutralize your colors and thereby reduce their saturation, try adding the complementary of the color you want to tone down – a touch of purple added to yellow will take the edge off this dominating color; green added to red, or vice versa, will do the same. In the chart on this page we explore these and other possible combinations.

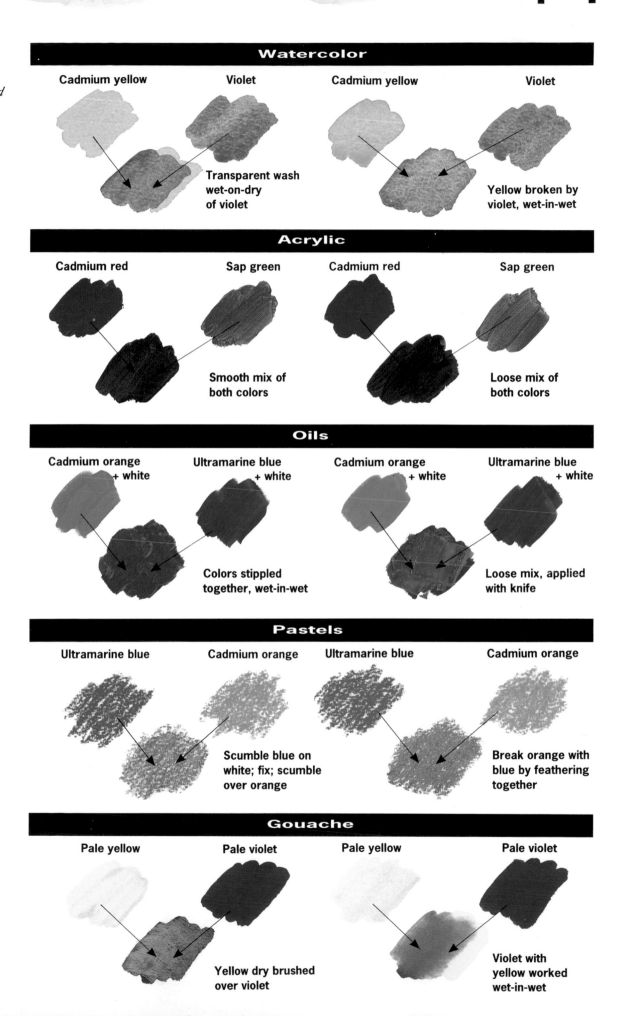

Watercolor

Cadmium yellow — Violet — Cadmium yellow — Violet

Transparent wash wet-on-dry of violet

Yellow broken by violet, wet-in-wet

Acrylic

Cadmium red — Sap green — Cadmium red — Sap green

Smooth mix of both colors

Loose mix of both colors

Oils

Cadmium orange + white — Ultramarine blue + white — Cadmium orange + white — Ultramarine blue + white

Colors stippled together, wet-in-wet

Loose mix, applied with knife

Pastels

Ultramarine blue — Cadmium orange — Ultramarine blue — Cadmium orange

Scumble blue on white; fix; scumble over orange

Break orange with blue by feathering together

Gouache

Pale yellow — Pale violet — Pale yellow — Pale violet

Yellow dry brushed over violet

Violet with yellow worked wet-in-wet

Contrast and Color

Don't reject tube greens – they can save you a lot of time

THE VARIETY OF GREENS seen in nature is amazing, and one of the trickiest aspects of landscape painting is learning first to assess these different colors and second to mix them. On the following pages, you will see how to mix a wide range of greens from blue and yellow, but here we look at some of the many ready-made greens. Most artists' palettes include a few greens, as they are useful for modifying other colors or for mixing further greens, and are also a timesaver when you are working fast outdoors – mixing greens "from scratch" can be time-consuming.

Learning about your medium There are considerable differences in the characters and hues of colors between both different brands and the different media, even when they have the same name. This can make life difficult if you are changing from one medium to another. Sap-green oil paint, for example, is transparent, while in acrylic it is much more opaque. A summary of the color characteristics of ready-made greens is shown in the chart, opposite.

The relative transparency of colors is important because it affects the way they behave in mixes or when one color is laid over another to mix on the surface. In oil and acrylic painting, transparent colors are particularly useful for glazing techniques. Note that pastels are always opaque.

Sometimes you will have to discover these things by trial and error, but some paint manufacturers help you by printing full information on the tubes. The Liquitex range of acrylics is graded "transparent," "translucent," and "opaque," while Winsor and Newton gouache paints range from "completely opaque" to "wholly transparent." Other tube information relates to the relative permanence of colors (some are less lightfast than others) and whether or not they are considered harmful.

Another factor that affects color mixing is the staining power of the pigment. Some pigments are very strong and will overwhelm any

Mixing media

Sometimes a particular effect or color is achieved by combining two or more different media. Here the deep green of the cedar tree came from superimposing pale green pastel over black gouache.

1 • Tonal underpainting

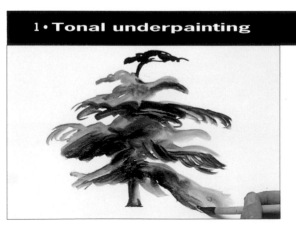

2 • Pastel texture

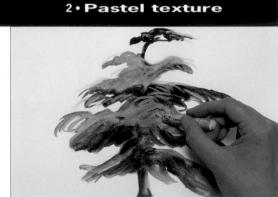

	Oil	Watercolor	Gouache	Acrylic	Pastel
Terre verte *A dull, earth green useful for underpainting and color modification.*	■	■			■
Sap green *A good medium green, and a useful all-rounder, but needs modifying.*	■	■	■	■	■
Oxide of chromium *An opaque, cool, bluish green, excellent straight from the tube.*	■	■	■		■
Viridian *Very strong, transparent bluish green. Too powerful to be used on its own, but good for mixing.*	■	■	■	■	■
Permanent green, deep and light *A yellow green which tends toward viridian in the deep shade.*	■		■	■	■
Olive green *Deep, earthy green. Transparent or semi-transparent – good for glazing.*		■	■		■
Cadmium green *A bright yellow-green – excellent used straight from the tube for small color accents.*	■				
Chrome green *A warm yellow-green, weaker than sap green.*	■				

color they are mixed with unless used in much smaller proportions. Also, if another color is superimposed on a strongly staining one, it may "bleed" through. This information is found on some but not all tubes.

▲ **Ready-made greens** *Pastel greens vary according to the individual manufacturers, as do the naming and manufacturing systems. Rowney pastels, used here, have traditional pigment names and are produced in tint variations numbered from 0 (pale) to 8 (dark).*

**Stream Near
Luxulyan, Cornwall**

Don Austen • oil

*By using lots of
impasto, the artist
perfectly captures
contrasts in texture and
subtle transitions of
color in trees and
foliage. You can almost
hear the rustle of the
trees.*

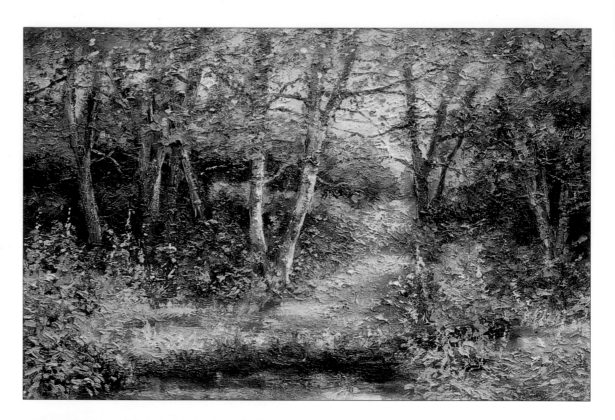

Contrast and Color

Mix Fresh, Vibrant Greens by Combining Colors

A SOLID BANK OF trees in your middle ground will look dull and lifeless if painted in the same colors and tones. You need to be aware of contrasts in texture, varieties in shape and tone – all discussed elsewhere in this book. But of course the subtle transitions of color found in nature will greatly enliven such an area and will require some clever mixing.

Be aware, too, of how the colors of the foliage change according to the fall of light. Note the direction of the light source and paint your trees to look three-dimensional, with highlights where the light falls and shadows where the leaves are hidden from the light. Leaf colors are nearly always lighter at the edge of the canopy where the foliage is less dense and the light can shine through.

Keeping your greens fresh You will find your greens fresher and more natural if you mix the colors with a few deft strokes of the brush. Don't worry if the paint isn't mixed to a smooth, even color: you will find the colors more vibrant if yellows and blues can be seen within the greens. This is not so easy with watercolor, so try mixing colors on the paper by diffusing one color into another. You can do this wet-in-wet so that the two colors combine in parts, or if you want the yellow to shine through the blue, allow the yellow to dry, then wet the precise area you want to "green" with water, touching it then with a tip of blue which will quickly diffuse over the wet area but remain darker where the brush first touched the paper.

Pastels are mixed by laying one color over another to create a third. They can be blended together with your finger, a brush, or a cotton ball, but more lively colors are created by working the constituent colors together through linear marks – small dots, curved lines called feathering, thicker strokes worked one into another.

Mixing greens *Greens often look more lively if you mix them by layering, so that one color shows through another. Here we show you some of the techniques that enable you to "mix" greens on the picture surface.*

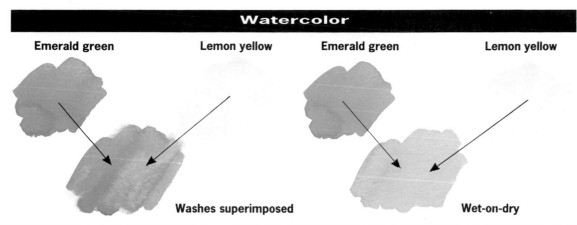

Watercolor

Emerald green · Lemon yellow · Emerald green · Lemon yellow

Washes superimposed · Wet-on-dry

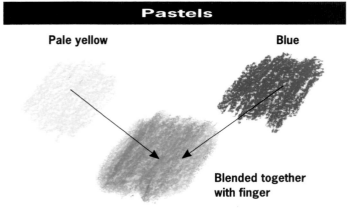

Pastels

Pale yellow · Blue

Blended together with finger

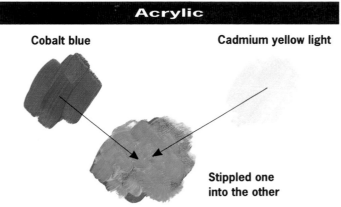

Acrylic

Cobalt blue · Cadmium yellow light

Stippled one into the other

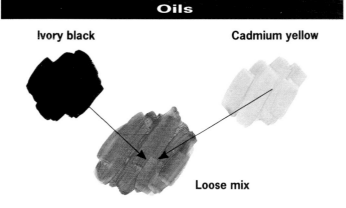

Oils

Ivory black · Cadmium yellow

Loose mix

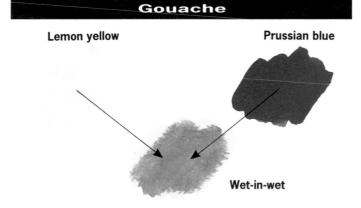

Gouache

Lemon yellow · Prussian blue

Wet-in-wet

Varying the proportions of the mix *As this chart shows, by varying the proportion of the new color added to the constant color, a wide variety of hues and shades of green can be mixed from only a few constituent colors. Using one constant color will help you to achieve color unity in your painting.*

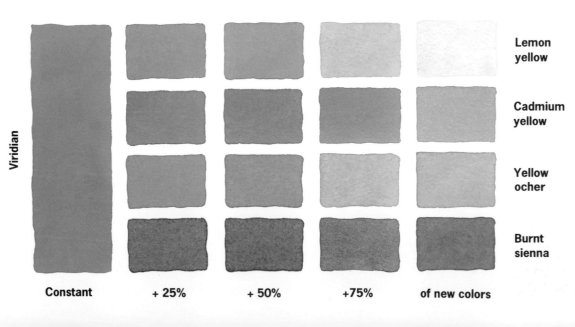

Viridian

Lemon yellow

Cadmium yellow

Yellow ocher

Burnt sienna

Constant · + 25% · + 50% · +75% · of new colors

Contrast and Color

USE COLOR TO LEAD THE EYE TO THE CENTER OF INTEREST

JEAN-BAPTISTE COROT (1796–1875), one of the greatest landscape painters, often included in his pictures a figure wearing a touch of red, carefully placed to lead the eye to an area of interest. Assertive, warm colors are often used in this way to lead the eye into and around the picture space. In Corot's case, he chose red because it is the complementary color to the foliage greens.

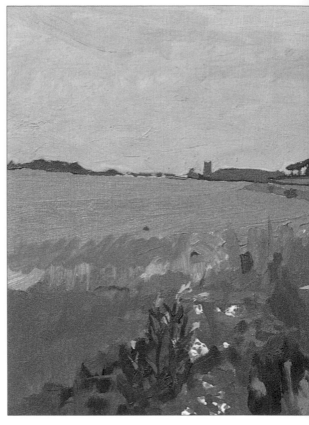

△ **Track Through Cornfields**

Jeremy Galton • oil

The artist uses red to great effect to guide the eye around this painting. The eye is drawn first by the figure in red, then diverted to the two simple patches of pure red poppies in the grain on the left, and finally to the distant muted red building.

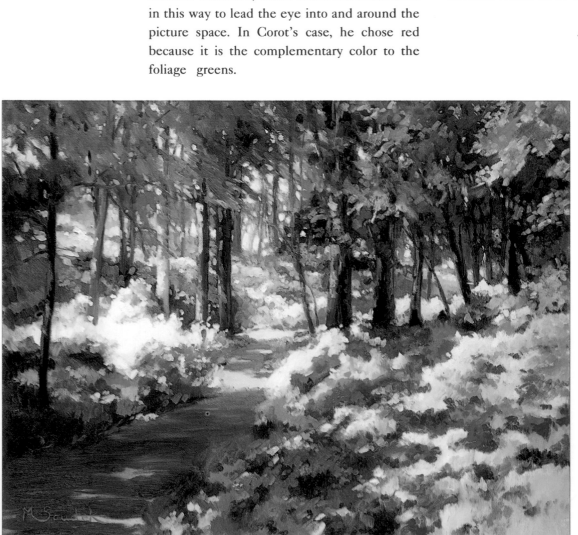

◁ **Winterthur's Azaleas**

Martha Saudek • oil

Muted versions of the pink, red, and orange found in the azaleas in the foreground can be seen not only in the background flowers, but also in the trunks and foliage of the trees.

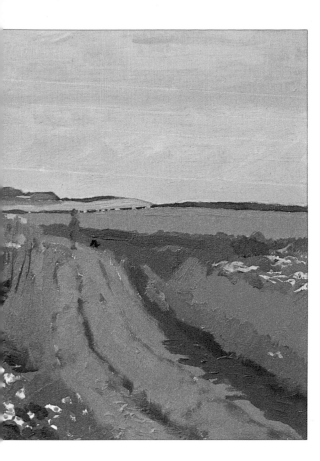

Carrying the color through When planning to draw the eye in this way, you may choose, like Corot, to include a figure, or perhaps a building in the painting's center of interest, but another way to manipulate color to keep up the interest is to carry a dominant color through the painting. For example, if your foreground includes red or yellow flowers, take a muted version of this color back into the shadows or highlights of the middle ground and distance, making a series of color links which the eye will follow into the picture space. This will also give a sense of unity to the painting.

You will find the method most effective if you choose a naturally advancing color like red or yellow which comes forward to the picture surface, but obviously you will have to be careful in the placing of such strong colors and find ways of balancing them with other colors.

This device, particularly if you are dealing with yellows, can be applied to patches of light in the middle distance. You may of course have to exaggerate a little, or even invent, but this is artistic licence – the artist always interprets reality in the interests of the painting. Corot may have seen his red-clad figure once, but it is unlikely that he existed every time the artist painted such a landscape.

Dominant colors *A maple tree in dramatic fall colors is captured expressively in acrylic and pastel, with an emphasis on color and light. Patches of bright red and yellow lead the eye around the picture space.*

1 • Acrylic underpainting

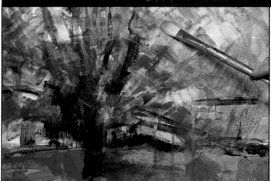

◀ *Working on canvas, the artist begins by making an underpainting in acrylic.*

2 • Pastel broken color

▶ *Using the side of a yellow pastel stick, she strokes it lightly over the dry acrylic.*

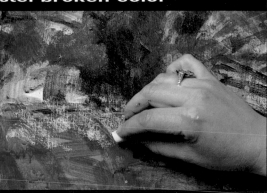

3 • Creating a focus

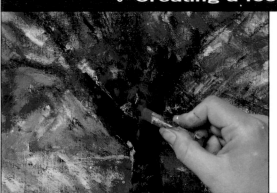

◀ *The focus of the painting is in the middle, and here she adds dots of pure bright red, twisting the stick as she brings it off the surface to leave intense points of color.*

4 • Carrying color through

▶ *By restricting her color scheme mainly to shades of red and yellow, she has created both unity of color and excitement.*

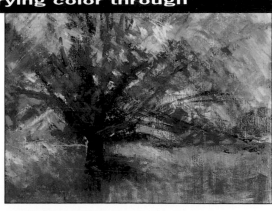

Scale and Proportion

Understanding the Basics of Perspective Can Save Hours of Confusion

PEOPLE OFTEN AVOID PAINTING buildings and urban scenes because they know they will have to cope with the intricacies of linear perspective. Landscape, they believe, won't throw up any such problems. But although you won't need a detailed knowledge of perspective, bearing in mind some simple rules can save you a great deal of trouble and help you check where and why things may have gone wrong.

Getting the size right The basics can be summed up quickly. You cannot fail to have noticed that things appear smaller the farther away they are; the problem is judging how much smaller than a similar element in the foreground. You can work it out with the help of simple linear perspective. All receding parallel lines draw closer and closer together until they meet at a point called the "vanishing point," which is on an imaginary line drawn across the picture at your own eye level (called the horizon). Imagine standing in the middle of a road which has a line of trees on each side and drawing one line along the bottoms of the trees and another along the tops. The two parallel horizontal lines would appear to come closer and closer together, and the trees will become smaller and smaller.

If you are dealing with manmade objects such as buildings, all the lines will be straight and the parallels truly parallel, so you can plot perspective by drawing a series of lines to the vanishing point. Landscape seldom contains such regular features and very few straight lines, but perspective is still useful for helping you to get the relative sizes of features right. Suppose, for example, you have one tree in the foreground and another of the same species and size in the middle distance; lines drawn

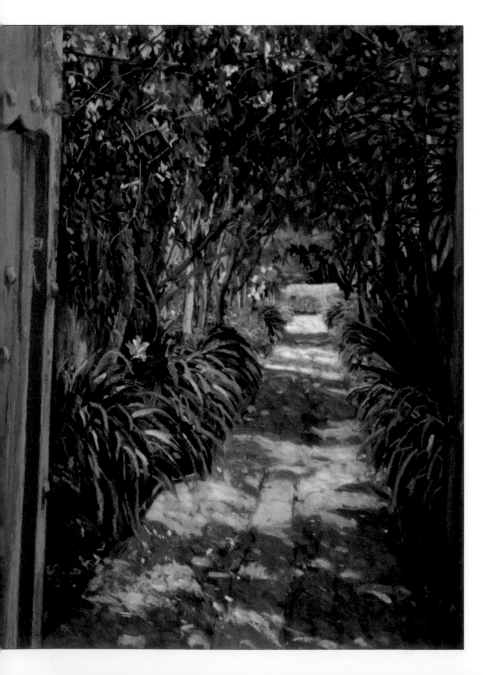

Blue Doors with Fuchsia and Geraniums

Elsie Dinsmore Popkin • pastel

Applying the rules of simple perspective, with parallel lines converging over distance, provides a structure for the artist to work on.

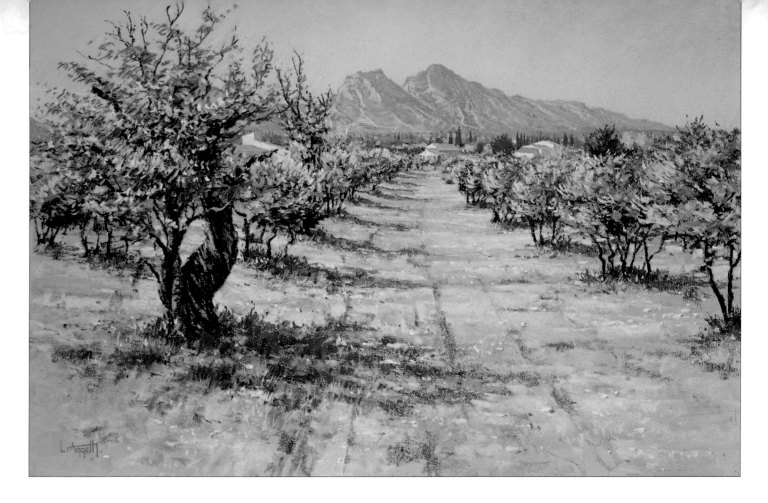

along the tops and bottoms of both would establish the size of the more distant tree. It is also useful for establishing the sizes of such features as fields, paths, fences, and hedges.

Up and down hill Often your landscape will include hills, which alter the perspective. On rising ground, the receding parallels will meet on a vanishing point above the horizon; on a downward slope, the vanishing point will be below it. The easiest way to visualize this is to think of a plowed field, or a hill striped with grapevines, and imagine it first flat, then tilted upward, and then downward. The steeper the incline, the less the parallel lines will converge. The lines of vines will appear closer together on the brow of the next hill and even closer on the one beyond. On the downward slope, the lines will converge much more rapidly than they would on the flat.

Olive Grove, Les Alpilles, Provence

Lionel Aggett • pastel

The curving wheelmarks between the rows of trees help to establish a sense of traveling into the picture space. For this space to be properly defined, it was essential that both these and the rows of trees were in correct perspective.

▶ *Even if you don't start with a structure of perspective lines, you may find it useful to check your drawing at some stage, particularly if it doesn't look quite right. Check that parallel lines recede to a point on the horizon, and so on, as shown here.*

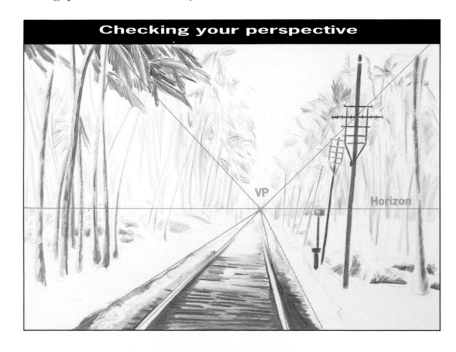

Checking your perspective

VP

Horizon

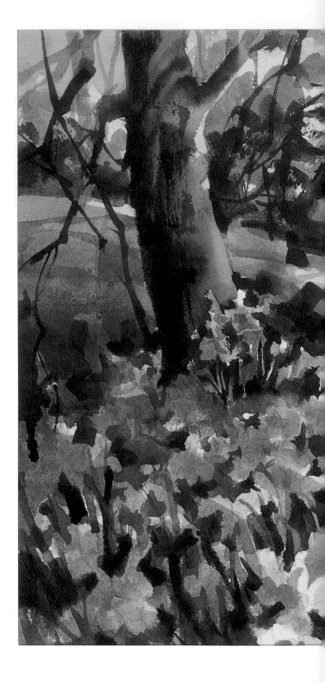

Scale and Proportion

KEEP MIDDLE-GROUND
FLOWERS "IN THEIR PLACE,"
AVOIDING TOO MUCH DETAIL
AND BRIGHT COLOR

BECAUSE FLOWERS ARE SUCH a delightful and colorful subject, it is easy to treat them in too much detail in the middle ground, or to make the colors too strong. If you have similar flowers in the foreground – perhaps a field of poppies or other wildflowers stretching right back into the picture plane – you must progressively "knock back" the colors, reserving the vivid ones for the foreground. Remember also that the flowers will appear smaller and closer

Generalizing middle-ground flowers

Brilliantly colored flowers such as this bougainvillea will have to be generalized and the colors balanced by equally vivid foreground colors if they are to remain in the middle ground. Here the colors are built up in watercolor, used both wet-on-dry and wet-in-wet.

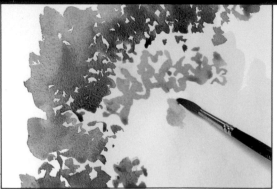

1 • Wet-in-wet	2 • Medium tones

▲ *Dappled foliage is painted around the edge of a dry pale pink wash in a graduated blue-gray, with darker gray touched in wet-in-wet to create soft shadowed areas.*

▲ *Brushstrokes of medium-tone pink are now laid over the first pale wash, and touches of the same color blended into the foliage wet-in-wet to tie the two areas together.*

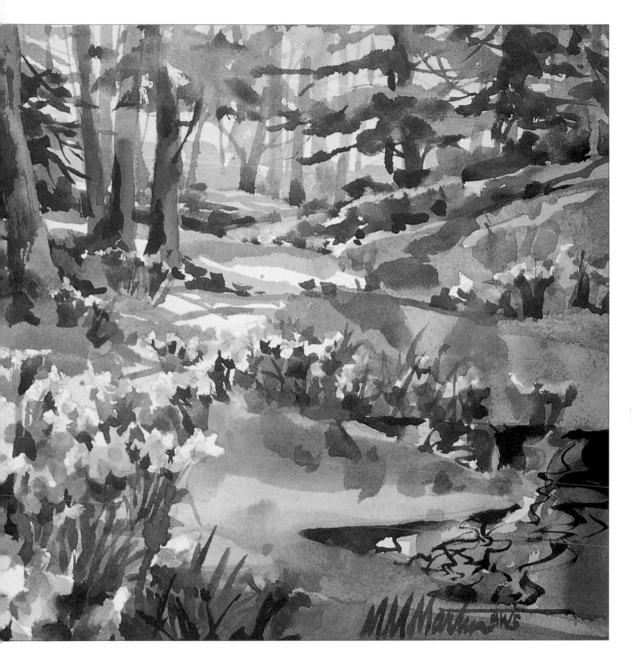

Spring Crowds

Margaret M. Martin • watercolor

The oranges and yellows of individual daffodils are visible in the foreground, but in the middle ground, detail is reduced and the range of color limited to pale yellows. Daffodils in the distance are merely hinted at by means of a specific distribution of tone and color.

3•Adding darker tones   4•Creating color links

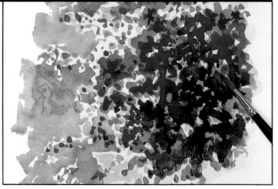

▲ *Darker washes are laid in and around the two previous washes, using the same pattern of dappled marks. This buildup of tone creates an impression of light filtering through.*

▲ *Finally, a darker version of the blue-gray used for the background is introduced into the shadow areas. This has the effect of "tying" the foreground and background together by means of a color.*

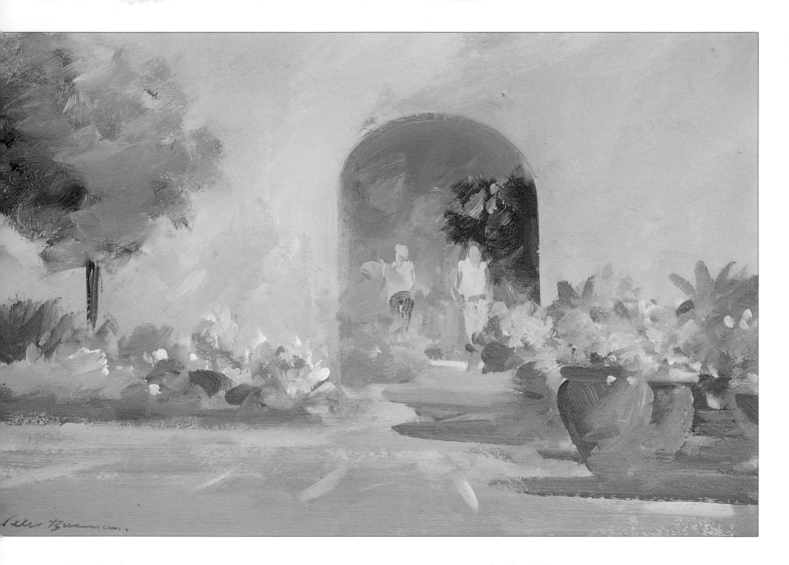

Garden in Provence

Peter Burman • oil

With a narrow range of color and tone, the artist hints at a wide range of flowers and foliage in the middle-ground area in front of the house.

together the farther away they are due to the effects of perspective, as explained on the previous pages.

Color control If the flowers are in the middle distance only and the foreground is relatively featureless, you will have to be tough with yourself. You know that colors become less saturated and the tonal range narrower, but if you put that into practice and dull the color, you may feel that the whole point of the flowers is lost. It won't be, though – if you capture the fall of light and shade successfully and suggest the blooms with texture, the eye will read the flowers as clearly as if you had painted each petal.

Large, brightly colored flowers such as sunflowers can be a problem because you can distinguish them quite clearly and thus may find yourself expressing them too vividly. Yellows and reds, as we have seen, are strong colors which come forward in the picture plane, draw the eye, and need to be treated

Balancing color and tone *Controlling tone can be difficult in pastel, as the colors can only be mixed on the paper. There is a potential problem in these middle-ground blossom trees, as the "white" blooms against the dark and light pinks provide too great a contrast.*

1 • Scumbled side strokes

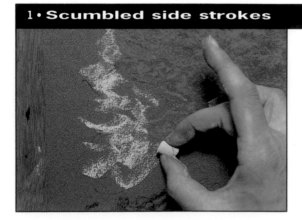

▲ *In order to "knock back" the whites, the artist works lightly, with a small piece of pastel held on its side. Because the coverage is so light, the color of the paper shows through the strokes.*

Prince Valley

Joyce Zavorskas • oil bar

These trees in bloom are created with many shades of "white" – pink, green, blue, yellow. The colors are built up in a delicate layering technique, and the marks of the oil bar (a larger, softer version of oil pastel) give a strong sense of movement.

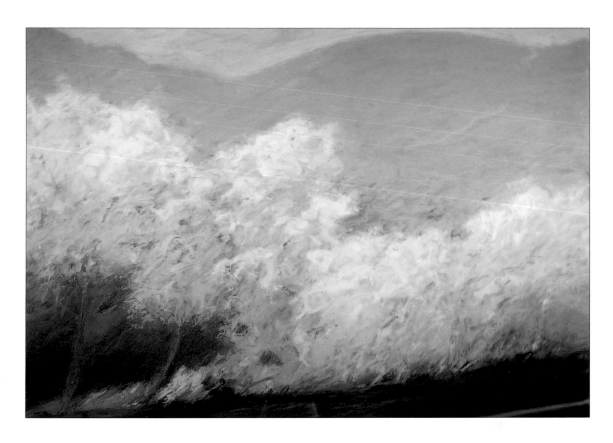

carefully. In such cases, if you want to retain vivid colors in the middle ground, you will have to make more of the foreground – or less of it, deliberately allowing the middle ground to be the center of interest.

Painting blossoms Trees in flower should be treated in the same way as trees in leaf; the blossoms will form a mass of color just as the leaves do. Again, don't overplay the colors – in the middle-ground planes, the delicate colors of pink blossom will barely exist, appearing as white modified with the merest touch of red. For a soft effect in oils, try working wet-in-wet; in watercolor leave the highlights as white paper, then wash in palest pinks and superimpose foliage greens. In pastels, try laying in the darker tones, then spraying with fixative before superimposing small marks in paler colors.

2 • Linear strokes

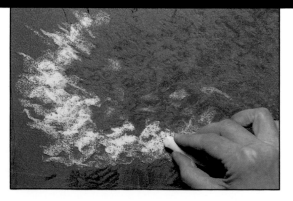

▲ *Using a blunt pastel, soft linear marks are worked into the scumble. The blossom is still too bright, however, and comes forward in the picture space.*

3 • Fixing between stages

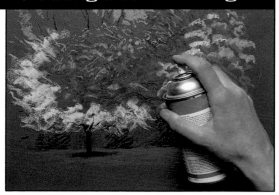

▲ *Adding light pink highlights to the dark pink cherry and building up the tree on the right have helped to reduce the contrasts. The picture is fixed at this stage to allow more colors to be laid on top.*

MIDDLE-GROUND TREES

FOR HER PAINTING OF A sunlit olive grove in Italy, Jane Strother uses oil pastels spread with mineral spirits, a technique she likes because it gives a freedom not usually associated with pastels – mistakes can be easily wiped off with spirits and color moved around the paper. She is not afraid of strong color and begins with a bright yellow base color. For this she has used oil paint mixed with linseed oil, which gives a slightly slippery surface, making it easier to manipulate the color.

Materials: pink colored pencil; flat bristle brush; rag; linseed oil; mineral spirits; Indian yellow and white oil paints. **Oil pastel colors**: white, flesh pink, Indian red, violet, peacock blue, pale turquoise, olive green, gray-green, cadmium yellow, lemon yellow.

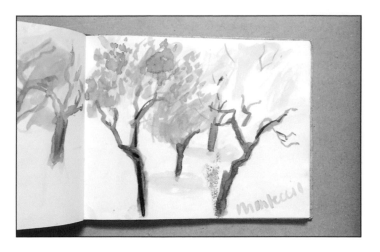

1 *A quick on-the-spot watercolor sketch was the basis for this studio painting completed at a later date.*

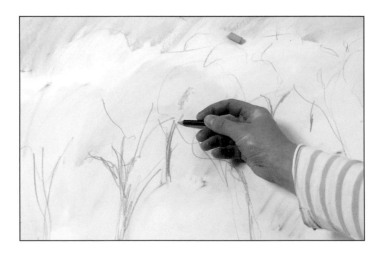

2 *Indian yellow oil paint mixed with a little linseed oil has been spread on gently with a rag, and a pink colored pencil is now used to draw in light guidelines for the trees.*

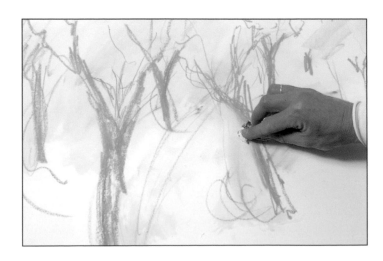

3 *The artist establishes the tree shapes with a dusky pink oil pastel, using loose, directional strokes. Any unwanted lines can be removed with mineral spirits.*

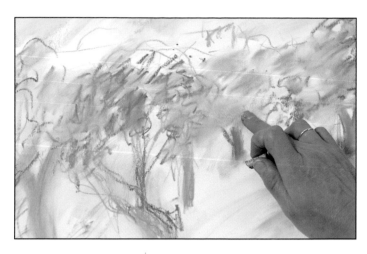

4 To create soft medium tones, she draws in foliage marks with a soft blue-green pastel and then smudges the color with her finger. The background foliage is more thoroughly blended.

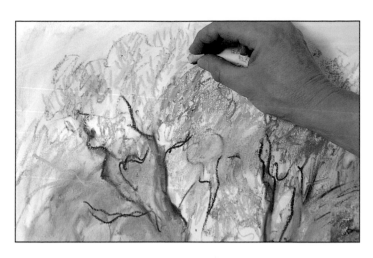

7 The leaves of the foreground are expressed with short sharp strokes which are left unblended in contrast to the softer treatment of the middle ground.

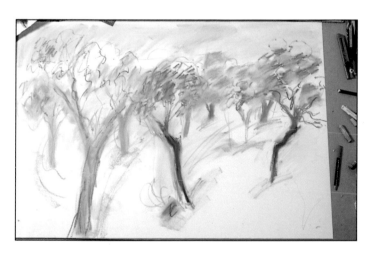

5 At this stage, although the trees are developing, there is little differentiation between the foreground and background. The tones and colors in the foreground need strengthening.

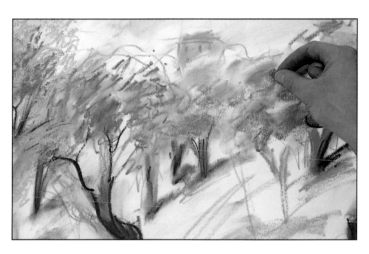

8 A distant house establishes a background focus and helps to define the middle ground, which is now built up more positively. A soft scumble with the pastel stick varies the foliage texture.

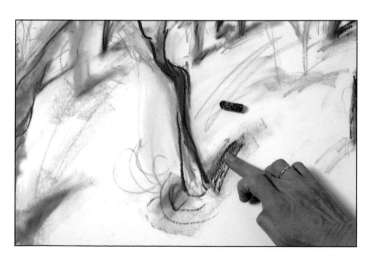

6 Increasing the contrasts in the foreground pull this tree forward, and the strong cast shadow takes the eye into the picture space. The edge of the shadow is softened by finger-smudging.

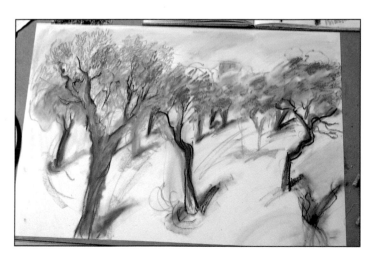

9 At this stage the painting is assessed to decide what still needs to be done. The different planes are better established, but the foreground and middle ground still lack "bite."

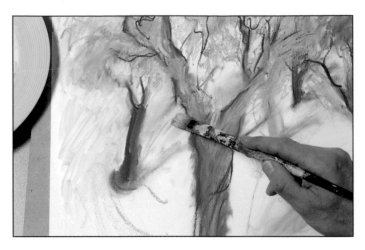

10 More of the Indian yellow oil paint is brushed on to suggest shafts of sunlight coming through the trees and set up a complementary color contrast with the shadow purples.

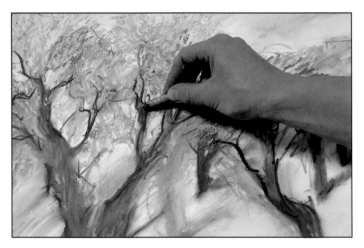

11 Now the darks in the foreground are intensified. Here a warm Indian red is used to bring the tree forward.

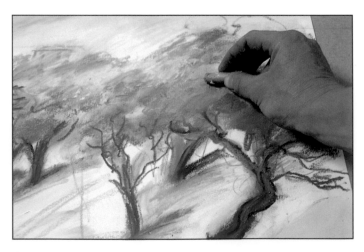

12 A paler version of the foreground Indian red is dragged lightly over the earlier colors to create a relationship between the two areas. White pastel has been used to "knock back" the trees.

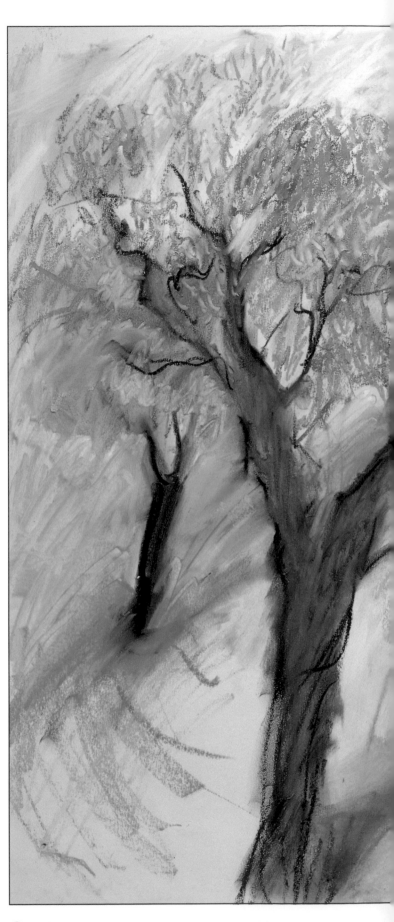

13 The artist has taken care to treat each tree differently and yet to pull them together with color, making effective use of yellow-purple complementary contrasts.

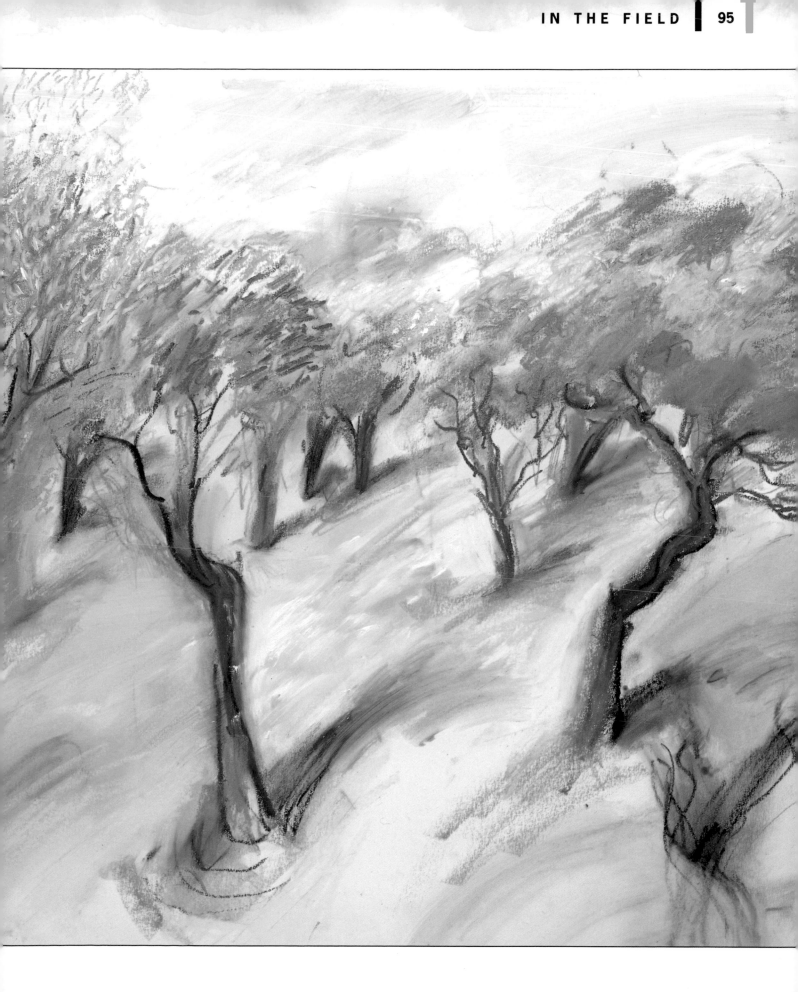

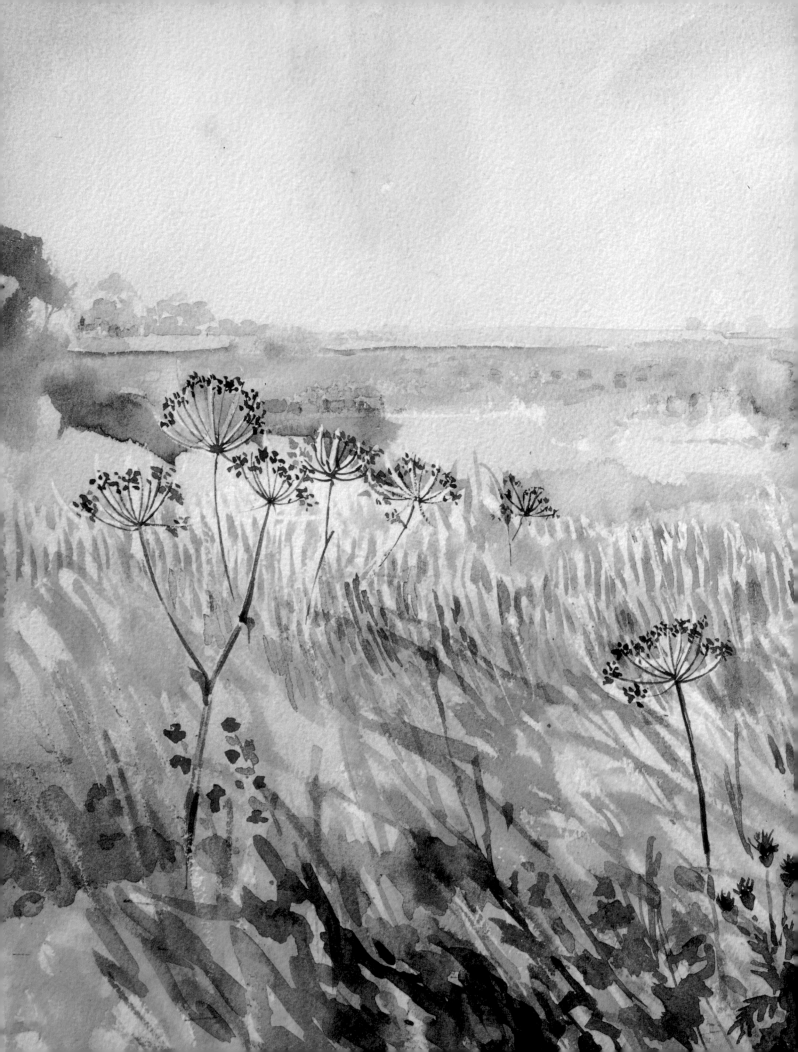

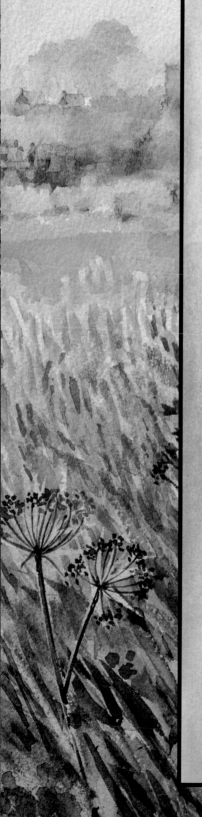

Chapter Three

DISTANCE

ABOUT LOOKING   98

CHOOSING AN APPROACH   100

DETAIL AND EDGE QUALITY   104

CONTRAST AND COLOR   110

SCALE AND PROPORTION   116

IN THE FIELD   118

WE NOW TRAVEL FURTHER into the picture space, continuing beyond the middleground into the distance. This area of the landscape, where the land meets the sky, is often the most exciting part of a scene, but it is also challenging, requiring an understanding of color and tone and an ability to manipulate your chosen medium. Here we look at ways of meeting the challenge and creating the effects of space and recession so vital in landscape painting.

After Harvest, Norfolk

Maurice Read • watercolor

About looking

SEEING DISTANCE

IN THESE PHOTOGRAPHS you can see how changing weather and light can alter the distance in your view. Being able to compare the same scene at different times of the year will help you to see the effects of such changes on the composition and mood of your painting. By introducing such effects as the blurring and bleaching qualities of mist or the stark tonality of snow, you will discover new challenges. And you do not need to travel far – try your backyard, as the photographer did in this case, or a local park.

On these two pages the focus is on the distance.

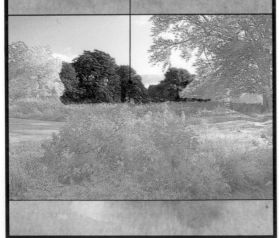

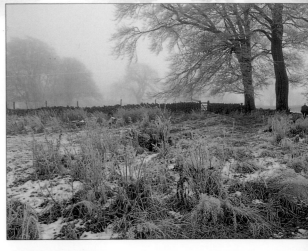

▶ *In the same scene on a foggy winter's day, the distance becomes the soft shapes of the misty trees seen beyond the wall.*

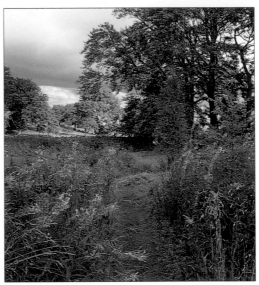

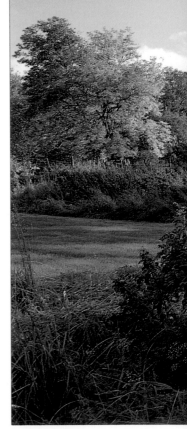

▲ *Moving back on the general view (center), with a high viewpoint, the distance is spotlit by a shaft of sunlight breaking through the clouds, creating a study in sharp contrasts.*

▼ *The same view again, but now in the fall. The shadows cast by the trees behind the photographer are an important part of the picture.*

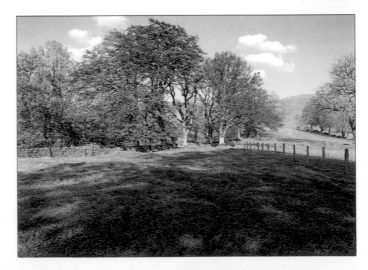

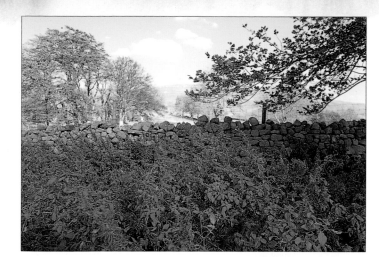

◄ *A closer view in the fall reveals the distant trees and hill beyond the wall.*

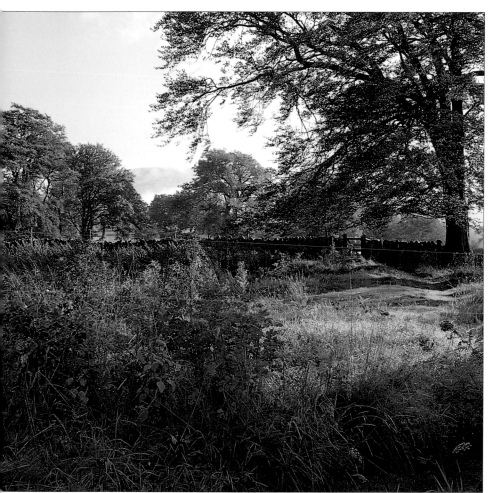

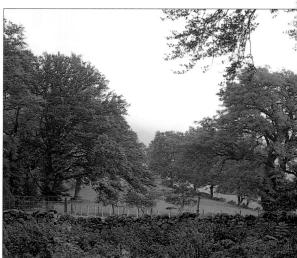

▲ *The photographer now moves right up to the wall to view the scene beyond through the wire fence. The distance becomes a misty frieze of trees.*

▶ *Stepping beyond the wall, the line of posts takes the eye into the distance.*

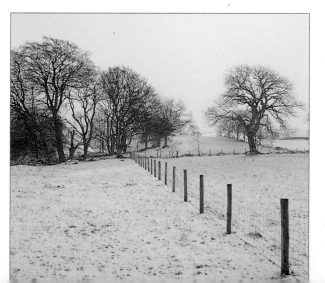

▲ *An overcast summer's day gives a blue cast to all the greens. Note how the sense of space is reduced because the contrasts in tone between foreground and background are less pronounced.*

Choosing an Approach

IDENTIFY THE AREA OF DISTANCE IN YOUR COMPOSITION BEFORE YOU START TO PAINT

FIRST LET'S DEFINE WHAT is meant by distance. Like the middle ground, it can be a large area of your picture space or a small one, and unless there is some clear natural division, it will merge into the middle ground. The distance could be the view over a backyard fence a few hundred yards from you, or a mountain range more than 100 miles away, forming a dramatic backdrop to an extensive middle ground. But however near or far, it is the land

View from Froghole

Brian Yale • oil

The distant patchwork of fields are enveloped in misty rain, which exaggerates the effects of aerial perspective. The high viewpoint chosen gives prominence to the distance, to which attention is drawn by the curves of the foreground fields and lines of the hedges.

May Tree in Blossom, Rainy Day

Patrick Cullen • oil

This view over vegetable gardens seen from an upstairs window leads the eye over trees to misty woods beyond. The eye is arrested in the middle distance by the subject and focal point of the painting, the May tree, but the distance extends far beyond this, melting into the cloudy sky on the horizon.

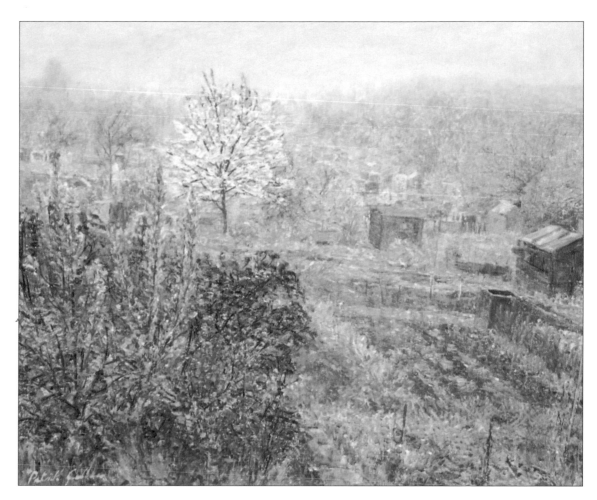

that we can see that is furthest away from us.

In order to give the viewer of your painting a sense of progressing into space, you will need to consider the effects of aerial perspective on this area of the picture, and it will help you if you identify this background area in your composition before you start. Where the sky meets the land will demarcate the farthest boundary, and sometimes you can find another, such as a high wall in front of distant hills, or the top edge of trees in a middle-ground woods, as the nearer boundary.

The effect of viewpoint Treatment of these distant planes will depend very much on how far away they are, and this often depends on the viewpoint. A high viewpoint will allow the artist to see more – if you are sitting on top of a hill, you will see much farther than if you are halfway up.

Nearer distance If the ground is flat and you can't see far, a line of trees a few hundred yards away may well represent your background, or distance, but you must still try to

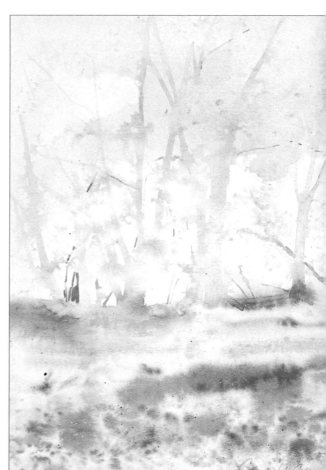

Bluebells at Freers Wood

Clarice Howitt • watercolor

In this sketch, the artist has chosen to "fence off" the distance with a line of trees, thus concentrating attention on the bluebells. Yet even though there is only white paper, there is a strong feeling of misty distance beyond the trees.

Creating distance *If your chosen subject includes converging parallel lines, you will be at least halfway to creating distance, but it is also conveyed by the cooling of colors and the diminution of detail and tonal contrast. All these effects are combined in this colored pencil drawing.*

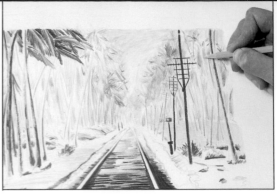

1 • Mapping out

▲ *The composition is mapped out in pale purple pencil, with the railroad tracks placed almost centrally so that the eye is taken along them into the distance.*

2 • Increasing contrasts

▲ *In the foreground the trees and telegraph poles are darkened with Prussian blue. In contrast, a much paler turquoise blue is used both between the poles and in the background.*

create a feeling of space in your painting – every landscape has space, no matter how small. If your background is a border of trees running right across the picture, you can create a feeling of distance through your treatment of the foreground and middle ground. Try lowering your viewpoint so that you have the feeling of struggling physically through the foreground

countryside – perhaps wet, muddy pasture or a richly plowed field, creating distance with the receding furrows of earth. The eye cannot go beyond the distant line of trees, but it will have traveled far before reaching it. Distracting the eye with patches of light and color in the foreground will also increase the feeling of distance.

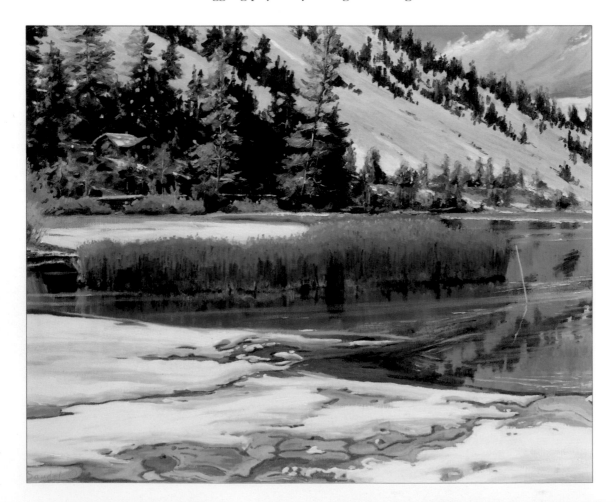

Coming of Winter

Martha Saudek • oil

Here you can see a dramatic difference in the amount of color and detail in the middle-ground trees and those on the more distant hillside. This is what creates the feeling of space in this painting.

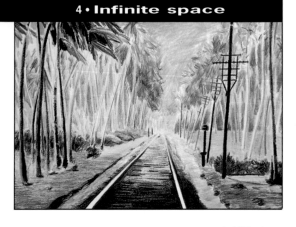

3 • Increasing color

4 • Infinite space

▲ *The range and intensity of colors in the foreground are gradually increased, pushing the distance farther back in space. Notice that the colors in the distance are cooler as well as paler.*

▲ *The finished drawing creates a successful illusion of space, with very strong contrasts in the foreground and accurate use of linear perspective.*

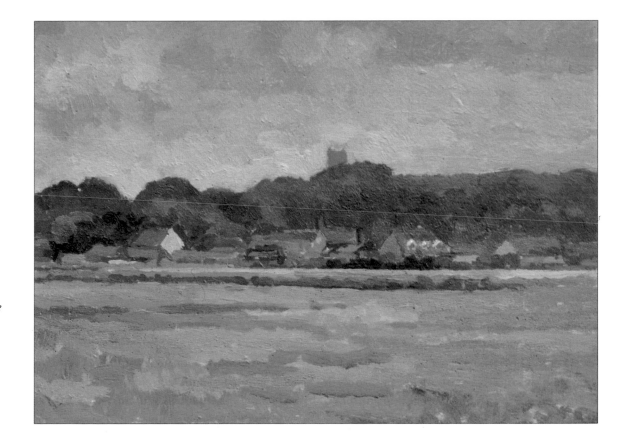

Distant Village

James Horton • oil

Blocks of subtle color and patches of light in the foreground expanse of marshy ground help to "entertain" the eye and create a sense of space in front of the distant line of trees and houses.

Focus in the background The distance does not have to be a dull area; you can set up a focus of interest within it, leading the eye toward it through the middle ground. The focus might be a clump of trees or a ruined building breaking through into the sky, a distant lake catching a shaft of sunlight or an intriguingly shaped rock silhouetted against the sky. You will have to be careful, however, not to get carried away by the subject of the focus; if there is too much color, detail, or tonal contrast, it will no longer read as distance.

If you want to make the distance the most important part of the painting, you could try "framing" it with a group of foreground trees, which introduces the view and gives a feeling of coming upon it by chance. A similar device much used by landscape painters is to work from the interior of a room, using the window frame, bars, and perhaps a swag of curtain as a frame within a frame to draw attention to a distant landscape.

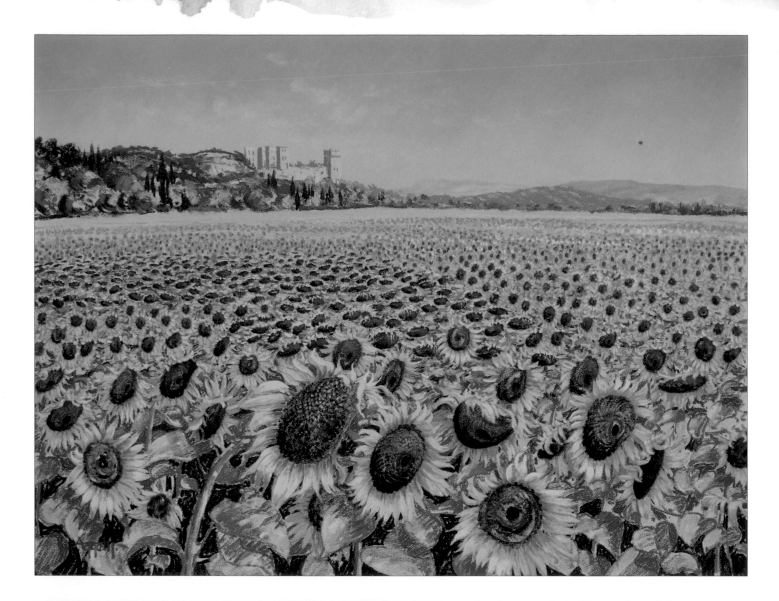

Les Tournesols de Montmajour, Arles

Lionel Aggett • pastel

The effects of both linear and aerial perspective are well illustrated in this picture – over distance, the shapes become smaller, the colors less intense and cooler, and the tonal contrasts narrower.

Detail and Edge Quality

USE ARTISTIC LICENSE – IF THE EFFECTS OF AERIAL PERSPECTIVE ARE NOT OBVIOUS, EXAGGERATE THEM

IF YOU STUDY A variety of landscape paintings, you may be surprised by the variation in the treatment of the distance. Often a line of hills can be summarized in a few strokes of paint, guaranteeing that the focus of interest is elsewhere in the painting. Sometimes the distance is dealt with in considerable detail, but whatever the treatment, the artist always makes sure that it reads as the farthest-away part of the landscape.

How much detail The amount of detail you include in the distance depends very much on how far away it is. If it is relatively near, you can put in a good deal, but you must always remember to reduce contrasts. When you look out of your window or at a view of a park or gar-

Diminishing detail *In this simple oil sketch of a Caribbean beach, a line of palms stretches into the distance. By reducing the trees to a basic shape and making sure that there is a contrast in detail between those closer and those farther away, an illusion of distance is created, helped by the roughly parallel curving lines converging on the far side of the bay.*

den, the effects of aerial perspective on the more distant trees and foliage is not always that obvious, but it is there, and the job of the artist is to point it out.

Obviously the greater the distance you are dealing with, the more pronounced are the effects of aerial perspective – everyone has noticed how blue and hazy a far-away range of hills looks on a clear day. So if you want to give the impression of large distances, you will need to exaggerate the lack of detail, the loss of any formal edges, the narrow tonal range, and the blue cast of the colors.

You can experiment with a middle-ground screen of trees, behind which you add a bluish-purple line suggesting more trees. Now add some rising ground in a paler version of your bluish-purple, and so on. You will be amazed how far back you can take the eye in this way.

Unifying the picture Another matter you will have to consider is the sky and how it relates to the far distant land. This can be a problem, but one usually caused only by lack of observation. The sky is darkest at the top, above your head, and it becomes progressively paler at the horizon, with sky and land sometimes appearing to melt together into a single pale tone. If there is too much color and tone in this area of sky, it will fail to link with the land, and the picture will "fall apart."

Often some landscape element can be found to "tie" land and sky together, such as trees breaking up into the sky. These could just pierce the sky area on the horizon in the far distance or they could be larger and more positive, set closer to the viewer but overlapping the horizon line.

If you are using opaque paints or pastels, you might consider painting the tree or trees first and then working the sky around and into the form, rather than the other way around. This has the effect of locking the two areas together more strongly.

1 · Capturing shapes

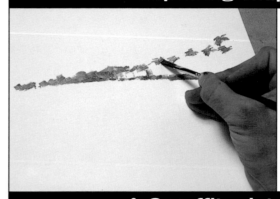

◀ *The line of palms is painted with a ¼-inch long flat brush which will give an impression of palm fronds with one touch. The color used is sap green.*

2 · Sgraffito detail

▶ *The trees closest to the viewer need to be more clearly described. The end of the brush is used to scratch into the paint, making a series of white lines.*

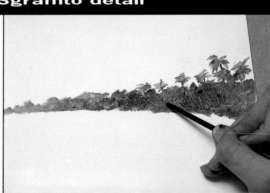

3 · Balancing the contrasts

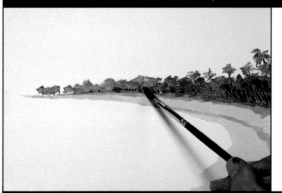

◀ *Touches of raw sienna are now introduced into the trees, with the colors kept close in tone to avoid strong contrasts.*

4 · Softening tree edges

▶ *The sky has been worked around the trees, allowing the blue and green to blend slightly. Oil paint dries slowly, allowing you to exploit such wet-in-wet effects for some time.*

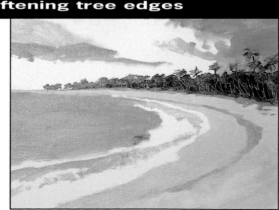

Detail and Edge Quality

EVEN SUBTLE CHANGES IN LIGHT WILL ALTER YOUR VIEW, PARTICULARLY IN THE DISTANCE

▷ **The River Lagan, Ireland**

Paul Kenny • oil

The whole scene is bathed in a misty evening light, softening edges and detail and reducing tonal contrasts. The painting is carefully structured, with patches of golden light leading the eye along the river.

EVERYONE WHO IS INTERESTED in landscape will have noticed how a scene changes as clouds are blown across the sky, cutting out the sun in one place and then another, and suddenly directing it like a spotlight on a distant hillside. The weather – and hence the light – not only affects the key of your painting, determining whether it is in an overall light or dark "key" or a patchwork of sun and shade, it can also alter the structure of your view even

within one painting session. Even on a clear day when there are no dramatic weather changes, subtle color shifts caused by the movement of the sun will alter your view substantially, and nowhere is this more obvious than in the distant features of a landscape.

Focus on the distance In the foreground and middle ground, changes of light obviously alter the strength and direction of shadows, but they don't in general affect the clarity of landscape features. In the distance, however, they do, particularly in a large panorama where the distance is far from you. Take a distant range of hills or mountains, for example. In the early morning when the sun is low, it will be hazy, with perhaps a pinkish tinge from the rising sun, and details that may be visible later will be impossible to distinguish in the subtle merging of pale color and tone. As the sun strengthens

Solid Geometry and Sunlight

Brian Yale • acrylic

The combination of the bright sunlight and the strong geometric shapes of the hedges gives a dramatic stage-set appearance. How different this scene would be on an overcast day, without the stark tonal contrasts.

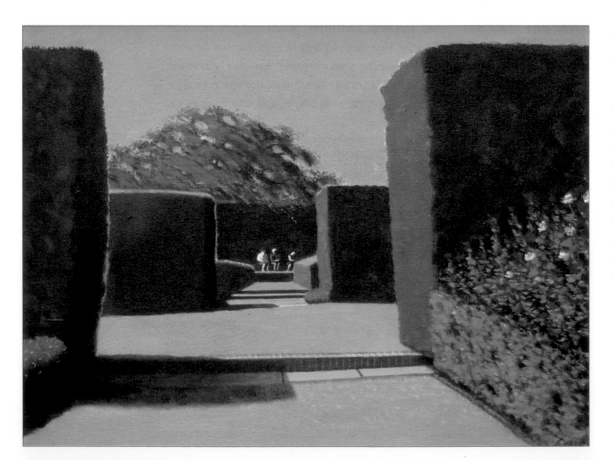

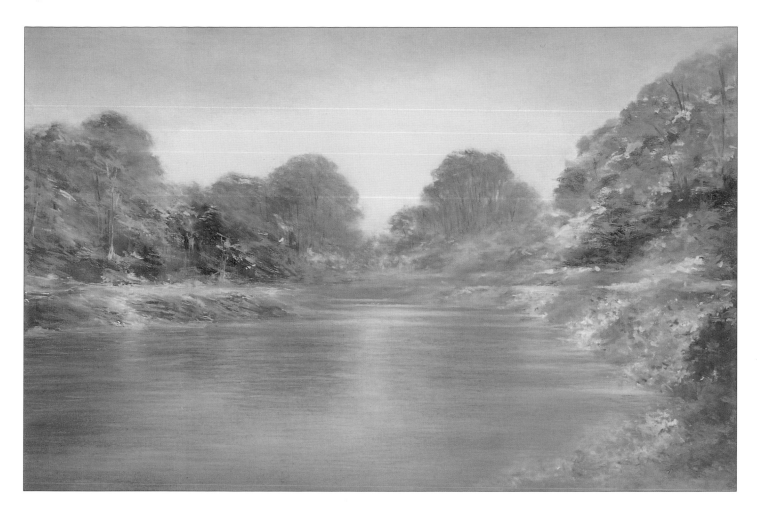

and rises in the sky, these same hills will come into focus; and if clouds are present, you will see patches of shadow and sunlight defining forms and picking out individual details. In the evening light the distance is reduced to a haze.

Painting changing light So how do you deal with this when you are painting? One answer is to work in short sessions, working on two or more paintings at the same time, the procedure followed by the great Impressionist painter Claude Monet (1840–1926). You have to be tough with yourself and stop painting as soon as the light begins to change, but it is surprising how much you can do in an hour or two. Another way of dealing with this problem is to make quick color sketches or drawings with written color notes.

Changing weather *A change in the weather always means a change in the light, which will have a dramatic effect on the visible structure of your view. Painted in short sessions, these two watercolor sketches of the same view clearly demonstrate these changes.*

1 • Cloud and snow

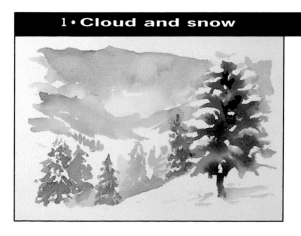

▲ *Snow reflects what light there is and makes it seem brighter. Here the light is dull, resulting in an almost monochrome landscape.*

2 • Evening sun

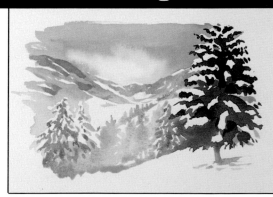

▲ *In a brighter light, more of the distant mountains is visible, and there are greater contrasts of color and tone as well as more detail.*

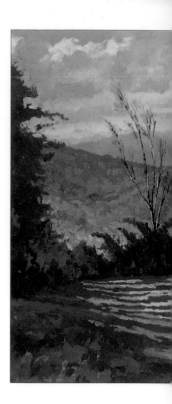

**View from
Les Planes**

James Horton • oil

*There is a lot of
interest in the
foreground, with the
shadows of unseen
trees creating a strong
tonal pattern. Thus,
although the feeling of
distance beyond the
mountains is
important in the
composition, the
mountains do not take
too much of the
viewer's attention.*

Detail and Edge Quality

ASSESS THE SCENE BY LOOKING THROUGH HALF-CLOSED EYES TO REDUCE DETAIL

IT HAS ALREADY BEEN established that painting landscape is not always a matter of painting exactly what you see. The artist is always editing, refining, and making decisions about each area of the picture. When you are dealing with distance, you may need to suppress detail deliberately in order to throw a center of interest in the middle ground or foreground into prominence. You won't want to make your distant planes too featureless, however, so consider ways of hinting at detail without describing it literally. Trees in the background – clumps of pines on a hillside, for example, or fir trees in the Rockies – can be suggested by one or two upright brushstrokes or pastel marks contrasting with horizontal or curving treatments elsewhere. The shape of the tree seen against a light sky will be clearer, giving you a chance to portray individual features – but only with a touch of the brush.

Help yourself to reduce detail Leaving out something you can see, or generalizing it, is easier said than done, but it may help to impose some physical restrictions. If you use a small brush, you will find yourself naturally adopting a detailed approach – so don't. Try a larger one, and try also holding it differently.

Use a long-handled oil or acrylic brush held at the end so that you can stand as far away as possible from your working surface; this will also restrict your ability to describe detail, as you will have a less tight control over the brush. Keep standing back from your work, and look at both it and the actual scene through half-closed eyes. This blurs the image and helps you to get an overall perspective on color and tone.

Creating soft edges Your distant view will only look distant if you paint it with softer, more blurred edges than those in the foreground and middle ground. With both oils and watercolors, you can achieve the slightly blurred effect by working wet-in-wet – in oils you can soften edges further by gently blending colors together with a fingertip. With pastels, fingertip blending, or blending with a rag or piece of cotton, is the usual method for merging colors and tones into one another, and you can also soften and unify an area by lightly drawing a veil of color over it using the side of the stick.

A particularly important edge in this context is the horizon line, where the land meets the sky – too hard an edge will destroy the sense of space, as any sharp contrast comes forward to the front of the picture. Even when the sun drops beneath the horizon and the con-

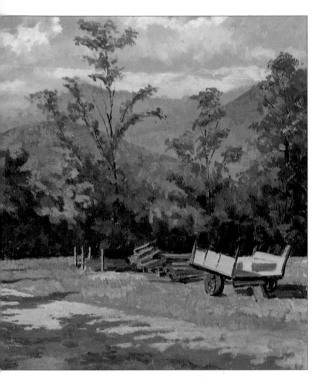

trasts between land and sky are sharpened, this edge will still be relatively soft.

Sometimes it is useful to transfer some of the land color into the sky area and vice versa. This can be done by using any of the methods suggested in the previous paragraph. In pastels you might also try dragging one color lightly over another with the side of the stick, or use the feathering method, which involves laying quick, light, linear strokes over an underlying color. Don't overdo feathering unless the foreground and middle ground are quite strong, however, as it creates a lively, busy effect.

Winter Sun, Delph

John McCombs • oil

The tones are carefully controlled in this painting. The artist has taken back the trees on the far hill with layers of lighter grays over dark, working the outline into the sky area to soften them.

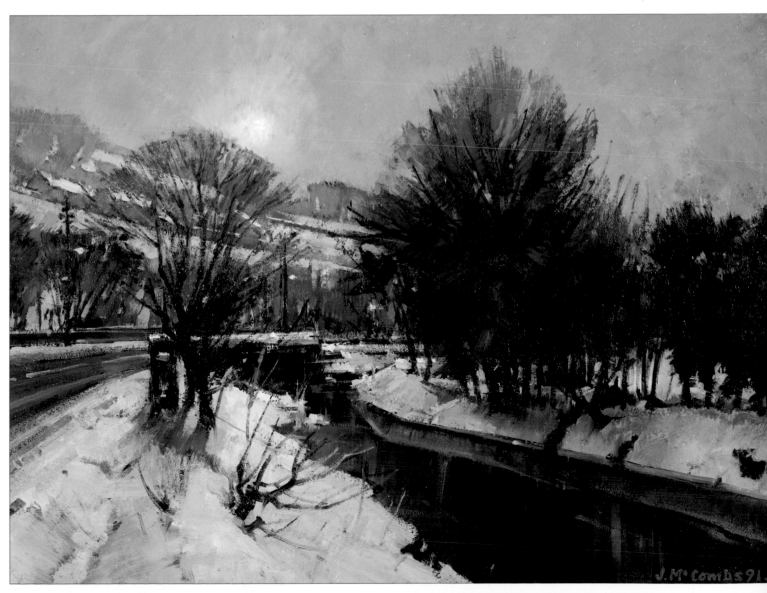

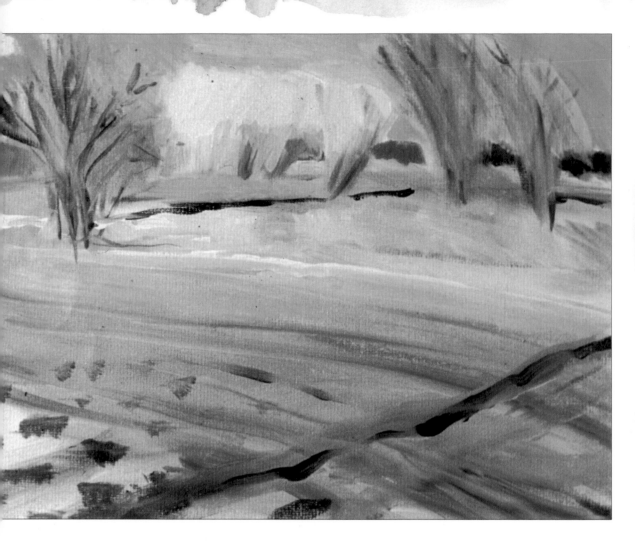

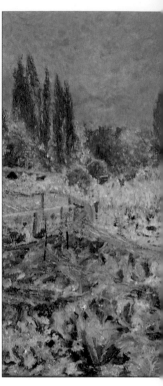

Contrast and Color

CREATE AREAS OF SUBTLE TEXTURE IN THE BACKGROUND OF YOUR PAINTING

△ **Lode, Cambridgeshire**

Jane Strother • acrylic

The sweeping curves made with the brush in the foreground lead the eye to the distant trees.

ONE OF THE WAYS in which you can increase the illusion of distance is by reducing the amount of texture that you include. This applies not only to the texture of features in the landscape, but also that of the paint itself. Thick paint, and obvious brushstrokes, have a strong physical presence and tend to come for-ward to the front of the picture. At its most extreme, this could mean working from impasto textural work in the foreground to areas of smoother, thinner paint in the background, but normally the contrast is less obvious.

Creating discreet texture It is, however, usually a mistake to remove all vestiges of tex-ture or to have too great a contrast between thick and thin paint – it is a matter of degree. Banks of trees in the far distance can be hinted at by discreet color and tonal changes. Distant hills painted in watercolor can be applied in pale washes, superimposing further washes until the required tone is reached. Try blotting areas of these washes with a tissue to create subtle areas of texture which might suggest wooded areas or patches of soft light. Or feed in a slightly darker color wet-in-wet.

Distance with knife impasto *Pages 46–49 show this artist's treatment of the foreground of his painting, but first he builds up this most delicate of distant views, which plays an important part in the composition. He uses a small painting knife to spread on the oil paint and then scratch into it. For the foreground he also uses a knife, but with thicker impasto.*

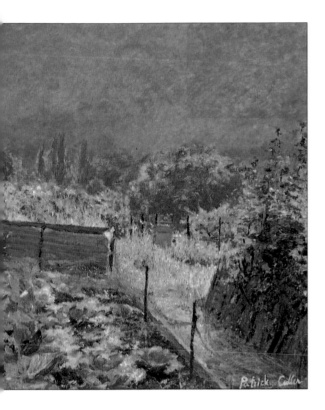

△ **Cabbages, June**

Patrick Cullen • pastel

In the distant trees, the pastel marks are closer and smaller than in the foreground.

With acrylic and oil paints, which hold the brushstroke, you can describe a patchwork of fields, wooded hills, or mountain crags with directional brushwork. For broken textures you could try leaving the paint to dry and then gently rubbing it with sandpaper to break up the surface. Another method is to scrape into opaque paint with the end of a paintbrush or a fingernail – Turner kept one especially long for this purpose. Such "sgraffito" marks can suggest details such as tree trunks without interfering with the color balance in the area.

Using soft brushes If you are working in oils or acrylics, you will find it easier to produce a smooth paint surface in the distant areas if you use soft brushes rather than bristle ones. Most artists have one or two sable or soft synthetic brushes for use in areas of a painting.

1 • Spreading the paint

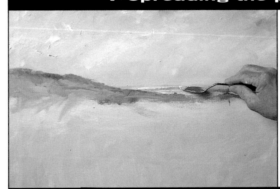

◄ *Using a small customized knife with the tip cut off and filed smooth, the paint is taken up and applied with the long edge. The knife is turned as the paint is spread.*

2 • Scratching into the paint

▶ *By drawing the edge of the knife along in the paint, the artist creates a series of ridges and delicate lines suggesting the edges of fields.*

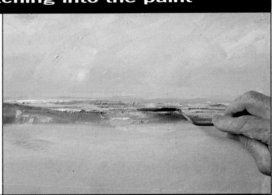

3 • A distant focal point

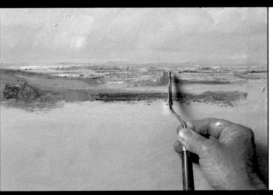

◄ *To draw the eye by creating a vertical contrast to the horizontality of the fields, a church is added by applying paint carefully with the tip of the knife.*

4 • Adding highlights

▶ *A very pale mixture of white and Mars yellow, with a touch of lemon yellow to cool it, has now been touched on in places to give a suggestion of patchy sunlight.*

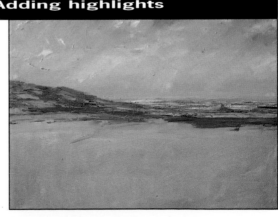

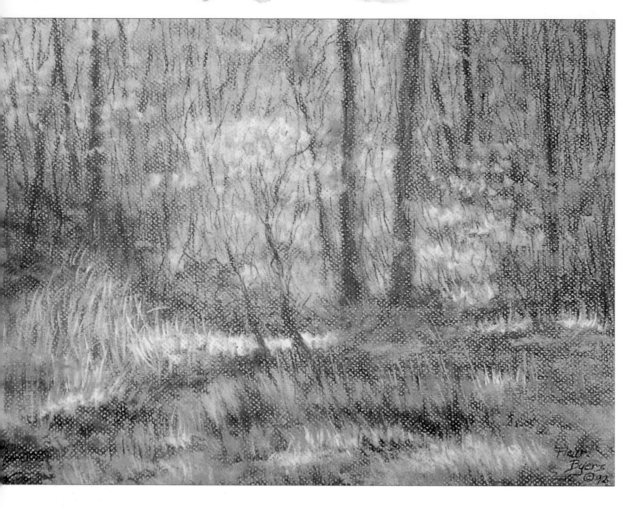

April in the Forest

Fleur Byers • pastel

Pale neutralized colors make up the background of these woods. Some are complementaries – pale moss greens and pinkish-browns – juxtaposed with delicate linear strokes to create a soft and luminous effect.

Contrast and Color

Cleverly juxtaposed neutrals can create lyrical passages in the distance

ONE OF THE MAIN problems with painting distant areas of landscape is keeping the colors unobtrusive enough to melt into the background while at the same time avoiding a muddy mess of characterless grays. As we have seen, the tonal range will be greatly reduced; indeed, there might be only one overall tone, but there will be small variations in color, pro-

ducing very beautiful and subtle effects.

Although colors in the distance will be paled and neutralized, they are still there, and you need to find a way of persuading the eye that a yellow field in the distance is actually the same yellow as one in the middle ground. This is done partly by controlling the tones and partly by very careful color mixing. The range of colors which come into the category of neutrals is more or less infinite, and if they are cleverly juxtaposed, they can create lyrical passages of color in the distant planes.

Complementary neutrals When Corot placed a red figure in a green landscape (see page 84), he was using the power of complementary colors to draw the eye. But they also have a part to play in color mixing, as these "opposites" form neutral colors when combined. Practice mixing them in different proportions and then adding a little white (the mixtures will be quite dark). In your painting, you'll find that if you place complementary neutrals close to one another – a mauve-biased neutral next to a yellow-biased one and so on,

Mixing neutrals for the background

Mixtures of two complementary colors produce a neutral color.

In this watercolor sketch, the foreground is painted in pure sap green. For the middle-ground hill and trees, cadmium red is added to darken and neutralize the green for the trees, and diluted with water for the paler hill. The distant hill has more red added and is further diluted.

This desert scene, painted in acrylics, uses mixes of ultramarine blue and cadmium orange with a little added white for the variety of subtle browns – leaning toward orange in some places and blue in others so that the painting is alive with juxtaposed versions of these complementaries. Breaking up the color and superimposing light on dark adds to the range of tones.

Pastels are blended on the paper or the colors mixed optically – scumbling or stippling colors together. For the distant hill here, the sense of distance is created with pale tints of complementary violet and lemon yellow, with some white.

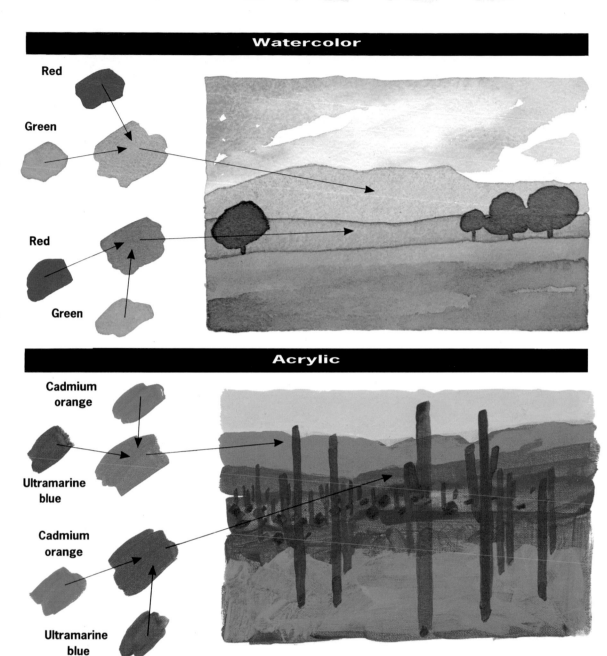

Watercolor

Red
Green

Red
Green

Acrylic

Cadmium orange

Ultramarine blue

Cadmium orange

Ultramarine blue

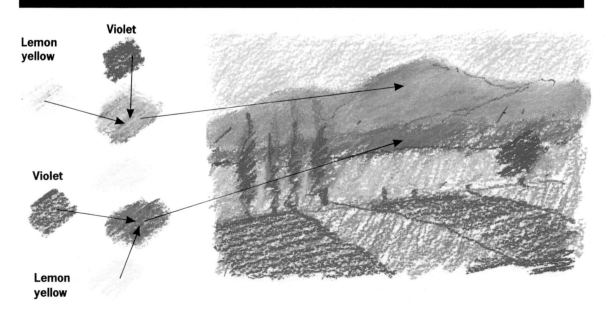

Pastels

Violet
Lemon yellow

Violet

Lemon yellow

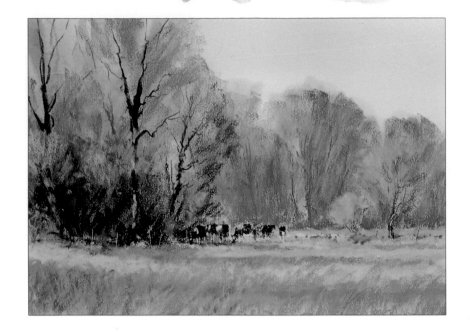

Spring Meadows

Alan Oliver • watercolor and pastel

Notice the wide variety of colors, scumbled and blended over the watercolor underpainting, which have gone to make up the "blue" of the distant trees.

the area will be alive with color even though it is very weak.

Distant blues The distant blue which is caused by aerial perspective can be a problem, as it is easy to make it too bright. Which blue to start off with in a color mix will depend on the overall "temperature" of your painting, that is, whether you are using predominantly warm or cool colors. Ultramarine is a warmer blue than cerulean or cobalt, so it is not the best choice for the background of a green landscape. It might work in a desert scene, with a dominant red-yellow theme, but even so it would need to be neutralized.

It would be nice if there was a recipe for

mixing distant blues, but unfortunately it all comes down to color relationships. If the vivid blue of the distance is what most attracted you to a scene, you might try painting this first so that you can then heighten the middle ground and foreground colors to balance it. It takes practice to get this kind of approach right, but it can produce exciting results.

Often it is more satisfactory to achieve the effect of "bluing" the background colors by mixing on the working surface. In oil and acrylic, for example, try laying thin glazes of blue over soft neutral tones, or scumbling one lighter semi-opaque color over another. In pastel the same effect can be created by lightly dragging the side of the stick over existing colors, which can first be sprayed with fixative. These methods allow you to introduce the blue as one of the constituent colors without blending it fully. Turner created the foliage of his trees with successive glazes of blue and greenish-brown oil paint, increasing the blue as he progressed into the distance.

Distant blue hills

Here it is the vivid blue hills which attract the eye, so in order to make them recede, the other colors have to be "keyed up." Oil pastels, which create both texture and vivid color, are used on oil sketching paper and spread with turpentine, allowing the artist to manipulate and blend the colors.

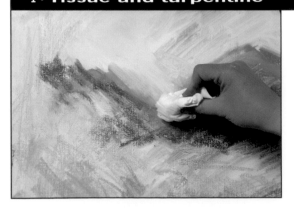

1 • Tissue and turpentine

▲ *To create the soft effect of mountains merging into sky, the artist uses a tissue dipped in turpentine to spread the oil pastel, making broad, sweeping marks.*

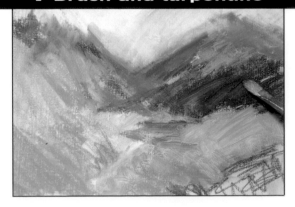

2 • Brush and turpentine

▲ *In the closer, darker-blue mountains, the pastel marks are blended with a bristle brush dipped in turpentine. Some of the pastel marks are left showing, complementing the gestural brushmarks.*

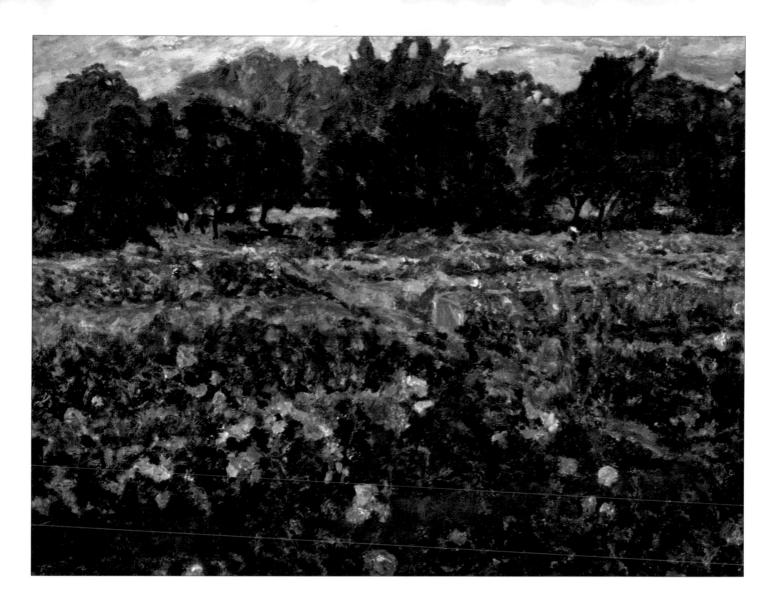

Roses, Evening

Patrick Cullen • oil

*In the distance the greenish-grays are infused with
touches of pink reflecting the foreground colors.*

3 • White highlights	4 • Warming the foreground

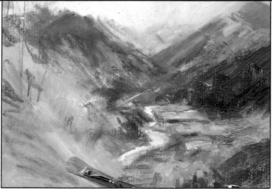

▲ *Using a white oil pastel stick and starting from
the back of the painting, the artist works into the
earlier colors, blending in places and leaving the
marks of the pastel stick in others.*

▲ *The foreground needs pale, warm colors to
contrast with the cool blue distance, and a brush is
once again used to create a generalized area of color
in the immediate foreground.*

Scale and Proportion

To set the scale of nature, contrast it with an element of a known size

End of the Day, Baggator

Roy Winstanley • watercolor

At first sight, the building appears substantial and the trees mighty, but the figures and the wheelbarrow beside the building explain the relative scales.

ONE OF THE THEMES of the Romantic movement in Europe in the late 18th century was the grandeur and omnipotence of nature and the power of nature over humanity. In many cases, notably in Turner's paintings, the monumental scale of nature was put across through the inclusion of one or more figures, shown dwarfed by trees and huge mountains.

If you want to express the size of anything, you can only do it by contrast. A human figure is a known size and thus explains the scale of everything around it. This does not mean you have to include a figure in every landscape, but such devices can be useful – you might use a

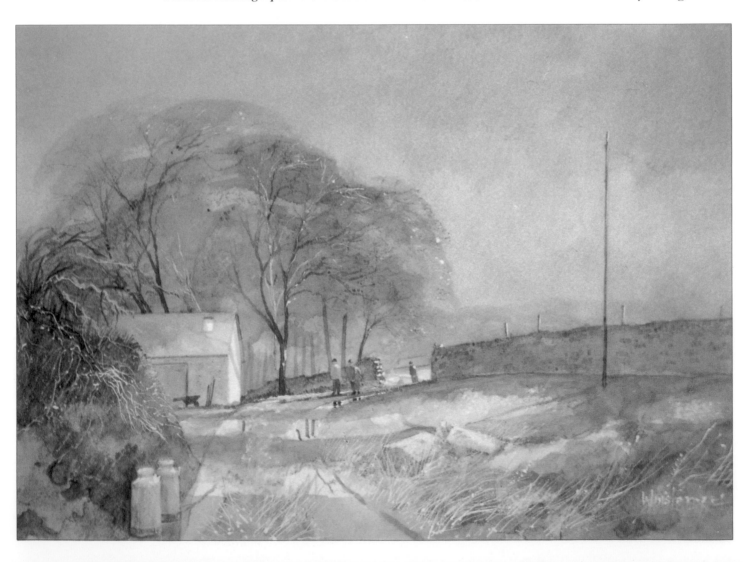

The Lake at Sheffield Park

Brian Yale • acrylic

It may take you a while to spot the tiny figures, even though the artist draws your attention to them with primary colors. Without these figures, it would be impossible to judge the size of the trees, but they set the scale.

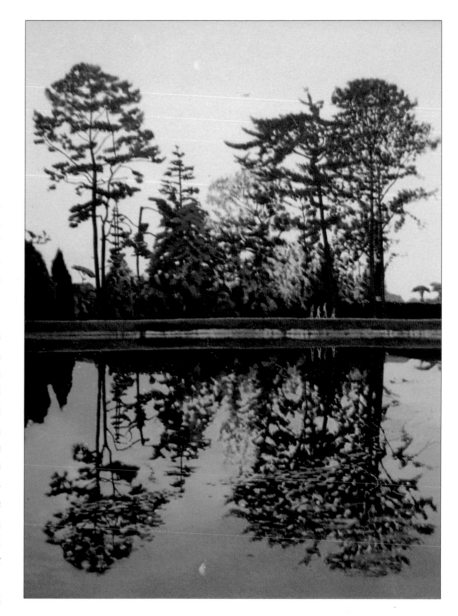

gate instead of a figure, or a building.

The Romantic painters often exaggerated the contrasts of scale between nature and humankind to express the drama of their theme. You can read a landscape in a certain way before you spot a tiny figure which forces you to reassess your original idea of the scale.

Setting the scale Contrasting opposites, such as small with large, is one way of setting scale, but you can also do this by comparing like with like. If you show a tree in the foreground and further similar trees set in the middle ground and distance, progressively decreasing in size, you will provide an important clue about the overall scale of the landscape – the distance from foreground to horizon. Repeating like elements in this way does not need to be static and predictable – the trees don't have to be in a neat row, nor need they be described in detail – they can be hinted at through shape, color or even similar brushwork.

If you have this kind of convenient placing

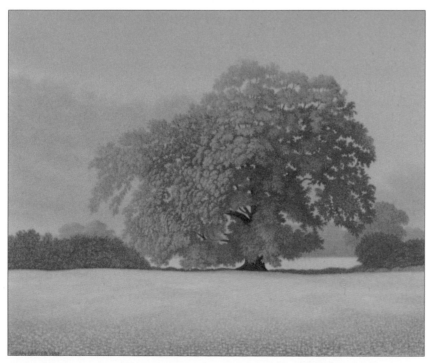

of trees, you will automatically be explaining the scale of your background, but what do you do if there is little to set the scale against? Perhaps you have only a single tree on the skyline and none in the middle ground. In this case, you will have to rely on your own observation and the use of the effects of aerial perspective, building up the planes in front through changing color, tone, and texture. A subject like this needs care, as it is easy to make a distant feature too large; and if it is out of scale with the rest of the landscape, it will have the effect of compressing the space.

"The Great Oak" in a Field of Buttercups

Jean Canter • watercolor and gouache

Although isolated, there is no doubt that this oak is indeed "great." The buttercups help set the scale, as do the distant trees.

In the field

DISTANT WINTER TREES

WORKING IN PALE watercolor washes, John Lidzey builds up transparent layers of paint until he is satisfied that he has captured the soft winter sunlight. He builds up the whole painting at the same time, never concentrating on one area for too long, and constantly assessing and balancing the tonal contrasts. The sense of distance is achieved through the gradual diminution of tone and color over distance, ending with pale neutral blue-grays on the horizon.

Materials: smooth (hot pressed) watercolor paper, stretched; sable brushes, cotton wool, dip pen. Colors: lemon yellow, cadmium yellow, aureolin yellow, yellow ocher, alizarin crimson, cadmium red, ultramarine, Payne's gray, indigo.

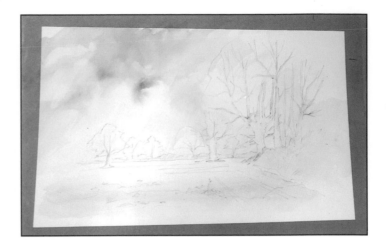

❶ *After making a careful pencil drawing, always necessary in watercolor work, the artist has laid light washes all over the paper with a large flat sable brush.*

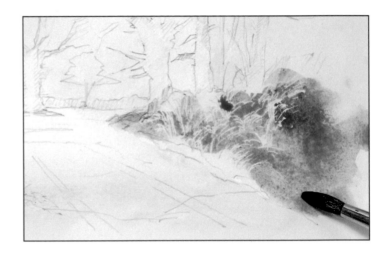

❷ *He now begins to establish the foreground, having used masking fluid to reserve details. A red-brown wash is dropped wet-in-wet into a mix of aureolin yellow and indigo.*

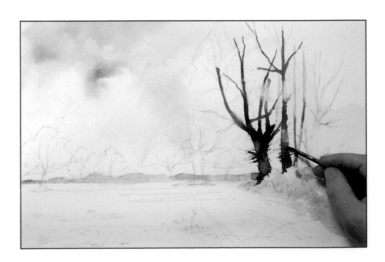

❸ *A dark mix of indigo, alizarin crimson, and yellow ocher is used for the foreground trees, with texture suggested by scratching into the wet paint with the brush end.*

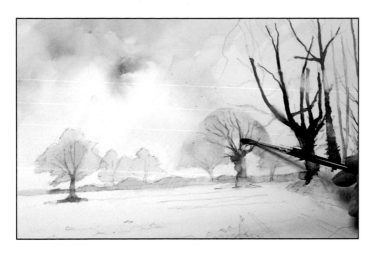

4 *Delicate washes of ultramarine "broken" with yellow ocher have been used for the most distant trees. The middle ground trees are a mix of Payne's gray, cadmium red, and yellow ocher.*

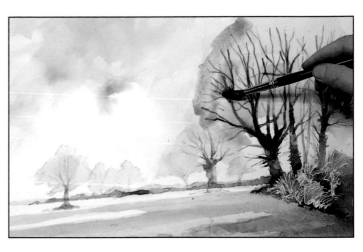

7 *A much stronger wash is now laid over the foreground tree to strengthen the contrast between it and the middle ground. If it is too strong, some of the color can be taken off with cotton.*

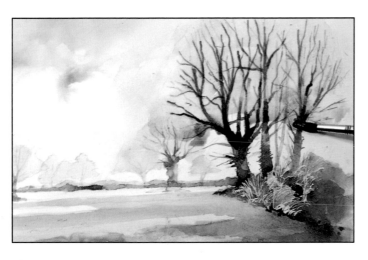

5 *Neutral blue shadows are laid wet-on-dry over the foreground bank and field, and darker mixes fed in wet-in-wet. Pale washes over the tree are controlled with the brush.*

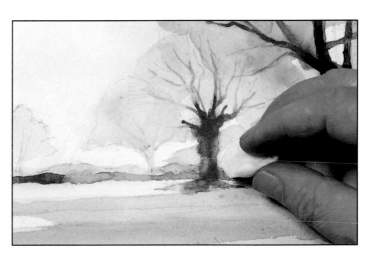

8 *The trunk of the middle-ground tree is now built up more strongly, but the edges must not be too sharp, so cotton is again used to lift out paint along the trunk.*

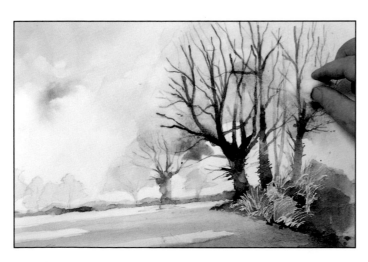

6 *Damp cotton is put to a number of uses: it controls the wash and prevents it from running; it takes off excess paint, and it adds texture to the wash.*

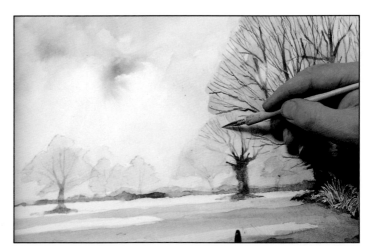

9 *The tracery of twigs is added with a fine pen, loaded from a brush charged with a paler mix of paint than that used for the foreground tracery.*

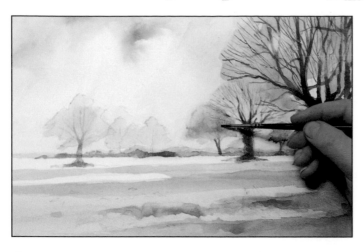

10 *The painting is now advanced enough for the artist to be able to assess the background trees and build up the tones to balance with the foreground. A number of superimposed washes create the effect of dense foliage.*

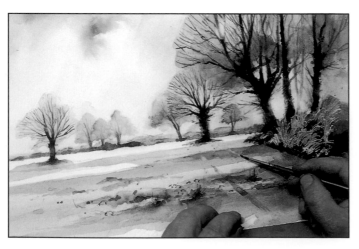

11 *In the foreground, some final dark washes are fed in, controlled with cotton and dried with a hairdryer; the hot air moves the paint around slightly.*

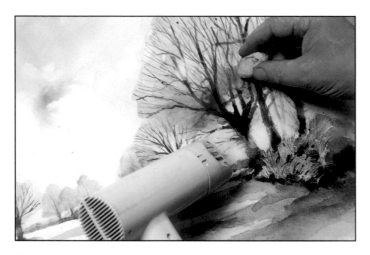

12 *The final touches have been added with a small sable brush, and here the same brush is used with water to lift out some of the paint. This light suggestion of tire marks helps to lead the eye.*

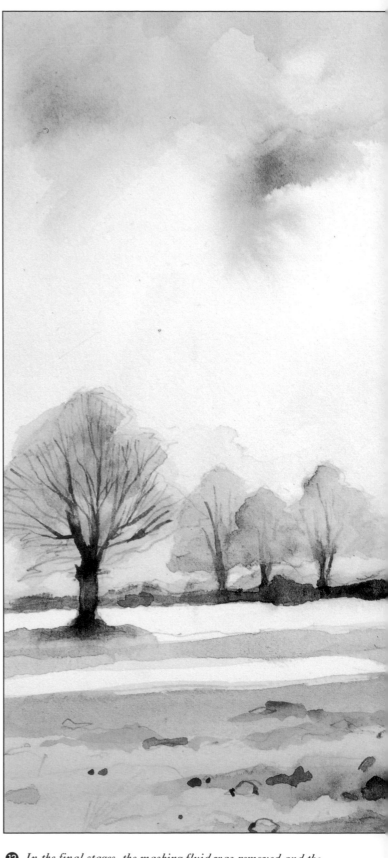

13 *In the final stages, the masking fluid was removed and the white areas reserved for the grasses toned down. The painting, with its strong contrasts of tone and its subtle colors, ably captures the mood of a misty winter's day. Even though the artist appears to have complete control over his washes, he still claims that chance plays a large part in watercolor painting.*

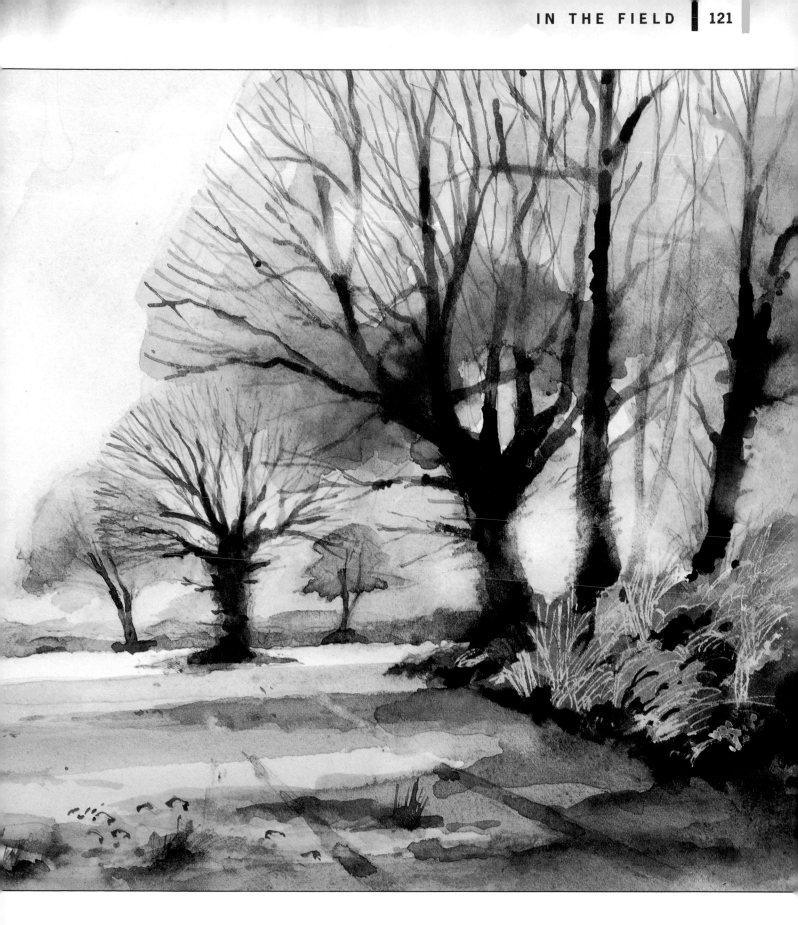

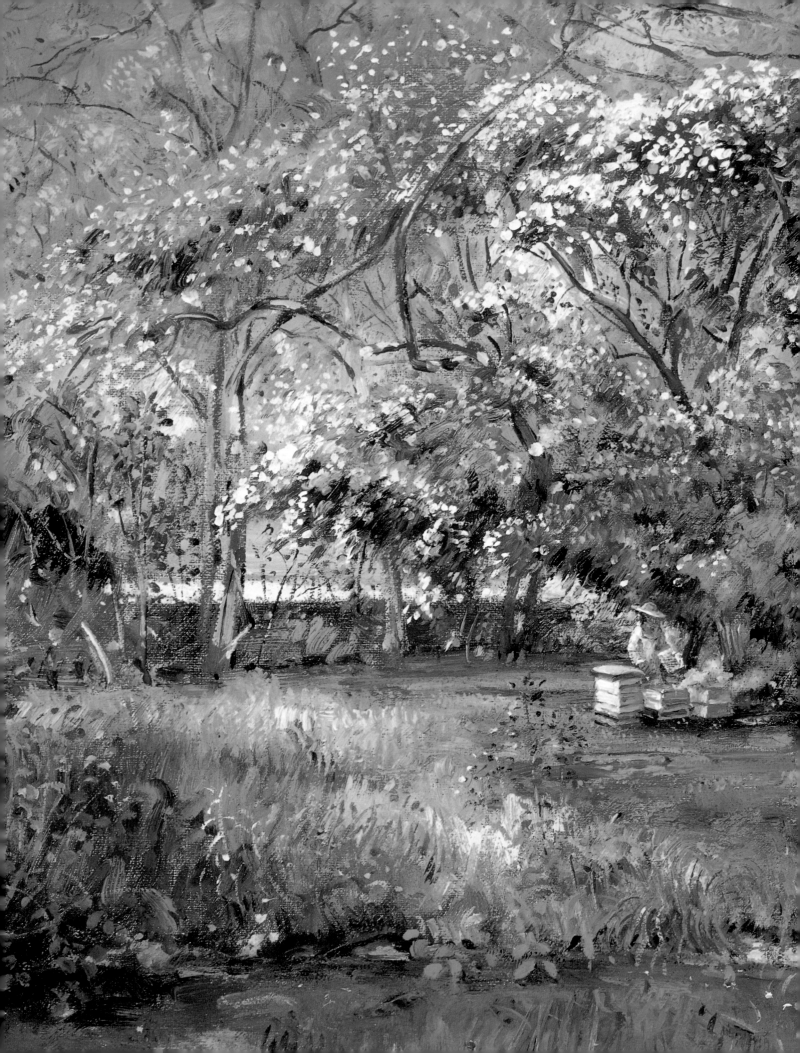

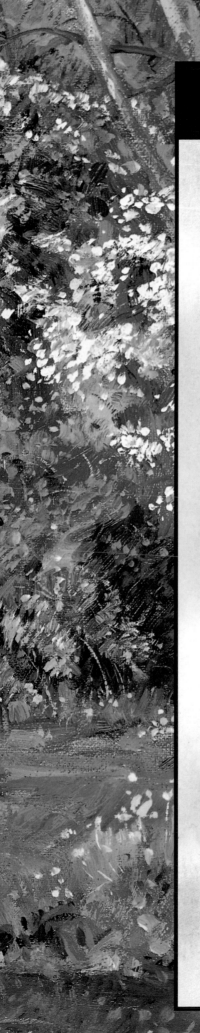

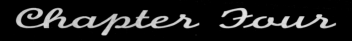

Chapter Four

PUTTING IT TOGETHER

CHOOSING AN APPROACH   124

THE PAINTING PROCESS   132

MAKING ADJUSTMENTS   138

IN THE THREE EARLIER chapters, we have considered trees, flowers, and foliage in the main divisions of the picture as foreground, middle ground, and distance. Although it is useful to look at these areas separately and consider how to make the best of them, the division is a somewhat artificial one, so now we focus on the complete picture, looking at ways of pulling it together, using annotated paintings to show you how.

Woodland Hives

Timothy Easton

Choosing an Approach

THE FIRST STEP TO SUCCESSFUL PAINTING IS TO ANALYZE YOUR OWN RESPONSES TO THE SCENE

Banks of the River Tame, Delph, Autumn

John McCombs • oil

This artist often keys down the tonal values in his paintings, with rich browns and blacks predominating. Here he has concentrated on the myriad of rich but subtle neutral colors provided by the golden autumnal light.

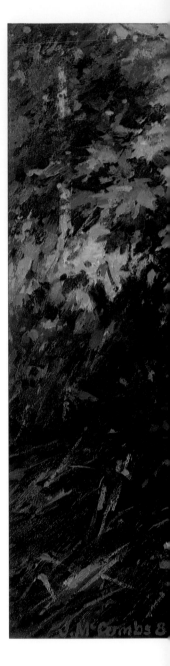

PLANNING YOUR PAINTING IS worth every minute you spend on it. At its most basic level, this process starts with checking that you have the right equipment and are wearing suitable clothes. Since you have limited time when you are working out "in the field," you may not want to spend too long working out the composition, but it will pay to take half an hour or so to sketch out some ideas and run through a checklist of points to consider – your center of interest, your viewpoint, where to place the horizon, and so on. Some artists enjoy the preparation and planning as much as the painting itself. It can be helpful, if your chosen painting spot is nearby, to make at least some of these decisions the day before; this gives you time to assimilate your impressions so that you arrive with a clear plan of action.

Interpreting the scene But before you begin to plan the composition, you will need to ask yourself an important question, because a lot

Surface pattern *In this watercolor the jigsaw-like layout of an Italian landscape makes an interlocking pattern on the surface. The bird's-eye view, with the sky outside the frame, creates an ambiguous sense of space.*

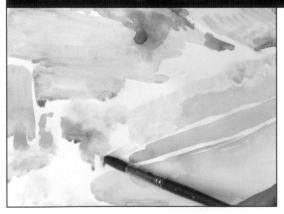

1 • Controlling watercolor

▲ *The composition is blocked in with pale washes of watercolor; some colors are kept separate and others encouraged to run together wet-in-wet.*

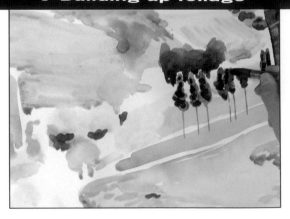

2 • Building up foliage

▲ *A line of cypresses is now built up with dark green washes laid over lighter ones, creating contrasts of tone which lead the eye to this area.*

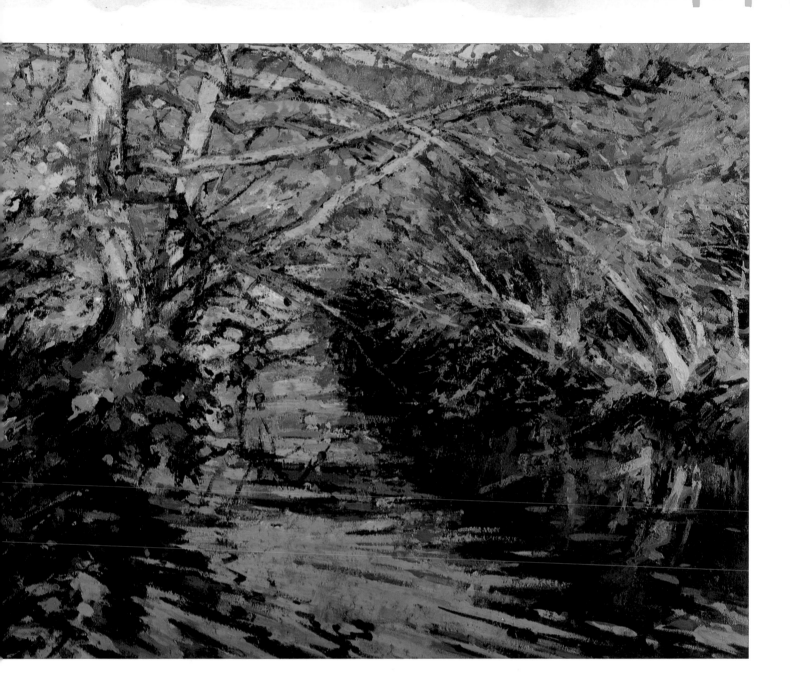

3 • Overlaid color

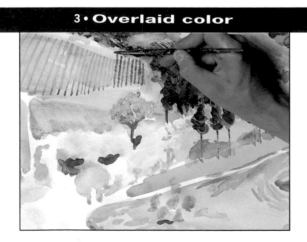

▲ With earlier washes and brushstrokes now dry, a darker, bluer mix is lightly rolled over the paper to create rough-edged lines.

4 • Broken color

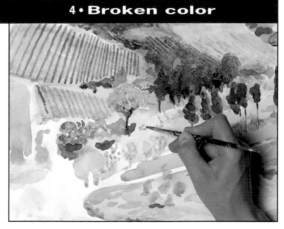

▲ The shadow area around the trees is applied with a stippling technique, using repeated small dabs of the brush to create broken color.

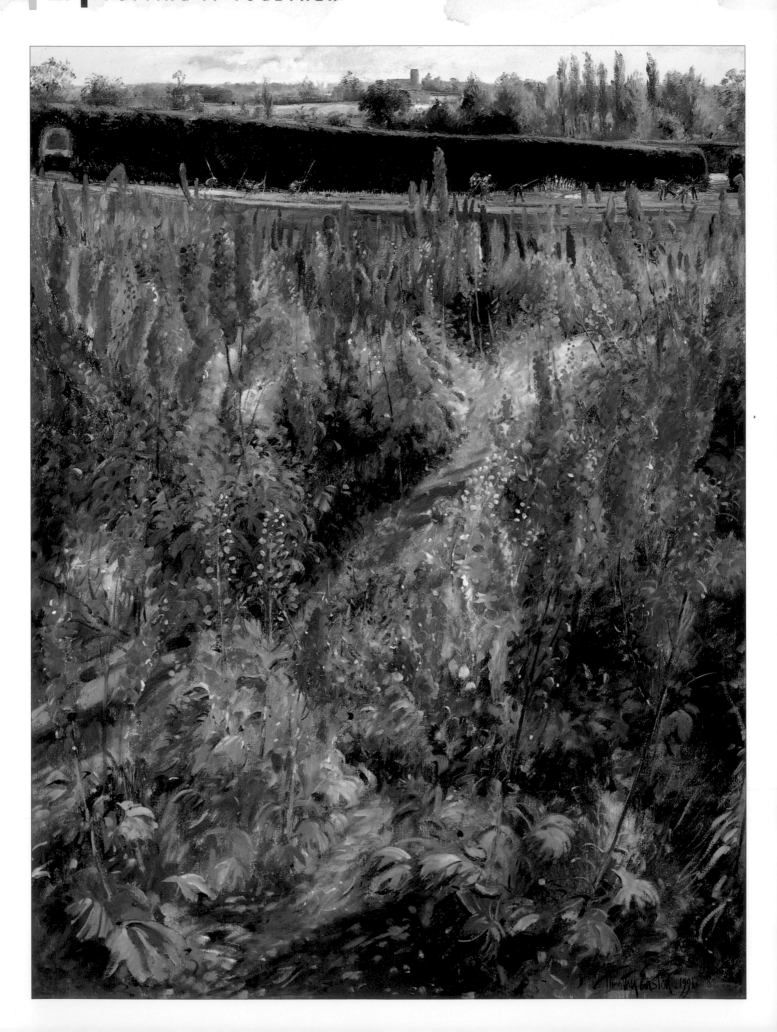

▷ **Romney Marsh**

Alan Oliver • pastel

A bright spring day with the clouds racing past overhead is captured with lively pastel strokes and in passages of light but vibrant color.

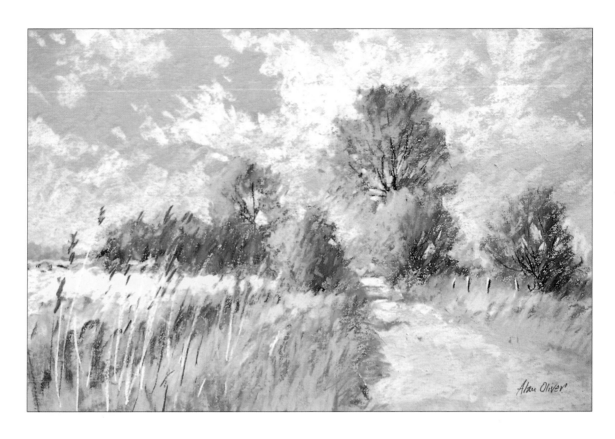

◁ **Delphinium Field and Hoers**

Timothy Easton • oil

This painting unfolds gradually as you look at it. First your attention is drawn to the vibrant colors of the flowers, then you catch sight of the workers in front of the dark yew hedge, and finally you move on to the view beyond.

hangs on the answer. What is it that attracts you about your chosen scene? Unless you face this question, you won't know what it is you are trying to express in your painting. In a garden, you may admire a particular bed of flowers and thus decide to make this the focus of your foreground. But this isn't really enough – you need to know more specifically what interests you. Perhaps it's the colors, the way they are massed, or perhaps it's their relationship with the landscaping of the yard.

A personal anecdote illustrates this very well. I remember looking across the Chianti Hills in Italy to a circle of umbrella pines on a hillside. Set among them was a small classical church, the dome just rising above the trees. I wanted to capture this idyllic and unexpected vision in paint, but my attempts were disappointing. It was only when the vacation photographs were printed later on that I realized where I had gone wrong – I had simply given too much prominence to this distant focal point. I had failed to grasp the fact that this

enchanting circle of trees was quite a distance away, and that part of its charm lay in its isolation in a hilly landscape.

The benefit of hindsight The best thing about failures is that they often show you how to get it right next time. So how should I have tackled this view? For a start I should have spent more time analyzing the view before painting. I should have exaggerated the sense of space and isolation in the picture, leading the eye across the empty, undulating foreground to the far distant circle of trees and "pushing back" the distant focal point by exploiting the effects of aerial perspective.

It would also have been worth my while to consider the different lighting conditions. I might have made a better picture if I had painted the trees at sundown or sunrise, darkly brooding as a silhouette against a bright sky. Equally, the golden light and soft tones of early evening might have deepened the sense of calm and isolation.

Choosing an Approach

MANIPULATE THE MOOD OF YOUR PAINTING BY ORCHESTRATING THE COLOR AND TONE

WHEN YOU NEXT VISIT an exhibition of landscape paintings, see whether any of the paintings evoke a particular feeling and analyze how the artist has put it across. Not all paintings have a recognizable "mood," but many do – some express tranquility; some have a joyous, celebratory quality, while others are somber and brooding. Color and tone play a vital role in a painting's mood – whether you use mainly warm or mainly cool colors, and whether the tones are predominantly dark or light.

Choosing a color "key" When you are planning your landscape, you need to decide on the overall temperature and color "key" of your painting. Do you want it to sing with bright

Tea in the Garden John Rosser • acrylic

Strong contrasts in color and tone make this a dramatic, almost disturbing, painting, in spite of the restful subject matter.

What pulls the painting together is the consistency of technical approach: thin staining washes of transparent color overlaid in places with thicker, richer dabs of paint.

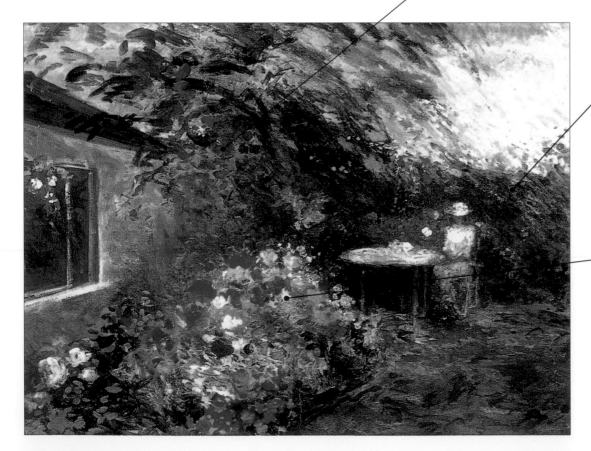

Another unifying factor is color. Even in this dark area, muted blues and reds are integrated with dark greens, echoing the brighter foreground colors.

Movement, created by both color and brushwork, is contrasted with an almost unearthly stillness. This floral riot of color dances before the eyes, with the still, pensive figure in the background providing an anchor for the surface activity.

Day's End in Winter Simie Maryles • acrylic and pastel

By keying down the tones, but not the colors, in this painting, the artist emphasizes the encroaching cold blue shadows of the night.

Touches of warm reds and pinks among the bare winter trees offer a telling contrast to the cold blue theme.

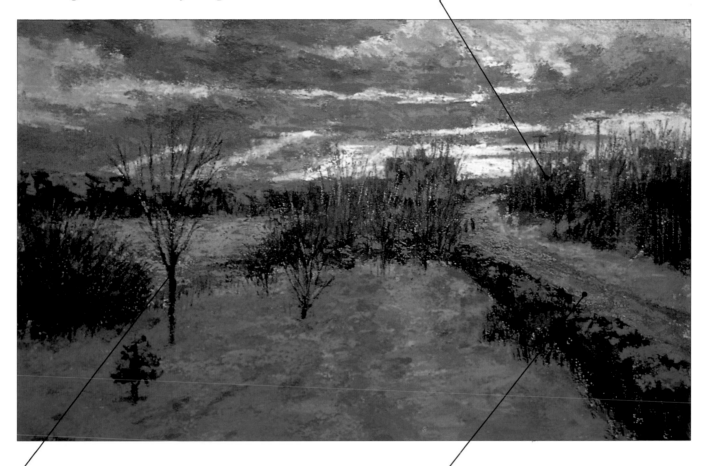

Trees are used to link the foreground with the sky area, with the bare branches "tying" the two together.

The snow-covered road, highlighted with reflected pinks from the sunset, leads the eye into the picture space.

colors – a "high-key" painting – or to be tempered with subtle neutrals – a "low-key" painting? Do you want to emphasize warm or cool colors? If you are painting on the spot, of course, the mood of your painting will be affected by reality, but you can still orchestrate the colors to make more of what you see.

Psychologists have shown that color can greatly affect the way we feel. Yellow, for example, is recognized as a cheering color, which is probably a factor in the popularity of the paintings of Vincent van Gogh (1853–90). Red naturally draws the eye, though it can be aggressive and overdominant if used in large quantities.

Blues and greens – nature's colors – are basically calm and tranquil, but they can be heightened and made more lively by juxtaposition with more assertive colors.

Dark or light Tones can also be described as high or low "key" and have an important influence on the mood of your painting. Here, too, you can control and edit what you see. For example, if you are painting a birch woods in summer and find that the shadows seem to outweigh the highlights, you might key your values to the higher end of the scale, lightening the shadows and playing up the patches of sunlight to produce a painting with a light, bright feel. Similarly, you might play up the darker tones in a cold winter landscape to give a feeling of bleakness, or exaggerate the pale colors of a misty morning by using exclusively light tones and brilliant colors.

Colors and tones can be manipulated by the artist to create landscape scenes which at first sight appear ordinary, but on closer inspection turn out to have a quirk of some kind. You

Tree Study Paul Powis • acrylic

The dark sky and unearthly light of an impending storm combine to create an unsettling effect.

Gentle scumbles of green and blue paint over a red underpainting build up a convincing impression of the wind-tossed tree.

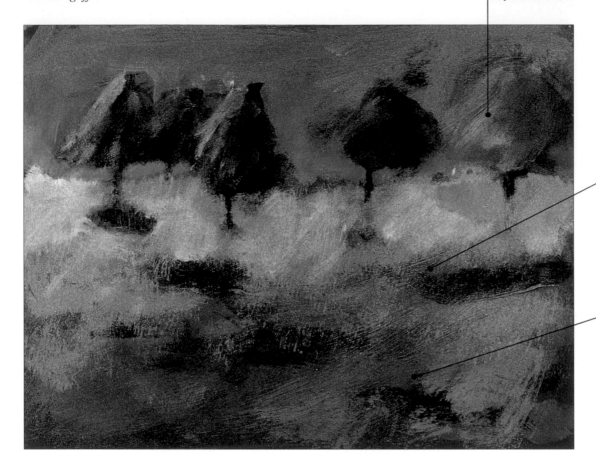

The patches of red underpainting visible in every part of the painting help to hold it together, as well as providing startling contrasts.

Loosely applied layers of broken color in the foreground make this area a positive part of the composition.

may see a painting which expresses a feeling of foreboding, or of unnatural calm, and wonder how this is done. Then you may notice that the lighting is unnatural, producing impossible extremes of tone. The Surrealist painters exploited these effects and used them to create paintings which unsettle the viewer and force us to reconsider fundamental concepts.

Nature's moods Often you will find that the mood has already been decided for you; all you need to do is recognize it and play it up if nec-

Light and mood *It is interesting to paint the same scene at different times of the day and in different seasons to see how changing light can affect the mood of your picture. This watercolor shows an exotic location, but you can choose whatever is at hand – perhaps the view from a window.*

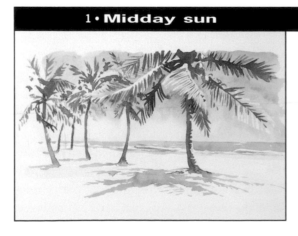
1•Midday sun

▲ *Bright light and strong shadows create a lively composition in which the trees appear to dance along the beach.*

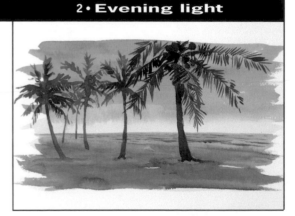
2•Evening light

▲ *Pink diffused light gives a feeling of calm and serenity. The line of trees is silhouetted, with no shadows to give them three-dimensional form.*

The Tree

Helena Greene • oil

Lively strokes of colored neutrals with dark linear marks create an impression of life and movement.

Building up from thin washes of neutralized pinks to bolder strokes of thicker, slightly brighter color.

Most of the tree branches are cropped by the frame, but in this area layers of fragmented strokes pull the small branches away from the frame, adding to the sense of movement.

Contrasts with background shadows help to "find" the edges of the trunk and lower branches.

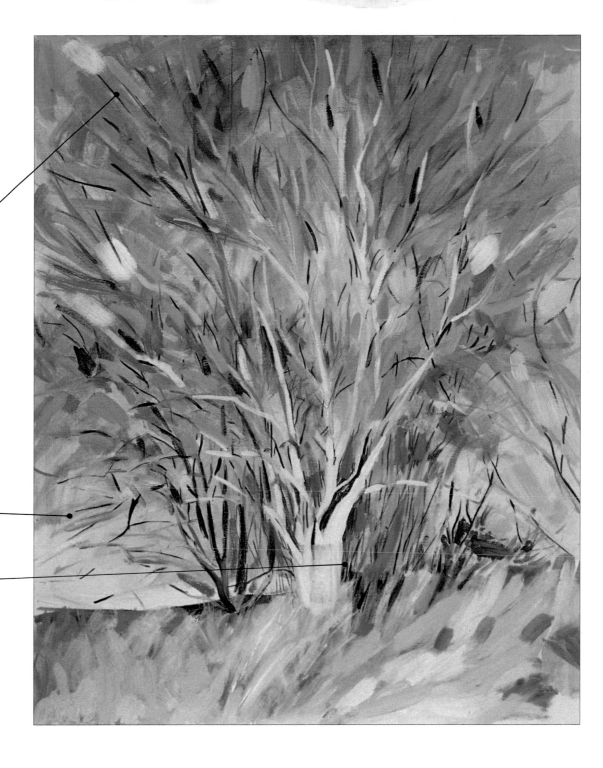

essary. We have already seen how much light and weather affect the landscape. Light can be hard and strong, warm or cold, dramatic or gently diffused, and a change in the quality of the light will completely alter your response to a particular landscape.

Creating movement Your emotional response to a painting can also be affected by what can be called the "tempo." The artist can ex-press a feeling of stillness and quiet or one of energy and movement. Movement is not necessarily

physical – if you are painting a windblown landscape, you will want to show leaves fluttering, trees bowed by wind, and so on – but even in an apparently still landscape, it is important that your painting itself has movement. Lively brushwork and carefully placed color which lead the eye from one part of the painting to another can give this feeling. Fragmented color, extremes of tone, and paint applied in small strokes all produce a lively effect which keeps the eye alert, while flatly applied paint has the opposite effect.

The Painting Process

UNIFY YOUR PAINTING THROUGH CONSISTENT BRUSHWORK OR PASTEL MARKS

ONE OF THE MOST important steps in becoming an artist is realizing that "rules" are made to be broken. Throughout the history of art, no sooner was a hard and fast "rule" laid down than the opposite was found to be equally true. A case in point is the "rule" of aerial perspective – it is possible to cast this aside and still

create a sense of space and recession. But once a tradition has been abandoned, something must be put in its place, and some other means devised to link the various parts of the picture to create a unified whole. Here we look at a number of ways in which the artist pulls the painting together, using annotated pictures to make the processes clear.

Surface pattern In landscapes there are usually natural repetitions of shapes, and variations on them, such as trees of different sizes, fields, and so on. The eye is naturally drawn to such "echoes," as to repeated colors, and will follow them into and through the picture surface. The artist can exaggerate such pattern qualities as painting a cloud to echo the shape of a tree.

Repeated shapes do not necessarily have

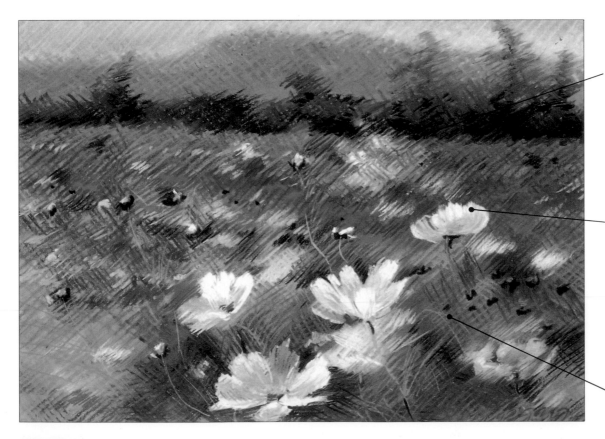

Background flowers become part of the basketweave, reduced to a pattern of tone and color.

The strong contrasts of tone and the more three-dimensional treatment make the flowers stand out from their crosshatched background.

The crosshatching in the foreground is crisper and more widely spaced than that in the background, helping to create an illusion of distance.

Title Unknown   Elizabeth Apgar Smith • pastel

Crosshatching has been used over the picture surface to preserve unity of technique.

At the edge of the painting, you can see how the dense canopy has developed from careful washes, layers of spatter, and dabs of paint.

The white paper has been allowed to show through the buildup of paint, creating discreet highlights.

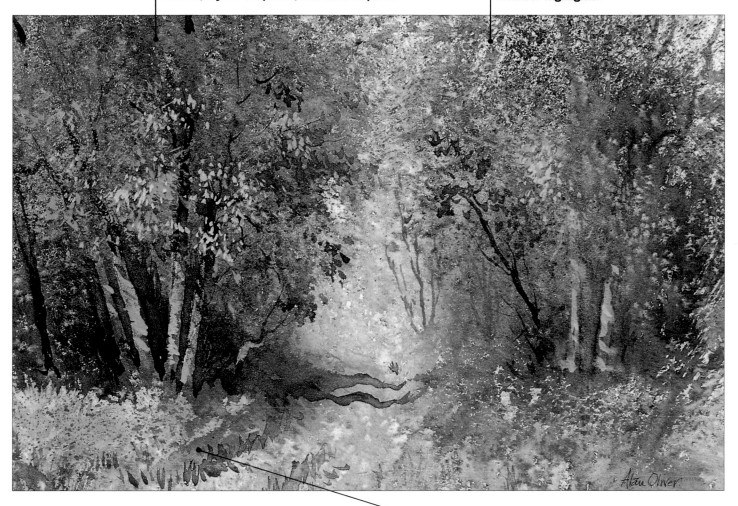

A blue spatter of paint in the foreground suggests patches of bluebells.

Woodland Path

Alan Oliver • watercolor and gouache

Taking the pattern "key" from the leaves, the artist has built up the painting with spattered paint and small dabs and strokes of color.

to be present in reality; they can be introduced into your painting by means of brushwork. At its most obvious, this could mean painting your picture with the brushstrokes all going the same way, which would have a barely perceptible effect while still acting as a unifying force. A more imaginative method could be to vary the brushstrokes, perhaps using sweeping horizontal strokes for fields and hills, and upright ones for trees, thus creating a series of different visual links.

Obviously, with opaque paints such as oils and acrylics, the brushwork can be seen in relief in the paint. Artists often build up their painting with many small individual brushmarks of the same size but different colors, which produces a busy, lively surface. With watercolor

and gouache, brushwork is usually less obvious, but if you intend to use a technique such as drybrush or spattering, be careful that you don't isolate it in only one part of the painting.

A repeated linear stroke is a natural way to work in pastels, as is a series of repeated side strokes, but you might also experiment with a more complex approach such as generalized crosshatching. What is important is that you use the same kind of technique all over the picture. An obvious difference, such as jagged brushstrokes contrasted with perfectly smooth passages, will create a disjointed effect. Smoothness itself can be the unifying factor, however. You can see such effects in some early Dutch landscapes as well as in Surrealist paintings.

The Painting Process

No TWO ARTISTS HAVE THE SAME WORKING METHODS – WITH PRACTICE YOU WILL DEVELOP YOUR OWN

THE WAY YOU CARRY out your painting will naturally vary according to the medium you use, but even then, no two artists will work in the same way. If you read descriptions of the working methods of famous artists, you will be surprised at their idiosyncratic approaches. There is a description of Turner putting the finishing touches to a painting on "varnishing" day at London's Royal Academy. Hunched over his painting, he worked mainly with a palette knife, at one time "rolling and spreading a lump of half transparent stuff over his picture, the size of a finger in length and thickness." Both Titian (*c.* 1485–1576) and Goya (1746–1828) used their fingers to blend and spread paint, and Courbet (1827–85) in his later work applied paint with a palette knife, a method which was less common then than it is today.

Watercolor and gouache Since watercolor is transparent, it must be worked from light to dark, so it is usual to begin with light washes of color in the palest areas – in a landscape, usually the sky and distant planes – and build up gradually to the darker ones, usually in the foreground. This natural progression imposed by the medium has in itself a unifying effect on the painting, but it is important to work across the whole painting at the same time rather than completing each area separately. You must always consider the overall relationships in the painting, and if you work "piecemeal," you will be seeing each area out of context.

The fact that watercolors dry so much lighter can cause problems with tonal balance, so until you become experienced, it is wise to try out colors on a spare piece of paper and let them dry so that you can judge the effect. Although you can darken colors by overlaying washes, it is not advisable to do so too often, as the colors will become muddy.

The velvety texture of gouache paints singles them out for certain effects, but, like acrylics, they combine the advantages of two media – watercolor and oils – because they can be used both thick and thin. If used opaquely, you can work gouache light over dark, which makes it a good medium for sketching where time for planning is limited. Additional body can be given to the paints by mixing them with acrylic medium.

Oils There are so many different styles of painting with oils that the whole book could be devoted to them. They can be used thick and juicy, applied with brushes or painting knives, or thinned with turpentine and put on as transparent washes, almost like watercolors. There is one important rule, however, which really must be followed if you want your work to last, which is to work from "lean" to "fat." This means that if you are building up a painting in layers, you reserve the thick, oilier ("fat") paint until last; otherwise, the paint will crack later. Apart from the technical consideration, it is easier to work in this way. The thicker the paint is, the longer the drying time, but the "lean" paint will dry quite quickly, enabling you to block in areas of color and then work over them, or to use thinned paint for the distance and thick impasto for the foreground. This creates a contrast of textures which will give your painting structure and interest as well as helping to create a sense of recession.

Acrylics So far in this book, oils and acrylics have been discussed together because they are similar in consistency and can be made to behave in a similar way. Yet there are consider-

Swamp Fever

Hazel Soan • watercolor

The artist starts with a drawing and then maps out the tonal structure so that she knows exactly which areas of paper to reserve for highlights.

Dark paint has been carefully painted around highlights with a small sable brush.

Small areas of foliage are added in the final stages with a sponge.

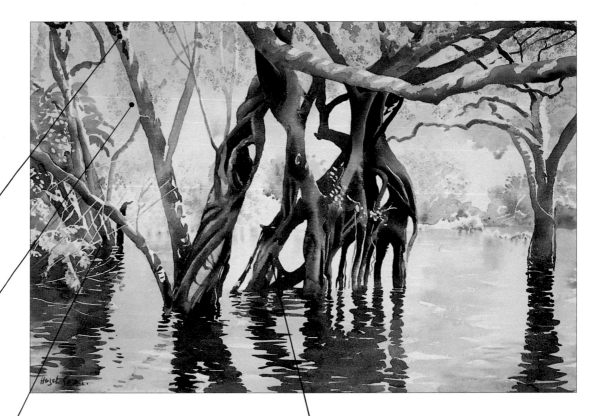

Fine lines were achieved by painting on masking fluid and removing it when all the colors were in place.

Controlled backruns create texture on the bark. Paint added to the still-damp first wash has dried with a dark, uneven edge.

able differences, as anyone who has used both will know. Acrylics are water-based and are diluted by adding more water. They dry very fast – as soon as the water evaporates. If you use the paint thickly, you can slow the drying time by adding a retarding medium, but this doesn't work for thin paint, with a lot of water added. So in general you need to learn to plan carefully and work fast. The great advantage of acrylics is that you can overpaint as much as you like; the paint is immovable once dry, so there is no risk of stirring up earlier layers and thus muddying the colors. One thing to watch is that acrylics dry darker, so it is not always easy to match your colors.

You can also build up surface texture much more quickly with acrylics than with oils. Paintings in thick knife impasto will dry in days, while a similar oil painting can take months.

Pastels and oil pastels Pastels cannot be premixed as paints can, so any mixing must take place on the surface of the paper. All pastels are opaque, so light colors can be laid over dark as long as there is not too heavy a buildup

of color beneath. It is possible to overlay colors quite extensively if you spray with fixative at regular intervals.

Because it is virtually impossible to cover the whole paper surface with pastel pigment, artists usually work on colored paper, areas of which are left uncovered. A gray-blue paper might be chosen, for example, and most of the sky left as bare paper, or small patches allowed to show through foliage greens. This has an important unifying effect on the picture, as it is a way of repeating colors without actually putting any color on.

Oil pastels are a particularly versatile medium. They can be used in the same way as chalk pastels, but they can also become something more like a painting medium, as you can spread them with turpentine (or mineral spirits), which "melts" the color. This can be done by moistening a rag or brush with turpentine and spreading the color on the paper, or by pushing the moistened brush into the pastel stick, just as you would dip it into paint on a palette, and then transferring it to the picture surface in a series of brushstrokes.

The Painting Process

OBSERVE THE EFFECTS OF LIGHT CAREFULLY – LIGHT ITSELF IS A UNIFYING FACTOR

LIGHT ITSELF IS AN ally in the business of unifying the picture. As we have seen, there are different kinds of light, which have their own color biases. An evening light, for example, is typically golden, and this affects all the colors seen under that light. Often paintings lack unity simply because the artist has failed to identify the quality of the prevailing light.

One of the problems here is that we are too influenced by what we know and thus don't look at things thoroughly enough. We know that roses are red, trees are green, branches are brown, and so on, so we assign them a generalized color that has little to do with reality. Never forget that color is light – without light color cannot exist. If you sat in

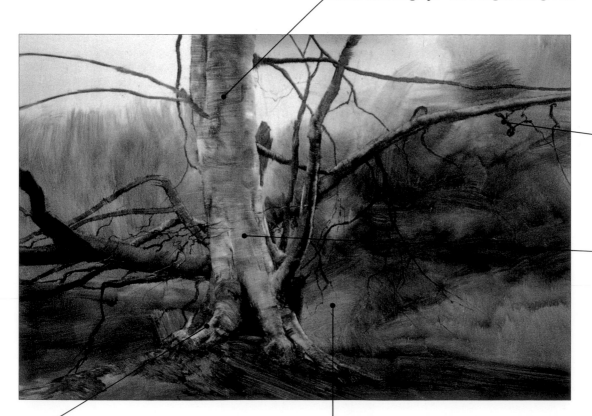

Reducing all colors to neutrals, the artist mixes careful colored grays – here tinged with green.

Beech Tree

James Morrison • oil

A dull winter light prevails, creating muted colors and dark tones.

Background woodland is generalized. Lively brushwork contrasts with the solid stillness of the beech trunk.

The horizontal markings on the trunk are created with thin, transparent paint applied with a bristle brush so that the coarse hairs leave a mark.

Highlights are formed by allowing the white-primed support to show through the thin paint.

Using oils thinly everywhere, and working from light to dark, as in watercolor, suits the misty light and helps to unify the painting.

Summer Mist, Corn Hill

Simie Maryles • pastel

A pinkish mist casts a unifying light.

In the background trees, pale pinks and blues are laid over green. The mist exaggerates the effects of aerial perspective.

To link this area to the foreground and distance, pinks have also been worked into the bulrushes.

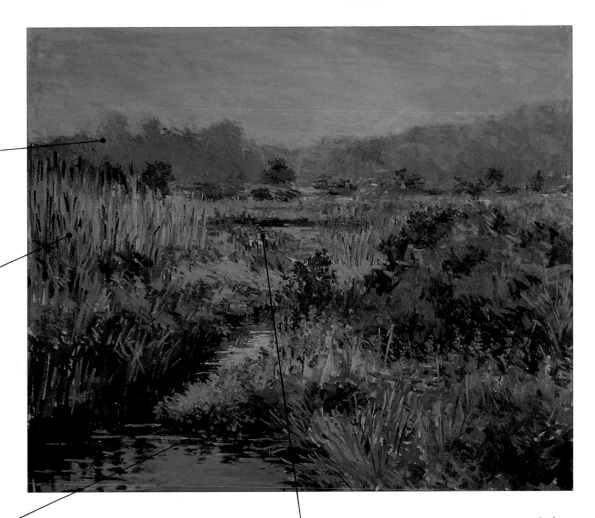

A patch of reflected pink in the foreground water establishes the predominance of this color in the landscape.

Shades of the same pinkish mauve are carried right through the painting, appearing again in the flowers.

front of a red flower for a whole day, you would notice how it changes color in different lights; and if you observed the same flower in different weather conditions, you would see further changes dictated by the prevailing light. Once you learn to identify this color bias of the prevailing light, you will find you can mix colors to create an overall unity while still expressing the "local" – actual – colors of flowers, leaves, and branches.

Taking the colors across Although it should theoretically be possible to unify your painting entirely by accurate observation of color, you will often need to resort to a little artifice as well. One of the most successful methods of pulling the painting together is to take colors across the painting, which means to use similar colors in different parts of it. You can do this irrespective of the overall color bias. For instance, you may have a bluish color bias for a

painting with orange flowers in the foreground, in which case you will need to search for highlights in the middle-ground trees where this orange can be accommodated in a neutralized form. It could then be carried into the distant planes by using it in mixes for the warmer tones and even into the cloud highlights in the sky. Similarly, you can carry patches of the blue used for the sky into other areas of the painting, used in a more intense form for the foreground and slightly neutralized for the middle ground.

As explained on the previous pages, pastelists often unify the picture by working on colored paper, and colored grounds are frequently used for oils and acrylics for the same reason. To prepare a ground for either of these media, you can paint over a white primed canvas with watercolor or diluted acrylic. Thinned oil paint can also be used for oils, if you prefer, and will dry very quickly.

Making Adjustments

FOR AN OBJECTIVE VIEW, REASSESS YOUR PAINTING AGAIN AFTER A FEW DAYS

DON'T THINK THAT JUST because you have finished a painting session that you have necessarily completed the painting. Often something that isn't quite successful can be pulled around by making a few adjustments. It often helps to look at the painting later, away from the scene, as this allows you to look at it objectively and see whether it works properly in pictorial terms. You may notice that there is insufficient contrast in the foreground, for example, or that a color in the middle ground is too bright and needs to be "knocked back."

Some landscape painters abhor the idea of "fiddling around" with a picture in the studio, but others see it as a necessary part of painting. The skill lies in recognizing what you need to do, so don't start making adjustments unless you are sure which passages of the painting are not working, and why. If a color looks too bright, you could find that instead of toning it down, you can add some vivid accents of color elsewhere – perhaps it is the other colors that are at fault, not this one.

Alpine Vineyard III William Shumway • acrylic

The warm greens in the foreground bring this area forward.

The distant hill is knocked back in space with a blue glaze over the dry green paint below.

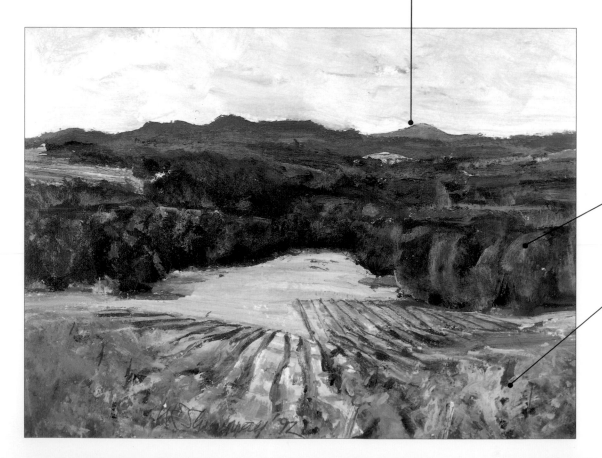

Thin paint scumbled on modifies earlier colors and creates form and texture.

The greens in the foreground are warmed with yellow, but there are echoes of the blue-greens used in the middle distance.

Blow and Make a Wish

Pat Pendleton • oil pastel

Color accents lead the eye around this picture, with warmer reds and yellows in the foreground and cooler blues in the background.

Background trees are loosely filled in with a dark green, allowing an earlier pale color to show through and break up the color slightly.

Small accents of pink create links between different areas of the painting.

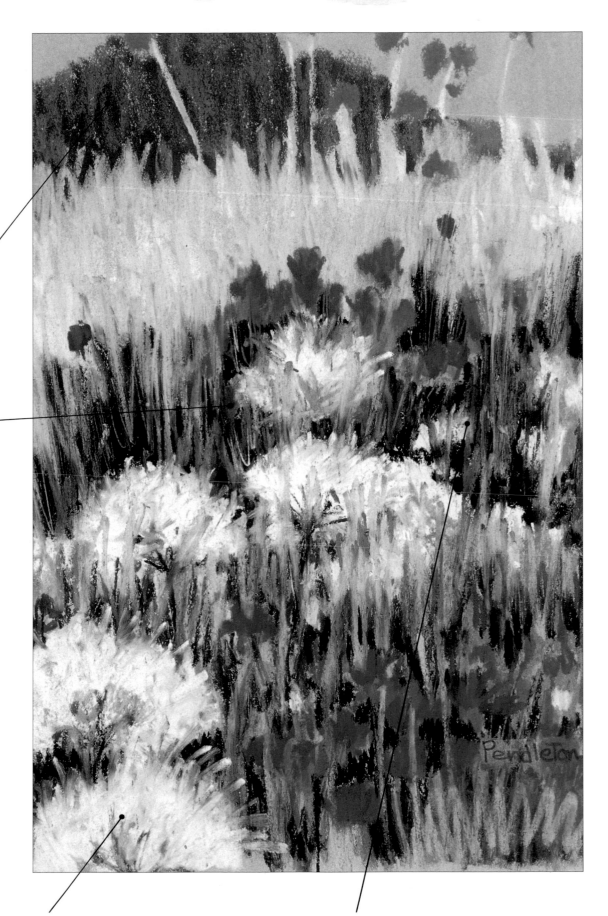

The white dandelions march into the picture so that the viewer follows them from foreground to middle distance and proceeds on to the patch of white just visible in the background (top right).

Strong vertical feathered strokes of yellow over green link this bank of greens in the middle ground with the yellow grass above.

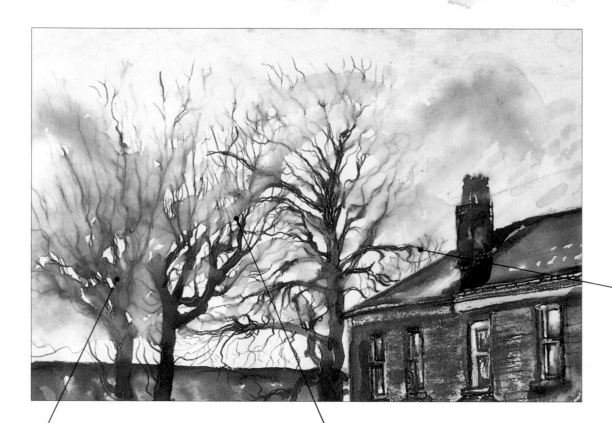

The branches and twigs have been mapped out in a dark neutral blue.

The water wash has been encouraged to run across the page by tilting the paper. Backruns become part of the image.

A heavy water wash dilutes the watercolor, softening the crisp branches, creating a maelstrom of wind and rain.

Putting matters right How you tackle your adjustments will, of course, depend on the medium you are using. With oils, you can be quite drastic as long as the paint is still wet. If necessary, you can remove whole areas of paint with a rag soaked in mineral spirits. If the paint is too thick and rich in one area, try the method called tonking (after Sir Alfred Tonks, one-time head of the Slade School of Art in London). This involves pressing a piece of newspaper over the offending area, which removes the top layer of paint and provides a good surface for further work.

If you want to make alterations after oil

Lifting out *The trees in the background of this gouache painting (see page 76) are too close in tone to the topiaried yews on each side, so the artist lightens them by removing some of the paint, a method known as lifting out.*

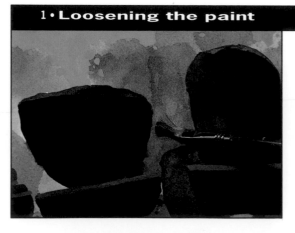

1•Loosening the paint

▲ *With a soft brush moistened with water, the paint is gently loosened with a circular motion. The same method can be used with watercolors, but gouache paint comes away more easily.*

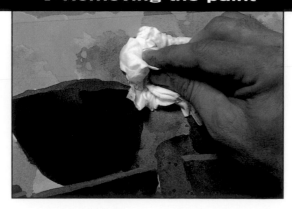

2•Removing the paint

▲ *A clean dry tissue is now used to mop up the wet paint, taking care not to rub the paper, which could easily be damaged.*

Making adjustments.
In this gouache painting (see page 41) the artist has covered the whole picture area, fully establishing the composition and color scheme. When a painting is nearing completion, it can be reassessed and final adjustments made to pull it together.

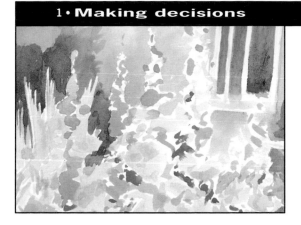

1 • Making decisions

▲ *The foreground flowers don't stand out well enough from the background. Colors could be made brighter and tonal contrasts increased, but the artist likes the flowers the way they are.*

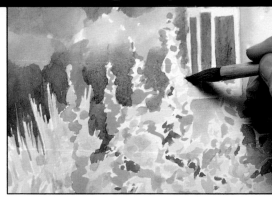

2 • Solving the problem

▲ *She quickly finds the answer. Building up the contrasts around the flowers so that the edges are more clearly defined makes them stand out from the darker wall behind.*

paint has dried, you will have to overpaint, and the same applies to acrylics. With both of these media, you might try adjusting tones and colors with a glaze or scumble, light over dark, or for an overbright color, lay a thin layer of the complementary color on top. If you find you have to remove a dried layer of paint, you can sometimes do so with fine sandpaper, but such major alterations are seldom necessary.

In watercolor, tones are easy to darken, simply by putting on more paint, but harder to lighten. This can be done, by gently dabbing with a damp sponge or wetting a soft brush with water, going over the area with a circling motion, and then blotting with tissue. This is difficult to do well, however, and should only

be attempted as a last resort. Colors can be "taken down" by overlaying washes of a neutral or contrasting color, but be careful not to overwork. Often all that is wrong with a watercolor is lack of sharp detail in the foreground, and this is easily put right.

An overbright pastel color can be reduced by lightly feathering over it with another color, perhaps the complementary. To lighten a color, fix the area with a fixative spray, allow it to dry, and then scumble a paler tint over the top. Pastels sometimes become too "wooly," particularly if you have overdone the blending techniques. If this is the case, a spray with fixative and a little linear work on top will work wonders.

3 • Letting the paper show

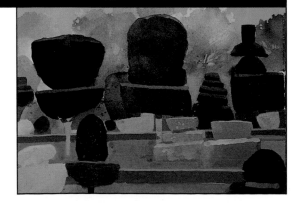

▲ *Removing some of the color in this way allows more of the white paper to show through. The lifting-out technique is often used for soft highlights in both watercolor and gouache.*

Softening edges *An atmospheric pastel of light shining through the trees (see page 74) is now given its finishing touches. Sometimes edges need either softening or sharpening to define the spatial positions of the various elements.*

Blending with a cotton swab

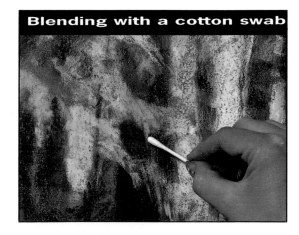

▲ *Highlights on the foreground foliage appear too stark against the deep browns of the tree trunks, so a cotton swab is used to blend them into their surrounding colors.*

INDEX

Note: Page numbers in *italics* refer to illustrations

A

acrylics
  alterations 141
  brushwork 133
  building up picture *21*
  greens *81, 83*
  impasto *26-7*
  lightening colors 77
  mixing colors *73*
    neutrals *113*
  neutralizing colors *79*
  oil glaze on *32-3*
  softening edges *64-5*
  techniques for flowers 35
  textures 111
  transparency of colors 80
  working with 134-5
adjustments to painting 138-41
aerial perspective 38, 76, 101,
  104-5, 132
Aggett, Lionel
  Olive Grove, Less Alpilles,
    Provence 87
  Sunflowers at Bonnieux,
    Provence 29
  Les Tournesols de Montmajour,
    Arles 104
alla prima painting *61*
atmospheric perspective *see*
  aerial perspective
Austen, Don
  Path to Heligan, Mevagissey 25
  River at Lanhydrock, Cornwall
    68-9

B

background *see* distance
Baptist, Gerry, *Mid-day in*
  Provence 7
Bartlett, Paul
  My Parents' Garden in Winter
    54
  Stormy Weather in Lime Grove
    (detail) 140
Bennett, Brian
  Ashbridge Beeches 70
  Bluebells in Ashbridge 20
  Foreground flowers,
    demonstration *46-9*
  Hogweed 26
  Honesty 39
  Wild Parsley and Chestnuts 74
Bernard, Michael, *The Blue Tree*
  21
blues, in distance 114, *114-15*
brushes 69, 108
  for leaves 30-1, *30-1*
  for texture 111
brushwork 133
building up
  color *23*, 42, *42*
  glazes *33*
  tones *61*
Burman, Peter, *Garden in*
    Provence 90
Byers, Fleur, *April in the Forest*
  112

C

canvas
  painting edges on 29
  preparing ground 137
Carter, Jean, *"The Great Oak" in*
  a Field of Buttercups 117
Chamberlain, Trevor, *Sheep on*
  the Meads, Hertford 62
Clinch, Moira, *Peach Tree in the*
  Rhône Valley 23
color(s) 9
  balancing 90-1, *90-1*
  blues, distant 114, *114-15*
  broken 42, *42*
  building up *23*, 42, *42*
  combinations 40-1
  complementary 42-3, 112-14
  detail 18-19
  differences between media
    80-1
  dominant 85, *85*
  greens, ready-made 80-1, *81*
  high and low key 128-9
  keeping fresh 42
  knocking back 88, *90*
  lightening 77-8
  mixing 40, 42, *72-3*, 78, 82, *83*
  mood expressed by 128-31
  neutral 112-14
    mixing *113*
  neutralizing *79*
  pigments 40
  planning 17
  staining quality of pigments
    80-1
  to draw eye 84-5, *85*
  tonal values
    increasing 78
    reducing 77-8
  tones 128, 129-30
    range 76-8
  unifying picture 137
  warm and cool 41-2, *41*
Constable, John 61
contrast 9
  diminishing 38, 76-8, *76-7*
  of edges 66
  in foreground 36-9
  light and 36-9
  lightening colors by 78
  to show scale 116-17
  in tree painting 60-1, *61*
Corot, Jean-Baptiste 84-5, 112
Courbet, Gustave 134
cropping 44-5
crosshatching *132*, 133
Cullen, Patrick
  Cabbages, June 110-11
  May Tree in Blossom, Rainy Day
    101
  Roses, Evening 115
  Row of Poplars, Stormy Day 60
Curtis, David
  Late Autumn, Clumber Park 19
  Pinewood in the Peak 58
  Poplars in a Breeze 8

D

Dawson, Doug
  Fall in the North Woods 30-1
  Kipling Woods 73
detail
  decreasing over distance 62-7,
    104-5, *105*
  degree of 7, 9
  in distance 104-11
  reducing 18, *18*, 108-9
  selection 18-21
  suggesting 20-1
distance 96-121
  choosing approach 100-3
  color and contrast 112-15
  creating *102-3*
  detail and edge quality 104-11
  focus in 103
  interpreting and editing 98,
    98-9
  nearer 101-2
  scale and proportion 116-17
  texture in 110-11
  trees in, demonstration *118-21*
drawing
  brush drawing *61*
  outlines 28
  underdrawing 28-9
dropping in color *23, 34, 35*
dry brush technique 133
  building up color *42*
Dutch landscapes 133

E

Easton, Timothy
  Delphinium Field and Hoers 126
  Delphiniums at Dusk 16
  Mid-day in the Lane 63
  The Morning Letter 32
  Woodland Hives 122-3
edges
  contrasts 66
  effect of light on 26-7
  finding *23*, 24-6
  impasto *26-7*
  lost and found 23-4, 45, 66
  painting on textured surface
    29
  quality 9, 22-9
    describing 24
  softening *64-5*, 108-9
  over distance 62-6, *64*
Elliot, John, *Queechee Trees 65*
exploring view 16-17, *17*

F

failures, benefiting from 127
feathering 109
fixing *91*, 135, 141
flowers
  color balance 9, 88-91, *88-9*
  generalizing *88-9*
  light on 34-5, *34-5*
  in middleground 88-91
  techniques for painting 34-5
focal points 84-5, *111*
foreground 10-49
  choosing approach 14-17
  contrast and color 36-43
  demonstration *46-9*
  detail and edge quality 18-35
  interpreting and editing 12,
    12-13
  as pointer to middleground 56
  scale and proportion 44-5
  as subject 15

G

Galton, Jeremy
  Autumn Shadows, Hampstead
    Heath 66
  Provençal Meadow 54-5
  Track Through Cornfields 84-5
glaze, oil *32-3*
gouache
  brushwork 133
  diminishing contrasts 76-7
  greens *81, 83*
  mixing colors 72
  neutralizing colors *79*
  techniques for flowers 34-5
  transparency 80
  working with 134
Goya, Francisco Jose de 134
Graham, Peter
  Bluebell Wood 43
  Indian Summer 38
  Picking Gooseberries 9
Greene, Helena, *The Tree 131*
greens
  differences between media
    80-1
  mixing 82, *83*
  ready-made 80-1, *81*
    color characteristics *81*
grounds, colored 137

H

highlights *111*
hills, perspective on 87
horizon 105, 108-9
Horton, James
  Distant Village 103
  View from Les Planes 108-9
Howitt, Clarice, *Bluebells at*
  Freers Wood 101
Hutchings, LaVere
  Autumn Shadows 57
  Ballet 27

I

impasto *26-7*, 35, *111*, 134, 135
Impressionists 42
interpreting scene 12, *12-13*,
  124-7
introducing painting 14-15

J

Johnson, Sandra, *Delphiniums 29*

K

Kenny, Paul, *The River Lagan,*
  Ireland 107
knife impasto 27, *111*
knives, painting with,
  demonstration *46-9*

L

leaves
  brushes to use 30-1, *30-1*
  colors 31
    variations 82
  light on *32-3*, 33

CREDITS

movement 33, *33*
shapes 31
sponging *66-7*
Lidzey, John
distant trees, demonstration
118-21
Road and Trees, Northam 55
lifting out *140-1*
light
contrasts 36-9
effects of 26-7, 106-7, *107*, 131
on flowers 34-5, *34-5*
on leaves *32-3*, 33
mood and 129-30, *130*
quality 36-7
identifying 136-7
tones of 17
unifying picture 136-7
linearity 28
Lorrain, Claude 70
Luck, James, *Coach Whips 24*

M

McCombs, John
Banks of the River Tame, Delph,
Autumn 124-5
Winter Sun, Delph 109
Martin, Margaret M, *Spring*
Crowds 88-9
Maryles, Simie
Corn Hill 4
Day's End in Winter 129
Gardener's Yard in Summer 78
Summer Mist, Corn Hill 137
masking fluid *22*
middleground 50-95
choosing approach 54-61
contrast and color 76-85
demonstration *92-5*
detail and edge quality 62-75
extending 59
focus on *56-7*
identifying 54-6
interpreting and editing 52,
52-3
scale and proportion 86-91
tonal changes 76-8
mist 98
Monet, Claude 42, 107
monochrome sketches 38-9
mood
color and 128-31
light and 129-30, *130*
Morrison, James, *Beech Tree 136*
movement, of leaves 33, *33*

N

Napp, David, *Flower Pots and*
Apricots 28
neutral colors 112-14
complementary 112-14
mixing *113*

O

oil glaze *32-3*
oil pastels
blending *114-15*
working with 135
oils
alterations 140-1
brushwork 133
greens *81*, *83*
lightening colors 77
mixing colors *73*
neutralizing colors *79*
techniques for flowers 35

textures 111
transparency of colors 80
wet-in-wet technique *105*, 108
working with 134
Oliver, Alan
Romney Marsh 127
Spring Meadows 114
Woodland Path 133
outlines
drawing in 28
in underdrawing 29
overlapping subjects 45

P

paper, unifying picture 135, 137
pastels
alterations 141
building up 42
fine lines with *28*
fixing *91*, 135, 141
greens *81*, *83*
mixing colors *72*, 82
neutrals *113*
neutralizing colors *79*
oil
blending *114-15*
working with 135
opaqueness 80
softening edges *64-5*, 108, 109
techniques for flowers 35
using 69
working with 135
pattern, surface *124-5*, 132-3,
132
Pendleton, Pat
Blow and Make a Wish 139
Full Bloom 40
perspective 9, 44, 86-7, *87*, 88
aerial 38, 76, 101, 104-5, 132
creating distance *102-3*
photography, interpreting scene
by 12, *12-13*, 52, *52-3*, 98, *98-9*
pigments 40
staining qualities 80-1
planning 124-7
Popkin, Elsie Dinsmore
Azaleas and Dogwoods on Glen
Echo Trail 35
Blue Doors with Fuchsia and
Geraniums 86
Diana with Cedars and
Columbine
(detail) *18*
Reynolds Gardens – Pink Cannas
and Mexican Sage 44
Powis, Paul
Montadon 56
Northill 59
Tree Study 130
West Malvern Spring 41
proportion 9, 44-5, 86-7, 116-17

R

Read, Maurice
After Harvest 96-7
Hogweed, Norfolk 7
reassessing painting 138-41
Romantic movement 116-17
Rosser, John, *Tea in the Garden*
128
Ruskin, John 70

S

Saudek, Martha
Coming of Winter 102
Descanso's Woodlands 67

El Viejo 50-1
Winterthur's Azaleas 84
scale 9, 44-5, *45*, 86-7
setting 116-17
scumbling 74
sgraffito 42, *105*, 111
shadows
building up 37, 38, *43*
colors in *37*, 38
composition 37-8
shape, capturing likeness 21
Shumway, William, *Alpine*
Vineyard III 138
'signposts', leading eye round
painting 14-15, 58-9
sketches/sketching
exploring ideas by 16-17
monochrome 38-9
sky, effect of distance 105
sky holes 72-4, *72*
Smith, Elizabeth Apgar, untitled
paintings *42-3*, *132*
snow 98
Soan, Hazel
Behind Closed Doors 36
Pathway to the Sea 68
Relaxing 15
Springtime, Chelsea 10-11
Swamp Fever 135
Wiltshire Garden 22
spattering *18-19*, 133, *133*
sponging *66-7*
Stedman, Daniel
Silver Birches 71
Summer Shadows 77
Summer Winterbourne 75
stippling 20, *43*
Strother, Jane
Gubbio 39
Lode, Cambridgeshire 110
trees in middleground,
demonstration *92-5*
studio landscapes 61
surface pattern *124-5*, 132-3, *132*
Surrealists 130, 133

T

Tarbet, Urania Christy, *Sunrise,*
Sunset 14
texture 20
by sponging *66-7*
creating illusion of distance
110-11
Titian 134
tonal studies 38-9
tonking 140
Tonks, Sir Alfred 140
trees
characteristics 9, 70-5
color transitions 82
in distance 108
demonstration *118-21*
in middleground,
demonstration *92-5*
as 'signposts' 59
sky holes 72-4, *72*
trunks 74-5, *74*
variety in 60-1, *61*
in winter 75
Turner, J.M.W. 70, 111, 116, 134

U

underdrawings 28-9

V

Van Gogh, Vincent 129
vanishing point 86, 87
viewframe 17
viewpoint
choosing 16
effect of 101

W

watercolors
alterations 141
brushwork 133
darkening colors 78
glazes *33*
greens, mixing *81*, 82, *83*
lightening colors 77
mixing colors *73*
neutrals *113*
neutralizing colors *79*
techniques for flowers 34
textures 110
wet-in-wet technique *34-5*,
108
working with 134
weather, changes in 106-7, *107*
wet-in-wet technique *21*, *61*, 88
controlling *34-5*
impasto *26*
mixing colors 82
in oils *105*, 108
in watercolors 108
wet-on-dry technique *21*
Winstanley, Roy, *End of the Day,*
Baggator 116
working methods 134-5

Y

Yale, Brian
The Lake at Sheffield Park 117
Solid Geometry and Sunlight 106
View From Froghole 100

Z

Zavorskas, Joyce, *Prince Valley 91*